For Martin

'A Man's A Man for A' That'

Robert Burns - 1795

NOT ANOTHER WALTZ

(I, NAUSIUS)

KERRY GARDNER

A MEMOIR

Published by
Filament Publishing Ltd
16, Croydon Road, Beddington
Croydon, Surrey CR0 4PA UK
www.filamentpublishing.com

Not Another Waltz (I, Nausius)
© 2021 Kerry Gardner
ISBN 978-1-913623-57-9

Printed by 4Edge

CONTENTS

CHAPTER 1
Getting to Know You

Imagine, if you will, millions of 'things' assembled before coming into this world, just little wisps of being perhaps, and an angel addressing them:

'When you get down there, you might be lucky enough to have a happy start, and later on, life – as it's called – can be full of wonder and excitement. But then, later still, parts of you will start to malfunction, not too painfully you'll be pleased to hear – to begin with anyway – but as it goes on you won't be able to play the sports you loved or do anything strenuous which gave you such pleasure. In fact, you'll possibly be in pain, and everything you hold dear will have disappeared. OK – hands up those of you who want to have a go. Oh, come on, I have to send someone!'

I must have been volunteered.

Baptism Solemnized At: S. Paul's Cathedral, Calcutta A.D. 1937; **When Baptized:** July 23 1937; **Said to be born:** June 14 1937; **Child's Christian Name:** KERRY ALEXANDER; **Sex:** Son of **Parents' Names:** ALAN GEORGE / ELINE THERESE MEEK; **Abode:** Calcutta; **Quality, Trade or Profession:** Mercantile Assistant; **By Whom the Ceremony was performed:** M.G. SCOTT Cathedral Chaplain.

What happened immediately before and after this ceremony is a blank. I've even forgotten the angel's name.

I asked my mother through the years to tell me about my father, Alan George Meek, but was told to mind my own business. She must have believed she had a patent on my manufacture. So, here are some clues. I'll tell you what I've heard from others and some later-in-life admissions from my mother – which may or may not be true!

It seems she married a man I was never to meet face to face, and between them, they produced me, then . . . then she had another husband. I have seen a handkerchief bearing my initials followed by this second husband's surname: K. A. Oldrini. Was Oldrini married to her, or was his name stencilled on my school clothing to make me acceptable to the Darjeeling school authorities? I'm not certain I was introduced to number two husband either, but I do remember a tall male presence when I was tiny. This figure showed me his service revolver (the Japanese were expected to invade Calcutta at any moment, apparently), and it was so heavy that when he handed it to me, I dropped it. I would have remembered if it had gone off, I'm pretty sure, but I never saw him again. It seems my mother had two husbands before I was six.

As my mother thought her life was hers alone, she refused to answer any of my questions on my early fathers, assuring me I was much loved and wasn't that enough? Hmm. You be the judge of that. Tell me later.

This is my scenario from the little I've pieced together through the years – and try to remember my mother only dallied with the truth. So, here's how it *might* have happened:

A young girl below the age of consent found herself pregnant. Maybe the only truth she told me was that my father was in the army, so to avoid scandal this girl and her shotgun-wedded husband were sent overseas to a British Army regiment in India. Her local vicar back home in England helped obtain passports for her and her mother, so a few seconds after he married them, the couple were exported to India, my grandmother as nurse/companion to her pregnant daughter.

I can't imagine a British army wedding attended by the military and their wives, so I'm betting the only member of the bride's family at both the wedding in Blighty, and my christening in Calcutta, was her mother.

Sometime after their arrival in India, my father (who is now presumably in business, hence 'Mercantile Assistant' on my birth certificate) received a letter from his childhood sweetheart saying she'd been wrong to refuse him and was it too late to start again? (Do you think, as a well brought up and moral young lady, she knew anything of her adored one's child when she made the request? She surely knew of his wedding to another. Or was his disappearance from her life explained by her disapproving parents as a regimental posting?). The letter had its desired effect because he upped and abandoned the baby (me), his wife and her mother (them), returning to England to marry the first in the frame.

My suppositions barely make sense. My father came from an army background, did he? Did the army give this cad its blessing? Wasn't he cashiered for his ungentlemanly conduct? Or was his father a soldier who smoothed the way with the top brass? Or is none of it true? Don't ask me. And there must be something lacking in me that I don't care. I shy away from getting involved in the modern-day mania of digging up one's past when in this case, it includes my abandonment. What do I say to a complete stranger after I've tapped him on the shoulder? 'I believe we're related. You might well be my half-brother. Did you have a happy family life as a child? You did! I'm so pleased for you'. I've never found it practical to use one's past as an excuse for the present. It would be interesting to know what happened, but it's not essential for my well-being, I don't think.

Having said that, I had felt divorced from the melodrama as it was so long ago, but now, as I'm writing this down, it has made me more curious.

What else do I know of my father? My mother told me the last time she saw him was at a charity dance in a smart London hotel many years later. Did she go up to him and say hello? On another occasion, she mentioned to a friend of mine that he'd died of a complication of the legs. Should I avoid the tango?

And not many years ago, my brother found himself in the village in which we'd been told she was born. There was no sign of her family's existence nor of the marriage in the Parish Register. See what I mean?

I don't think my mother coped well with looking after me at that time. How could she? Aged twenty or so, with three mouths to feed, she must have been desperate. I'm pretty sure her mother had little or no money, so every waking moment she must have been searching for some means of support, other than what my father – or the army – provided. Mind you, this is all conjecture. She may have been fine. I do know my grandmother figured largely in my young childhood. She told me later she kidnapped me, that my mother wasn't equipped to bring up a child.

What memories of life in India with my grandmother? I remember my granny as a fierce woman, and even now can feel the back of her hairbrush thwacking me behind the knees. But she was kind too, and I remember her with affection. Because dysentery was rife, she would occasionally plonk me face down on an ironing board and plug my behind with an enema tube attached to the half can of water hanging from a hook on the door. I would expel the contents of my bowels into the lavatory sometime later. I remember one day I was about to explode when, looking down into the bowl, I saw a gigantic spider straddling the water. I was far too startled and scared to 'bomb' it! What if the spider could jump upwards? It didn't, and I did, so we both escaped a fate worse than death. I also remember my male childminder ('ayah') spilling methylated spirits into a corner of the lavatory and setting fire to it so I could see the 'spirits' dance.

It was with this same man that I had the first defining experience of my life. My grandmother lived on the top floor of a three-storey house. I don't think it was situated in a particularly salubrious part of the city. When I later travelled to Calcutta to visit my mother and her third husband, the streets were wide, and their block of flats had well-tended gardens. My granny's house, on the other hand, was on a busy road, the front steps coming down to the pavement. It was up on the flat roof of this building, with only a three-brick-high parapet, that I would go with my ayah to fly my kites. These wonderfully inventive things were made of tissue paper with colourful zigzag designs stretched across two cruciform struts of wood. I was aged four or five, and these kites were almost my size. Their string was wound around a slatted cane lozenge with a stick running through it for handles. And the first twenty feet of string had tiny shards of glass glued to it!

The thrill was this: when your kite was flying, say, fifty feet up and it was close to another flown from another roof (and the sky sometimes seemed filled with these garish swoops of paper), you would try and entangle your kite with another's line so you could saw it loose with your glass-string. Once it was cut through, you tried to hook the loose kite with yours and haul both back. Of course, it never got to that. Cutting the other kite loose, yes – or theirs yours – but trying to catch a free-floating kite drifting in every direction the breeze took it was nigh-on impossible. I saw it done, but it was way beyond me and my ayah, who would have me in his embrace, pulling the string for me, manoeuvring the kite, preventing my squirming body from falling off the roof. But if a freed kite landed on your roof . . . joy!

Teaching me the skills of kite banditry was not my ayah's only forte. He was also good at squatting down, parting his loincloth and offering his erection to be stroked - which was apparently something I could do because soon there would be a pool of liquid between our hunched figures. That was all. He never touched me. But I tried it on myself later in bed, and although there was an incredible sensation, there was NO WHITE STUFF. I must have gone on flying kites with him and I suppose I must have told my grandmother of our new game because he, like the other men in my infant life, disappeared.

What else do I remember from then? Everything was enveloped in heat and sunshine and sudden downpours. Tipping the egg seller's produce into a bucket of water to see which eggs floated (bad) and which sank (good). The man who was perhaps my first stepfather, the one with the gun; the methylated spirits dancing; and my mother in some block of flats climbing over the bannister screaming that she was going to throw herself down the stairwell if . . . my grandmother shouting at her and me wailing. The visits to the bazaar with its covered stalls, the tiny rooved cubicles selling brilliantly coloured cloth, spices, meat, vegetables, combs, needles, thread, picture frames, bangles . . . and the smells! In my mid-teens, revisiting Calcutta (nowadays Kolkata), I tried analysing those odours: sweat, spoiling meat, drying cow dung which was used for cooking, herbs, dust, and could it have been rose water? And the overall din; the beggars with missing limbs (often dismembered as children so they could beg more effectively) crying or murmuring low, their eyes beseeching, their bowls thrust towards you; the scabby barking dogs everywhere; the bicycle bells; the rickshaws with large adults aboard and skinny running men pulling them, weaving their way in and out of the honking cars; the sacred cows being shouted at but avoided; and the cajoling cries of the stallholders. All ear-splittingly exciting when the world is new.

In the hot weather, Europeans went down like ninepins as diseases like dysentery flourished, particularly in urban areas. So, the Brits would send their little darlings north, up country, to the mountains – to the Himalayas – to be schooled in possibly the most breathtaking scenery in the world. From here, I could see a far-off range of even higher mountains with Everest somewhere in there, and the snapshots in my adult mind are of a rare and beautiful sight. But a bit like dogs who are oblivious of their surroundings, as a child, I mostly remember the walks, churning through the leaves of wild strawberries looking for the fruit, which we ate as we moved along in file, two abreast, and the one or two black leeches on each leg after removing my rubber boots.

You always knew when you were coming to a waterfall because the air about you seemed to move, there was an increasing roar, and your world reverberated. Then the paths became narrow shelves in the openings of the steeply sloping forest, water crashing down from above on one side into a boiling pool which overflowed across your way – a flat racing stream, the pebbles underfoot – before it rushed over a sharp edge on the other side to fall and shatter again further down the mountain. Sometimes we had to turn back; the water ran just too thick and fast for safe crossing. Then there were the little opaque sacks of snakes' eggs – *aah*, the tiny worms in the gluey fluid!

The Haunted House just half a mile up the hill from our school – why were we scared, and who told us the house was haunted? And why did that word frighten us? Racing paper boats in the gully that surrounded the schoolhouse, which was a torrential river during the monsoon. The playground cut out of the side of the mountain with its climbing frame – I was fearless on that, and I was a daredevil on stilts.

I was soon removed from my first – huge – school because I seemed to always be in the sanatorium in those first nine months when I had every childhood ailment: whooping cough, measles, mumps and chickenpox (some of those, anyway!). My other memory of that school is that, to my shame, I peed into the shoes under my bed because I was too afraid to wander through the vast dormitory in the dark to find the lavatory. Walking was a bit squelchy the following day!

The second of my schools must have been small because it wasn't an imposing building and there were only three dormitories of maybe eight or ten children. I know I loved playing the piano, and apparently, I was good. Odd, isn't it, how as a child, you effortlessly master skills that later become problematic? For instance, in those days, I'm told I could speak Hindi every bit as well as I spoke English. Between leaving those schools aged six and now, the piano and I have been only cheerful acquaintances, and I can only remember the Hindi words for fresh lime squash.

The schools were a long day's train trip from Calcutta, so to save shuttling us little people back and forth, we were at school for nine months on end with a three-month holiday which included Christmas. Looking back on it, nine months seems a long time for a child of five to be away from its parents – or granny in my case.

Back in the smaller and happier mountain school, I was told one day my father – *my* father, what's a father? – was taking me back to Calcutta. Presumably my luggage was packed because I next remember this tall man in a dark blue overcoat (my 'father') shaking my small hand in a grown-up way and ushering me into this gleaming black car. ('You can call me Daddy'. Was his name really Daddy? Mr Daddy, perhaps? Where had he come from? What had he got to do with me?). The children and teachers waved, and we were off. But Calcutta was a million miles away, and we spent what seemed like hours in the car snaking down the mountainside to the railway station. Sitting next to him in the back, I was violently sick all over his smart blue coat. I remember my dismay and his revulsion. It wasn't the most auspicious start to a relationship.

I'll tell you now because I might forget later: this man married my mother because she was beautiful, a tomboy, a wonderful horsewoman, a keen golfer, and a good tennis player. Was she a natural at these in England before she came over, or did she learn them assiduously in India so as to join the social set and attract a wealthy husband? I'm asking because I have almost no idea of what my mother did between my ages of zero to seven (I was with my granny when I wasn't at school). I've been told often enough she could charm men, women and children out of the trees. Sounds risky – what are they doing there? – but that's how the saying goes. Mr Daddy was a well-to-do English businessman abroad who needed a hostess. He got himself a charming, fun and very attractive woman for his social obligations. He also got this woman's mother and a child – the latter not something he particularly wanted, but it was an all or nothing deal, I'm sure, so he agreed gallantly to the entire package. (She did all right for us all, did my mother. For instance, years later, when Lord Mountbatten came to Calcutta for the transfer of power to the Indians, as the wife of the leading businessman in the city, she was asked to be Mountbatten's hostess on board ship for the series of meetings and greetings of Indian dignitaries).

My latest father, Mr. Daddy, was an honourable man, and he always treated me well. Formally, but well. He spent a lot of money on my education, but thankfully, as far as he was concerned, proper schooling for the children of well-to-do English parents in India meant sending them five thousand miles back to the Homeland, England. So now we were well-to-do off we jolly-well-went. No, off I jolly-well-went. They brought me to England, stayed with me for a short while, and then went back to their lives in India.

Although the war with Germany was over, the Japanese hadn't surrendered, so it was thought safer to do the journey home by ship. We crossed India from right to left by train, in a roomy compartment with stable doors so one could see the passing hinterland out of the open top. If I looked back along the length of the train, I saw men and women on the roof and hanging off the sides, and endless countryside with glints of water fringed by palms, farmers in the paddy fields, harnessed buffaloes, and once a working elephant. At the stations where the train stopped, we were regaled with shouted offers of food, adding to the noise of the steam engine at rest.

The journey must have been a wonderful experience, but early on in the week, I was bored. If only I could do that trip now.

In Bombay (now Mumbai), we boarded a troopship, the *Britannia* – civilians in separate cabins on the top levels, and the troops everywhere else. I had the lower bunk in our tiny cabin, my mother in the bunk above, and across the narrowest strip of the aisle was another mother with her daughter. I was six going on seven, on a ship with nothing to do and nothing to look at except the sea, and then more and more sea. The only excitement seemed to be a chance we might be torpedoed. Why was that word frightening? 'Torpedoed', and 'haunted'. It must have been the way the adults looked when they said them.

But the trip through the Suez Canal was memorable. Moving the enormous ship slowly through this narrow corridor in the sand, seeing camels for the first time lolloping along the tops of the dunes on either side, sometimes higher than the decks and often so close you could hear them grunting. And then there were the little kids diving off their canoes to catch glinting coins which the boats' passengers threw into the water and the children's huge smiles as they surfaced, spluttering and holding the coin above their heads to show us how clever they had been. I could have watched the animals and children forever. And of course, the overboard shopping, just like at the railway stations, but now by rope. Small boats alongside our troopship filled to the brim with raffia-work and fruit – bananas still on their stems, green coconuts, grapefruit – and us passengers lowering hemp baskets on long ropes, then pulling up the fresh produce and sending the payment back down in the basket which of course was filled again by someone else: 'We don't want that, thank you very much'. Puzzled looks and ear-cupping below: 'No, no, we don't want any more fruit. Thank you'. The gully-gully men in their little boats were suddenly deaf. 'Oh, very well'. As the baskets belonged to the ship, they had to be pulled up again, and the unwanted goods paid for by lowering the now moneyed receptacle – which was immediately refilled! The trick was to swing the basket into the reach of the man to be paid, not another merchant, or you got yet more produce. But one needed to be mighty crafty to swing a light, almost empty bag with only a few coins in it and get it right. Us children were raucous with delight when our parents were outwitted by the natives! The most fun we'd had in ages.

And two moments of drama! My mother later told me that I had sleepwalked during one afternoon siesta, and in bright daylight, had climbed over the ship's railing. Hand over hand, I had travelled a longish distance along the ship's side before I was seen. Apparently, there was lots of alarm and shushing: 'Don't wake him! He'll fall into the sea'. I do remember the last part: I was hand-over-handing the other side of a lifeboat where I was inaccessible. Me, railing, lifeboat. Halfway, I woke up to see my brand-new father beckoning me kindly towards the far end. Looking down, the waves seemed miles below, but I don't remember being afraid. When I was hauled aboard, the usual anger and relief, and hugging went on. I *do* remember I enjoyed being the centre of attention. Made a nice change. *Aah*, poor little diddums. I can hardly remember him.

It took fifteen days by ship from Bombay to Liverpool. So, two or more weeks after the start of our travels, we arrived in England, my new home.

We docked oh so carefully, manoeuvring gently into the berth in the cold grey of the evening, with the clamour of clanking, hooting and shouting. I remember mostly the noise, but the chilly dampness in the unfriendly fading light I can feel right now. This strange cold was home, was it?

We were to spend the last night on the ship before disembarking early the next morning. That's when the second drama happened. I suppose I had been asleep because I drowsily remember my mother leaning down to me out of her berth above my head. Then there was a whoosh. I tried to sleep through the continuous noise that followed, and it wasn't until the next day when my mother, her head bandaged, came to collect me from the cabin that I understood what had gone on. Having tucked me up with difficulty from above, she'd overbalanced and fallen headfirst onto the cabin floor and had been transported to the ship's infirmary to be examined and dealt with. *That* explained all the racket. There I was trying to sleep! She seemed fine. But then isn't that often the way?

CHAPTER 2
Sinking Ego

The cacophony of disembarkation and the icy darkness smeared with sulphurous lights is what I remember most about the following morning. Where had all the colour gone? And the next thing I know, I've crossed another country by train, this time from left to right, from northwest England to East Anglia, finding myself in a tiny bungalow which belonged to Mr Daddy's recently dead mother. (For all our sakes, I'm going to call this stepfather, Geoffrey John Gardner, my father from now on. He did change my surname to his by deed poll, he did support me all the time I was at school, and he was around longest). But this stranger, my father, was only in Essex with us for a month before returning to his business in Calcutta.

My new home was a squat, square, thirties bungalow, surrounded by drab wintery fields, with only a couple of rather larger houses on the other side of the road, in an altogether flat landscape.

We rubbed along well enough, this now full-time mother and me. (My grandmother must have been left in India). I don't remember much merriment with this comparative stranger until later in our relationship. Still, we were both in the strangest of positions: she coping full-time with a youngster in a part of the world she didn't know, and me transplanted into a cold, damp grey autumn, weather unlike anything I'd ever experienced, with nothing but white faces around, and an icy coolth seemingly laminated to my skin however many clothes I had on.

This was 1945, and there was still a great shortage of food, so there was rationing. In exchange for coupons which my mother presented in various food shops in the nearby village of Kelvedon, we got an egg each a week, a small amount of milk, tiny cubes of cheese or a thin slab of butter and one piece of meat – whatever the butcher had left in his shop. Bread didn't seem in short supply. The fruit we could get was grown in England – nothing as exotic as bananas, papayas, or the heavenly scented little Indian mangoes that are still my favourite.

The tiny orchard which surrounded the house had maybe ten trees in all: apples, pears and plums – great for a small boy to climb but none of them fruiting when we arrived that late autumn. I can only remember potatoes and Brussels sprouts in the vegetable patch – the Brussels because they were these green sticks with knobs on; knobs which you twisted off and boiled and were very disgusting to eat. And we got some eggs from the half-dozen hens in a wire-netted enclosure at the bottom of the back garden and which wandered free during the day. I suppose they were my first pets, as it became my job to feed them morning and evening, release them after their breakfast meal of scraps, and collect them together at night to have their evening meal before shutting them into their wooden house with its flimsy wire-netting door.

Their eggs were hardly ever where they should be, in the nesting boxes or in our tiny garden, so it was a great adventure searching for them in the ditches and hedgerows around the surrounding fields. When triumphantly found, they were sometimes so old they were inedible. Those ones certainly bobbed about on the water!

Oh yes, and once, in search of more food, my mother shot a pheasant with an air rifle. She was hunting for rabbits. I don't suppose then there would have been a quibble about shooting game out of season so soon after the war.

In fact, that air rifle figured quite prominently in my mother's new English country life. The radio gave out the news that a Famous Murderer had escaped from his prison. I presume this prison was nearby because suddenly the house was an air-gun-toting fortress, and my mother would sit by an open window at night (I suppose this must have been early winter), challenging every noise the country makes, and occasionally shooting pellets into the darkness. She told me later that once, after a shouted warning and a pellet, she'd heard running feet! Perhaps it really was this dangerous man. More likely a scavenger. Whatever, she was protecting our castle and her child – who it seems had continued his sleepwalking, but now as a bear. What a dilemma for her: murderers outside and the high-pitched growl of a seven-year-old boy prowling around the house behind her. What to shoot first?

My father returned from India to be with us over the Christmas period, primarily to book me into the local village school, but much more important as far as I was concerned, to teach me how to ride my first bicycle. I was going to need that to accompany my mother into the village. The sight of this gleaming contraption with its shiny spokes, its high leather saddle, pedals that whirled, and a BELL thrilled me. I took to the task of learning to ride it rather as I did later with my pony in India: the same grim determination with lots of falling off! The determination one needs to keep two big wheels upright – no little safety wheels for me – and on a course that doesn't always fetch up in a ditch. The scrapes and bruises from the spills, the wild wobbling, the guiding hand on the saddle, the exhilarating triumph of a ride down the narrow country road unaided. Was any achievement in later life so exciting, or so completely fulfilling? (By the way, I don't want you to think they encouraged me to learn to ride on a busy road. They weren't trying to save on school fees. No, because of petrol rationing there were almost no cars about, except those driven for essential services).

To me, the Kelvedon village school means one big room, like the proverbial village hall, with eight or nine other children. We sat on the floor – I don't remember desks there – with our crayons, or recited our timetables, or read out loud, or looked at a map of the world (India was only a handsbreadth away from England – that didn't seem right) or played games. We brought our meals with us – a sandwich, a piece of fruit, sometimes a sweet. This last really is engraved on my memory: sweets were rationed and had to be eked out over a week – one a day if you were clever and had used your coupon for a roll of fruit gums. But if you chose any of the bigger sweets, peppermints, or lemon sherbets (for the lovely surprise of that taste explosion), these were in shorter supply, so one could only get three of those a week. Sweet coupons made me a sugar addict for life.

Then I was sent south.

I have absolutely no memory of getting to my boarding school proper in England, St Wilfrid's: my first day, my first impressions, nothing. This preparatory school was on the south coast, just outside the town of Seaford in Sussex, which is itself situated below the South Downs. These Downs were hills, not a fraction as big as the Himalayas I was used to, and we walked them regularly. And that's when I first learned that in this new foreign country of mine, England, downs as often as not meant ups!

After I'd been safely delivered like a parcel to my prep school (it must have been after my ninth birthday, so in September), my mother and father left the country to get back to their life in India.

The week before school started, so just before they left, I had been driven up to Norfolk and introduced to three elderly ladies who ran a home from home for 'Raj Orphans' like me, and at the end of that first unmemorable term at this new school in Sussex, the pupils were put on a train to London, where I was met by a brisk and efficient woman (a Universal Aunt as the company is called) who transported me across London to another large railway station. She saw me onto a second train, this one going up to Norwich in Norfolk. And waiting for me, there was Joyce, a gaunt no-nonsense woman, one of the three elderly ladies my parents had instructed me to call aunts (Joyce, Mary and Dorcas – I suddenly had aunts galore) and was bussed to their large Victorian house for the holidays.

I regret for all sorts of reasons that I have so few memories of my early years. Not for me the total recall of a relation's whiskery face bent over the pram. But as I grew older and became a little Englander, my memories come more sharply into focus. I know I enjoyed my first independent boys' school because I got on well with work, the other children, and my teachers. I was liked and liked back.

I was good at English, pretty good on the piano, and pretty ordinary at games which were new to me. Hold on, I was a whizz on roller-skates!

I do remember three faces from St Wilfrid's clearly.

My English master was a Mr Lousada. Of course he taught me the rules and intricacies of our language, but I'll thank him to my dying day for introducing me to classical music. He would play his hissy shellac records in a large mahogany wind-up gramophone in Musical Appreciation class. Mostly it was music with stories: be it Saint-Saëns's 'Danse Macabre' (the bones rattling as the skeletons danced, the sad violin strain for the dead lovers, the cock's crow at dawn); 'The Sorcerer's Apprentice' with the terrified lad watching the waters surge; *Pétrouchka*, the story of the puppet who falls in love with the ballerina doll, and is slain by the Moor in the middle of the frantic fair outside the booths; Mussorgsky's 'Night on a Bare Mountain'; or Beethoven's Pastoral Symphony with all its beauty and drama, the hunting horn calls, and the storm followed by one of the most beguiling waltzes that man has ever imagined. Nearly all the music Mr Lousada played us youngsters was melodic – the most notable exception being 'The Iron Foundry' by some Russian – with tunes that lodged themselves in my head and remain there to this day. (I truly believe that nearly all of today's 'serious' music composers will be forgotten in a hundred years' time. Except perhaps for their cleverness. Even Bach, with his reliance on mathematical structure, would not be remembered and revered if it wasn't for the marvellous melodies he dotted around like rich currants in his carefully contrived slabs of music).

Mr Lousada put me up for the reading competition, which I won. I read a long paragraph from one of Captain John's Biggles books which described a sandstorm. I had to ask him how to pronounce *c.h.a.o.s.* – the strangest word – change, chuckle, children, *kayos*? And it was also he who persuaded me to be the prosecuting counsel in a make-believe trial ('Had the Head Gardener stolen the carrots and sold them elsewhere?' Yes, argued I – with flair I thought. No, was the jury's verdict on this most likeable man).

And I loved my piano teacher, Miss Becks (or Becky), a large sweetly powdered woman, sitting close beside me at the piano, who reintroduced me to crotchets and quavers and staves and keys, those black and white squiggles on a white page with corresponding black and white strips of ivory to be struck, gently or firmly, in strict but loving order. With one finger, I could recreate melodies like the ones I heard in Mr Lousada's class.

The third face is of a boy whose parents would invite me out at weekends when they were down seeing their son. We were friends, he and I, but those visits twice or three times a term, every term for about four years, by someone else's parents who would take me out of school and treat me as one of their own, were acts of kindness and generosity which, thinking about it even now, can make me a little emotional.

I was bright enough at school to get by without attracting adverse attention, captain of my form; eventually a prefect, but in no way brilliant at anything – except roller skating.

By the by: I also had a crush on a lad whose name and face I can't for the life of me remember, but I do know I would sometimes, after everyone was asleep in the smallest school dormitory, creep over to his bed and try to inhale his breath – which smelled like boiled sweets. As an adult, I've thought of what would have happened if he'd woken up to see a face looming so closely over him. Aargh!

As for my home from home in Norfolk with the old ladies: my parents told me later their father had gambled all his money away, leaving them nothing but this large house. The only way the three women could think of to keep the roof over their heads was to take in children whose parents worked abroad. One of the three had once been married, I think, but the others were spinsters, and I'm not sure how much any of them really liked children. Not that they were unkind. Except for the food which Dorcas cooked – putrid – sometimes literally. My father once dislodged a clump of stinking hair from the spout of a coffee pot they used for guests. And the home-baked cakes with the suspicious green bits . . .?

The house was a three-storey building called Sankence, and I spent nearly eight years of my holiday life there. It had a large lawn in front, a sunken once-croquet lawn to one side, and an extensive overgrown vegetable garden behind – along with a yard full of turkeys and smelly border terriers. On the other side were stables. It was surrounded by fields, sparse of grass for the number of horses grazing them, and I suspect now they were all undernourished – needing oats, bran and beets as supplements. Facing the house, there were trees almost as tall as the house itself, easy climbers, and getting to the top made you the King of the Castle. You could almost see into the front boys' bedroom from up there, the attic where I slept with two others. (There were sometimes two more boys across the landing). The girls, the aunts, and any guests were in the six bedrooms on the first floor. There was also the bathroom where two of us children would share a bath twice a week. I don't remember any shenanigans.

The stables and vegetable garden were looked after by Baxter and Ruby – until one year Baxter left his wife and ran off with Ruby. After that, we groomed our ponies, cleaned their tack, took them to gymkhanas and horse shows, and in the winter, those of us who went hunting would ride to the meets. Those poor dear horses – we were never off their backs. They must have dreaded the holidays.

The one small grouse I have is that when I was living with the aunts, we were sent to bed at 6.30 every evening until I reached the age of sixteen. The only good thing about this was, after we'd been settled, the deaf old dears would retire to their sitting room on the ground floor to listen to the radio with the door shut. Twice a week when the programme changed at the local cinema, we'd go to bed fully dressed, and the moment we heard their downstairs door close, we'd be out of a ground floor window, up on our bicycles, and racing off to the flicks where, for thrupence, we could see John Payne and Maureen O'Hara battling giant squid, cowboys and Indians drummin' and thunderin', Lassie saving the world from villains, or soppy love stories. Afterwards, we'd get a bag of chips from the fish shop next door, and in the dark, wander down the road, walking our bicycles with one hand and lipping greasy potato chips from the bag into our mouths. Then, when we'd finished the chips, us boys would take it in turns to widdle our way down the centre line of the road as we walked the mile back to our beds. The girls, marching arm in arm behind us, would talk or sing, ignoring us louts. (Remembering them with arms linked must have meant that occasionally we'd take them to the town and back on the pillions of our bikes).

We got smiles but no love from our aunts, but I'm not complaining. I've been kissed throughout my life by elderly women, and they always, somehow, contrive to leave a streak of spittle on my face. Tell me if you know, just when is it polite to wipe it off?

Actually, I did get love from one of the boys. He and his sister's parents lived in the West Indies. I got on very well with Heather, but I was totally smitten by her brother, Richard. The only time I expressed my feelings overtly was when I kissed him on the mouth, telling everyone present it was how I'd like to kiss his sister. They might have believed me, but I'm not sure he was convinced. That was as far as it went, I knew nothing about the tongue thing then. I was fourteen or so, and it was my first sexually motivated kiss, but for this sophisticated lothario, daring in the ways of the world, bedtime was still 6.30.

I've worked it out that for those first nine years in England, between the ages of eight to seventeen, I spent eight months of the year at boarding school, and the two shorter holidays, two months in total, with my 'aunts' in Norfolk – and two months a year with my parents. I would either go to see them in Calcutta for the summer holiday, or alternately, they would come to England for those eight summer weeks. When they came over here, we would tour Europe most of the holiday, driving through France, Switzerland or Italy. Once or twice, we went to Ireland and stayed just south of Dublin, a place called Malahide. I have photographs of myself wrapped in a towel, having just emerged from swimming in the Irish Sea. You can tell my skin is blue even though the photos are black and white.

When I was twelve, I passed enough exams to get into a well-known boarding school in Wiltshire, originally funded for the sons of impecunious clergy but by then a posh public school for those with secular riches. This was Marlborough College.

My life changed dramatically for the worse.

At six o'clock one darkening September evening, having shaken my father's hand and given a last desperate hug and kiss to my mother, I was left outside a looming house at the top of a drive, my overnight suitcase in my hand, listening to my parents' car receding into the dusk as they disappeared for another year. I don't remember ever feeling so alone, and I was fighting tears. A new boy blubbing – I'd better not be seen doing that! As there were no lights on in the front of the building, I wandered through the dark around to the back into a courtyard. There was only one door into the house that I could make out, and I opened it, entering into a blaze of light and sound. This being the first day of term, the boys – almost all of them much older than I was used to – were rushing about, talking loudly, laughing, and, it would seem, having a whale of a time. Nobody took any notice of me, so after a few minutes, my suitcase still in my hand, I wandered into the empty locker room and sat down on the wooden bench. I felt abandoned, cocooned in misery, everything so alien. I hope I didn't cry. At last, it became obvious that the boys were darting back and forth unpacking their trunks, so without any helpful guide from anyone as to where to put things in this strange building, I tried to do the same.

I must have meshed into this new life, but I don't know how. I don't remember now a single interested or friendly face in my Junior House for the whole of that first year.

You'll need to know the formation of the college for what's coming next, so let me explain.

My prep school had had 120 boys aged between seven and twelve, but this new school, this college, had over eight hundred, aged twelve to eighteen. We were quartered in Out Houses and In Houses.

The Out Houses were for boys with parents who could afford to have their children some short distance away from the centre of the school; these Out Houses being large detached buildings set in their own gardens, so presumed more pleasant and rural. Two of the three In Houses, along with the dining hall, the chapel and most of the classrooms, enclosed a large grass quadrangle with its crisscrossed paths. That was the hub of the college.

The less well-off children were immured in A House, B House or C House and remained where they were their entire time at college. The Out Houses consisted of Junior Out Houses and Senior Out Houses, with names like Preshute, Cotton House, or Barton Hill (my Junior House) and Littlefield (my Senior House). Boys moved after three years from a Junior House to a Senior House. Rotten idea. Having eventually established some sort of identity for yourself, a place in the hierarchy of your Junior House, you were removed to your Senior House, not knowing more than one or two of the forty older boys. A 'squit' at the bottom of the heap again.

Back to Barton Hill, my first Out House. My mother, who with my father interviewed my House Master, Mr. Brown, before my arrival, must have patronised him in her usual way. It's the only explanation. My father was a courteous man, so it wouldn't have been him. Otherwise, I don't know the reason for what happened. Mr. Brown was a man with a trench down the centre of his forehead (a war wound, we boys were told), a man who disliked me intensely. I was an average, rather plump boy, who had been liked by his fellows till now, someone who did his best to get by – only occasionally thinking himself more important than others when he was on roller-skates. Why, then, did Mr. Brown take such a loathing to me?

To give you a slant on my mother's attitudes to her fellow human beings: she told me that years later in her life, when on a crowded London bus, she had slapped a black bus conductress for being rude and had her face slapped in return, she was outraged at the temerity of this Jamaican servant. Not to excuse her, but she came from a background in India where plenty of people were eager for the British penny. Although she and my father were very pleasant to this Indian man who made our clothes on a treadle sewing-machine on our verandah, or that Indian who tested my father's bathwater, dried him when he stepped out onto the mat and dusted him with powder before helping him on with his attire, these men – along with the chauffeur, the head manservant, my mother's personal servant, my servant when I was there, and the cook – were definitely lesser beings. My parents thought the British kindness towards them was compensation enough. (Included in the list of lesser beings out there were the Dutch, the Germans, and any other non-British race. We had our superior position in the world, and the others were patronised with polite smiles of recognition, but there was no social mingling. Brexit, anyone?)

So how did she talk to my new school's House Master before I even met him? I'll give you a clue as to the result. In their first term, the new boys, the 'squits', were sent out on a cross-country run. Bicycling along the road beside our panting, heaving, lumbering, not-yet-teen bodies, our breath steaming the air with every jolt of our feet, two senior boys with long canes encouraged us along with thwacks on our bare legs. We ran for a mile, nothing I'd ever attempted before. I was podgy, and I came in fourth last. Although we'd all been told beforehand it was only the last two boys who'd have to do the run again, my housemaster insisted I join them – but the third from last boy was excused.

Bullying was endemic. In my Junior House, a year or two before my arrival, a boy had been asphyxiated. He'd been put in a wicker basket by the seniors, then hung over a dampened fire. All he could breathe was smoke. He was taken unconscious to the sanatorium. The then House Master stopped that particular practice, but by the time I got there, there was another couple of tortures for the new boys. We bathed daily in hip baths, ovals of porcelain not much larger than a big basin in which only our bums and middle were in the water, our upper bodies slouched with our legs dangling over the edge. Every Friday night, the bathroom windows were left open, the baths filled with cold water, and large enamel water jugs, full to the brim, were left waiting. Any Saturday morning that dawned cold enough for the seniors' purpose, us twelve-year-olds were dragged out of our beds one at a time, thrown naked into a bath and jug after jug of water was poured over our heads without let-up. Sobbing for breath meant lungsful of water, so after what seemed an eternity, we were lugged out of the baths onto the floor, coughing and spluttering, while the next unfortunate was doused. That particular torture only happened to me once but, until then, us squits had been told every Friday night what to expect on Saturday morning, and we waited nervously for the first five weeks – until the morning dawned that was cold enough to be fun for the seniors.

And just before the end of that Autumn term, early December it would have been, the same boys – all but me – were dragged out of bed, stripped of their pyjamas, and forced naked out onto the fire escape. (There was no ladder, so the only way anyone could have escaped a fire was to have jumped down two floors). They were left there shivering in the early morning for twenty minutes. The senior tormentors had hoped for snow, but – sadly for them – it was just very cold. I never found out why, but the older lad in the next bed to mine (I don't believe I spoke to him the entire time I was there) told the raggers to leave me alone, so of all the squits, I was the only one to see their humiliation from the warmth and safety of my bed.

I tried to prevent these practices when I was a little more senior, which did my popularity no good at all, and the year after that, it was stopped altogether. My House Master let it be known to the prefects that it had been stopped because I had complained to my mother – which made me an outcast! It was a complete lie. It wasn't until the boy who *had* complained was taken from the school by his parents that the general realisation that it had had nothing to do with me came out. But why did Mr. Brown tell the seniors that? I hope you can see why I think it might have had something to do with my mother? Soon after the boy was removed from college, my House Master was sacked by the school board.

His temporary replacement just happened to be my piano teacher. Once he was installed as head of Barton Hill, if we were called to his study after games – and it always seemed to be after games because we were still in our shorts – he'd beckon us to stand next to him and absentmindedly run his hand up the inside of our nearest leg as he talked to us. His fingers never got very far, not with me anyway. I quite liked him, although, funnily enough, when I was sitting on the piano stool at my lesson, and he stood next to me, it never crossed my mind to run my hand up *his* leg.

I had left the sunny warmth and friendship of my previous school in the south of England for the dank unfriendliness of this huge institution in Wiltshire, and I found it hard to bear. (When I was about thirty, I told my mother I wouldn't have treated a dog the way they treated me over these years. She asked me on her death bed if I still felt that. Of course, I said no, but I was lying). Without relations or friends in the vicinity, I never had an exeat – a weekend away from the school. As a result of my wretchedness, my schoolwork suffered, and I dropped down from always being in the top three of my class in Sussex to always being in the bottom three in Wiltshire. Bloody place. I was there for four endless years.

And then, of course, there were the army games we played in the Cadet Corps. (National Service was still in force). We each had a uniform, along with gaiters, webbing belt, berets with cap badges, and boots which we attacked with red hot spoons (courtesy of Bunsen burners), spreading the black boot polish over the toecaps, spitting on them, scrubbing them with rags, trying vainly to produce black leather mirrors; Brasso for the badge and belt buckle. The material of the uniforms was so coarse I came up in a rash, so I was told to wear pyjamas underneath. Felt ashamed, a bit like a hot sissy, but rather that than itch. And we would march up and down with our rifles over our shoulders, or present arms, or stand at ease with our cleaned and polished rifles aslant, being barked at, pretending to be soldiers. You can see from the photo that even though our house team had won a cup, I have a pocket button undone. The enemy wouldn't have cowered at the sight of me.

In this murk of unhappiness, I found solace in sex. Sex with other boys was new to me, and it was plentiful in my Junior House. For a merciful while it filled your mind.

For some reason, at the very top of our house, under the eaves, there was a mattress on the floor, which always seemed to have a clean cover. It was where other boys with the same inclination as myself would find ourselves in break periods tossing each other off – this was a phrase I'd heard my first term, and with a dreadful excitement divined it was what I'd been doing ever since my Indian nanny had shown me his cock. So tweaking my nub had an officially recognised title: tossing off. Mind you, my nub, now I was back to noticing it, was a deal bigger, bigger still with a tweak – altogether odd.

A few of us juniors masturbated each other up in the attic on the clean mattress, under the beds in the dormitories – under because there was a patrol of these out-of-bound places during the day – and in the photographic darkroom, anywhere we could find privacy. These co-handlers weren't in any way friends. We were just excited boys attached to one another by hand and mutual need. Must tell you: before I'd left my Junior House, I was producing WHITE STUFF!

Once in my Senior House, we boys had separate studies, so mutual masturbation became easier. Strung along either side of a corridor, these studies were tiny rooms, with ninth-or tenth-hand furniture: a desk, a wooden chair, a small cupboard for books and things, with just enough room for a cramped armchair. Best of all, a visitor had to knock and be asked in before entering. When you were a prefect, you got a bigger room, with nicer furniture. However, the prefects were the ones you avoided. They were allowed to beat you at their own discretion; beat you on the bum with a slipper. Not a cane, but painful enough.

Back to the mundane. Here's an example of a day: up early in your eighteen-bed dormitory, ablutions (the lavatory stalls had no doors on them – for obvious reasons), get dressed, down to breakfast, then the half-mile walk to the chapel, the bell tolling all the time. If you weren't within the chapel gates by that last *dong*, you could expect punishment. Punishment meant learning and reciting twenty to thirty lines of poetry to a prefect. If at the end of your allotted chunk of verse there was no punctuation, no matter, you stopped. I still don't like poetry. Once inside the chapel, all eight hundred or so lads and masters with their wives sang together, accompanied by the large chapel organ. (In my last year, I graduated from the piano to that mighty organ). Afterwards, hurrying around the inner school, we would go to one class after another, a single toll of the bell marking the start and end of each period. At one o'clock, all eight hundred of us joined together in the Dining Hall for lunch. To a boy, we found the food unpalatable.

Then afternoon classes, same routine as the morning – except for Wednesdays and Saturdays, when we'd repair to our houses, don our sports gear, and walk miles to whichever pitch we were designated. Cricket in the summer, rugby in the autumn, and hockey in the winter. I enjoyed rugby; if you were roughed up in the scrum or on the field, that was part of the excitement (I was a hooker in the scrum, make of that what you will) – but hockey! Running alongside one of your team, and he lifts his hockey stick to pass or score a goal, you can lose an eye. I didn't sign up for that. Or we might go to the gym. I took fencing classes there, in foil, sabre and épée. I also once tried a handstand on the parallel bars unsupervised and getting my body erect went too far over and plummeted down to the base onto the top of my head. ('How many fingers can you see? What day of the week is it? Off to the San'). If we weren't doing one of the above, it was the time for piano practice, or we could book ourselves into a squash court or rackets court – tennis in the summer, too. (Never tried rackets: too bloody dangerous. But I enjoyed squash). Or one could take woodwork classes which I did for a time but nearly lost a finger at the lathe. (However, those carpentry lessons did enable me later in life to make my mother a fitted built-in wardrobe and myself some kitchen units). And casting pots was fun, the slimy clay spinning under your hands as you gently throttled it. If our house teams weren't playing the seasonal game that day, and we weren't doing anything else, we could go for bicycle rides. The only stipulation throughout this free period was that every boy had to stay outside his house for a minimum of two hours. Immediately after lunch, we could also wander into town and purchase whatever we fancied with whatever pocket money our parents gave us. (We were still hungry, so egg and chips with Tizer was a favourite).

Back to the house for high tea, free time, then prep in our studies. After prep, we'd have house prayers, at which I sometimes accompanied the hymns on an upright piano – I didn't offer, I was volunteered. Half an hour to get to our bedrooms, clean those bits of our bodies which came easily to hand, ten minutes reading, and then lights out. No talking. End of day.

I forgot to mention: if anyone was going to be slippered, it would happen immediately before lights out, within earshot. Nobody cried out – if they were in tears on their way back to bed, they couldn't be seen in the dark. For these small mercies, many thanks.

For four years nobody, but nobody at college mattered to me, nor I to them.

CHAPTER 3
The Tubby Chrysalis

Dogs and horses have always been my favourite animals, and at the age of thirteen, I thought I'd like to be a vet. I could have chosen those two specialities now, but in those days, if I'd wanted to train as a veterinary surgeon, I would have needed to specialise in one or the other: horses and cows, or dogs and cats. And to qualify, I'd need to take a seven-year course at the Veterinary College in Dublin. Seven more years of learning! Seemingly no longer bright, it did cross my dull mind to wonder if I could make it. I thought, perhaps, I'd get through on keenness.

However, when I was fifteen and in my Senior House, I put my name down to be in a play, *The Knight of the Burning Pestle*, a comedy set in Elizabethan London, which was to be performed in the Memorial Hall, an enormous school auditorium across the road from Barton Hill. It seated the entire school, masters and staff. I played A Citizen in the Crowd, without lines, just assenting and dissenting with grumbles and groans, making believe I was engaged in serious conversations with other Citizens. It was the most fun I'd had at Marlborough up till then! So, six months later, I enlisted to do Shakespeare's *Julius Caesar*, and this time I was given a part that made a contribution to the story. It had a death scene! In some town newspaper, I was picked out as 'also very effective in his role as Titinius . . . was . . .' *me*. People who hadn't noticed I was alive suddenly seemed more aware – my new Littlefield Senior House Master, Mr 'Jumbo' Jennings, for a start.

At the beginning of what turned out to be my final year, I was chosen to play one of the male leads in a very funny modern farce, *See How They Run*. On stage, I sang, I fooled about, made the audience laugh – and overnight, I became one of the most popular boys in the house. I acquired a nickname: Laurie – short for Laurence Olivier, but because I was still quite plump, one of the more unkind told me it was spelt Lorry. The farce was so successful, I found complete strangers smiling at me as I passed by on my way to classes, teachers patting me on the shoulder. What a popular fellow I was. I *was* liked. Suddenly. After four years of being a nobody.

Surprise, surprise, I changed my mind as to my future career.

The bit between my teeth, I recklessly entered the school piano competition. Not good enough. There was a moment in the Pathétique Sonata by Beethoven when I found my fingers cascading through the helter-skelter of notes, going unbidden into the minor for three bars. What the hell? And then all was well, my page-turning teacher beside me relaxed (I hadn't touched his leg), and I finished as suggested by Ludwig van. I didn't win, and I should have quit while I was ahead. (I left Marlborough working on Brahms's Second Rhapsody, just to give you an idea as to where I'd got to in my piano playing). I learned the clarinet for two terms but the only sounds I could produce from that honeyed instrument were a clack and a squawk. I was a treble in the school choir and sang *The Messiah* with a London orchestra and soloists; I was good at tennis and fencing – and found myself up in London at the Public School Championships representing Marlborough in foil and épée. Was there nothing this suddenly confident boy couldn't do? (Apart from the clarinet). Power-mad, I moved from the piano on to the other keyboard instrument that was readily available: the mighty chapel organ with its four consoles and pedals. Practising one afternoon during the rest period after lunch, I was inspired to pound out a popular song of the day called 'I Believe', which I'd heard sung over the radio by a sobbing crooner. As the words included 'every time I hear a newborn baby cry, or touch a leaf, or see the sky, then I know why I believe', I felt the sentiment expressed justified my belting it out in a church. So there I was, stamping away with my feet while playing all the keyboards, the air throbbing, the stained glass windows rattling, when a breathless master hurtled through the chapel doors and ordered me to stop –

and there endeth my only public organ recital.

My English teacher told me that if I wanted to be an actor, I should go to drama school – whatever that meant. So with his help, I applied to go to the only drama school he knew of, the Royal Academy of Dramatic Art, and shortly afterwards, he received two pages of around ten speeches through the post. The letter enclosed suggested I work on two contrasting speeches and bring a classical piece of my own choosing to the audition in six weeks' time.

I knew not what was wanted of this new adventure ('a classical piece of my own choosing'), but my teacher was seemingly so knowledgeable about this new career path I'd so impulsively chosen that I don't remember a moment of anxiety.

Algernon in Oscar Wilde's *The Importance of Being Earnest* could conceivably be played by a young man near my age, so the master suggested I do that (I hadn't seen the play), and because 'contrasting' probably meant something very different, I picked out one of the suggestions from the list which was a piece of high melodrama from a modern play called *A Bill of Divorcement*. In it, a middle-aged man calls his household together to berate his wife for her infidelity, his temper rising to a mighty passion – or that's how it read to me. I wasn't yet seventeen, and my teacher wasn't at all sure as to its suitability but went along with my choice. Oh, and the piece of Shakespeare of our choosing was again of someone young.

As a lad, I'd always been somewhat intimidated by my father. He was very proper. The sixteen-year-old me found the courage to ask him if I could go to drama school and was gratified he accepted the proposal without fuss. My parents were in India at the time, and he asked my mother to open an envelope he'd given her years before. On the piece of paper inside, he'd written, 'Kerry will be an actor'. He'd predicted this at a time I'd thought I wanted to be a veterinary surgeon. He told me many years later I'd been quite a show-off on our trips abroad, performing at the piano to strangers without prompting.

Already renowned in my mind, I went to Calcutta for my summer holiday.

My dad owned a string of racehorses – almost all of them bred in Australia. Trained by a family friend, Darell Farmer, who was also a jockey (a Gentleman jockey, mind!), they won a lot of races. My tomboy mother was the leading amateur female jockey in Calcutta and, sporting the Gardner colours of gold and turquoise, she won a lot of ladies' races.

In India, I'd been taught to ride at an early age by an Australian. This was how: I was plonked on the back of a pony with only a circle of rope around its neck, the gate in front of us which led to a sawdust corral was opened, the pony was given a thwack on the rump, we both leapt forward . . . and I fell off. That first session ended when I'd fallen off four times, the next week three times, then the week following twice. Four weeks later, my knees like limpets on the pony's side, I hadn't fallen off once. As a reward, the teacher put a saddle and bridle on the animal. I didn't jerk or pull on the reins because I'd learned to go with the pony's movements by then, and the stirrups seemed unnecessary. I was balanced without needing support under my feet, and once out of the corral, I found a use for the reins: steering.

I'd had my own pony in Norfolk when I'd stayed with the old dears; then when I'd outgrown it, I'd been given a horse (my parents made sure I lacked for nothing in the way of things), so I was never out of the saddle during the holidays. This particular holiday in India, I was given one of my father's racehorses to ride; he'd not long before developed a spavin, so he was being given a rest from racing while he mended. He was the most beautiful of horses to look at, but he was a pig to ride. His mouth was made of iron and to say he was easily startled is an understatement. A sudden noise, something unexpected coming into view, and he'd instantly be twelve feet away, sometimes leaping forward, but mostly sideways. But by that time in my riding career, I didn't dump easy. At my aunts' place, my first pony, Prince, the gentlest of creatures, had found every clump of spring primroses in the hedges threatening. They didn't move, but to him, they were obviously terrifying. We'd be trotting or cantering down a country lane, he'd suddenly stop dead – and I'd be thrown over his head. He used to do this to me once, twice every outing, every spring. I grew used to it. Keeping a wary eye out for those bloody primroses, I'd be lulled into five minutes of relaxed riding – then he'd suddenly stop, and over I'd go. Worked every time! But here in India, I was on a magnificent, prancing, snorting, nervous charger, a really beautiful beast, and I was on guard every moment, my knees clamped fiercely to his sides.

(I've never been afraid of falling off a horse – of falling generally. A tut of annoyance at myself as I tumble through the air completely relaxed, with as soft a landing as my tonnage can manage. Now that I'm older, the annoyance is usually at the mud all down my front. As an actor, later in life, I volunteered to be flung off an admittedly not very high 'rampart' in *Macbeth*, landing night after night on the stage some fifteen feet away without a bruise. *Bring me no more reports, let them fly all . . .*).

In Calcutta, we'd get up at 5 o'clock in the morning to go riding so that it would be done with before the day got too hot. My parents and I would be driven through the seediest part of town to the Tollygunge Club, an oasis of green, where we would find four or five of our racehorses, Darell, our trainer friend, and some Indian riders waiting. That holiday I only ever rode Belmore, my magnificent black steed (dark bay if you must be a stickler – you need to remember I'm a romantic) and my mother and father their hacks; the others, the young Indian jockeys and Darell, would exercise the remainder.

The Tollygunge clubhouse was situated in the middle of a racecourse with a nine-hole golf course looped through it, so for an hour, my mother, father, and I would ride around the perimeter of the club grounds, catching glimpses of our animals being trained on the track, the glass-topped high wall beside us deadening the sound of the extreme poverty on the other side.

Holding Belmore in check was exhausting for the first week

or so. Then, when he was used to me on his back, I took this beauty, trained only to race on the flat, over jumps. We rigged up poles and barrels, and although he was very erratic, he took to it like a balloon takes to a gale. But at least I stayed on him as we plunged in every direction. Then, although I'd never played polo and was never likely to, I borrowed a polo stick and, hardly ever connecting with the ball, swung the mallet around his body until he'd lost his fear of things whizzing past his ears – my father's idea.

I entered him in a jumping competition on the Maidan, the huge park in the centre of Calcutta, and after the admiring *Ooohs*, as we sailed over the first jump, he scattered each and every pole at the second. He scattered me too. When the obstacle, horse, and I were reassembled, he leapt the jump as though it was on fire and then finished the course like a thoroughbred. There was a run-off which we won.

(When I'd returned to college, Belmore, my broken-down holiday hack, had recovered and was entered in his first flat race for six months, which he won by four lengths. So, you can add trainer to my CV).

After the early-morning ride, the club members present would sit and have a drink (tea or coffee during the week, and a Black Velvet – champagne and Guinness – on Sundays), and I'd go for a swim in the huge indoor swimming pool.

Down each side, at regular intervals, ropes with rings attached were suspended from the rafters. There were six a side. You would stand at the end of the pool, lean over the water to grab the first ring, take a couple of steps backwards, then launch yourself forward, swinging to the next ring in line, grab hold of that, swing backwards with both rings in your hands, then when you were at the highest point in your backward trajectory, release the first ring. The momentum rushed you to the third, grab that . . . and so on. You've probably done it, but it was new to me. At the beginning of that holiday, I could do maybe two rings, three at the most, and then fall into the pool. After my experience of holding Belmore in check, by the end of the holiday, I was going backwards and forwards down that line of rings until I was bored and dropped into the water for a swim.

All this to tell you that I lost every vestige of fat, and from this tubby sixteen-year-old a lean and if I can cite photographs taken at the time, a rather good-looking young man emerged – even if I say so myself, (or you can look at the photo and tell me I'm wrong).

After the drink and my swim, we were driven home for breakfast. My father would leave for work, and we'd see him again in the evening. I would go to the Calcutta Swimming Club and remain at the outdoor pool till lunch could be summoned, and I'd eat with my mother at a table if she was there or with other youngsters on the grass surround. In the afternoon, I might be driven over to the Saturday Club where I'd play tennis. We would go to the cinema in the evenings, or perhaps give or go to a cocktail party, go to dinner or a dance, and eventually to bed.

I found myself in great demand on the social circuit in Calcutta the last time I was there and, delighting my mother, got myself a girlfriend, Jo. About my age, she was blonde, sporty and, to me, disturbing. She was the first female of my age I'd spent time with. She didn't ride, but we played tennis, danced, swam, did all the things that well-brought-up young people did those days to have fun. We even kissed – without tongues!

So, it didn't make any sense to me that I found myself more and more troubled by the husband of a married couple we'd see quite often, friends of my parents. They were a good-looking pair, both good fun, but I began to appreciate the way Clive found time to praise me quietly, or to pat my back, or admire my riding, or watch me quite openly as I swung up and down the sides of that pool on those rings. It was pleasantly strange, and I didn't understand how it was that a man, much younger than my father, but nevertheless OLD, a married man with a fun wife, could excite me inwardly. I would be dancing with Jo at the Saturday Club for instance, and I would find him watching me, his wife in his arms. A small smile from him, and suddenly I wasn't sure what to do with my feet.

Years later, my mother told me that Clive and his wife, Annabel, had asked if they could take me up the country for a weekend to their tea plantation. She'd been shocked at the impropriety and had refused. That was my last visit to India, so I never saw them again. Perhaps if my mother hadn't been such a prude, with their help, I could have been a stereosexual rather than the monosexual I am now.

So, the experienced me, suddenly refined of face, tall, slim, and popular – even attractive it seemed – returned to that hateful school with a look-at-me attitude.

I couldn't get away from Marlborough quickly enough, so when it was suggested I didn't take my A-Levels, but, with my parents' permission, leave college a year early and go to drama school, I was thrilled. (It didn't cross my mind that I wouldn't get into RADA – and I hadn't yet auditioned). Of course, my marks got appreciably better in class those last two terms. I worked towards my GCE O Levels with confidence, sure I would pass. I won the house tennis tournament. I made people laugh. The boys seemed to want to be my pals.

Funny. It should have been obvious, but I was inexperienced in the ways of the world – and I'd been a blob until only a moment before. Nowadays, I know, along with confidence and manners, good looks will get you what you want – almost always. Not necessarily what you need, but what you want. If you've got a bit of brain to go with the looks, all the better, though that's not essential.

The easy availability of casual sex at school ended in the middle of that last term. There was a sudden witch hunt carried out throughout the college, where boys were being asked if they'd 'known' any other boys in their house – or in any of the houses. As with any criminal investigation, we were taken aside separately, so no one knew what anyone else had confessed to. In fear for my life, I was called to Mr Jennings' study. I admitted to playing with some other boy a few years back, but because I wouldn't give his name, I was beaten – not with a slipper but with a cane. After three sadistic thwacks with five eternal seconds counted out aloud between each of the three, I was asked the name of the boy again, and got another three of the best for still refusing to name him. (What does the saying, 'six of the *best*' relate to? Moments to cherish in one's life?).

A month before the end of that summer term, my parents, who had come to England early, took me to the entrance auditions at RADA. We waited in a small room with a few others, and I can't remember being nervous. I had been to Public School. We had been trained to rule the world. Of course, I was excited. Eventually, I was ushered into a long room, at one end of which sat four adults behind trestle tables. 'When you're ready . . .' and it was time to show off. The witty piece of Wilde from *The Importance of Being Earnest* went well, even got a small chortle, I think, and then I was getting het up with a group of invisible onlookers nearby, railing against my invisible wife in some dramatic lines from *A Bill of Divorcement*. The bitch was leaving me, and I was only seventeen, no, no, right now I was in my late fifties. My classical piece was Orlando's forest speech in Shakespeare's *As You Like It*, during which I was able to show some youthful ardour. I stopped. Fearful silence. By this time, my heart was pounding.

'Thank you. Can you wait just a moment?' Conferring in hushed tones . . . then, 'Well, Mr Gardner, you can wait for the next round of auditions for the scholarship in a month's time, and you . . . *may* . . . get it. But if you can afford the fees, we can accept you here and now.'

In those days, first names weren't immediate, so Mister Gardner asked as nonchalantly as he could if he could go and consult with his parents, flew to them across the corridor and, still airborne, back to the four invigilators behind the tables to say: 'That will be fine. Yes, please, I'd like to do that. Yes. They said yes.' The judges smiled. They seemed pleased. I felt sick with elation.

In my school report that term before leaving, Mr Jennings wrote of my upcoming O Levels Exams: 'Gardner II won't get Geography, but his facility with English will get him through History'. I passed in Geography but wrote fluently for an hour on the wrong period in History. I didn't remember the eighteenth century started in 1700! I passed in seven of the eight subjects I sat for in my O Levels. You can say I came from behind to win by a brass neck. That's what appreciation can do for you.

CHAPTER 4
The Gift of Tongues

I'd had intimations on that last visit to India that all was not well with my parents' relationship. Lo and behold, when my father returned to Calcutta, having established my mother and me in a Kensington house for my first year at drama school, Darell, our Calcutta racehorse trainer, materialised in London. Nothing was said. He simply took my father's place at the table and in her bedroom. It was bewildering. I was as disapproving of them as she had been about Clive and Annabel.

So, my mother was in love again. My father, always the gentleman, bowed out.

This man who adopted me had always been courteous and kind, and although he didn't love me, he did try to show warmth. But he was of the old school and wasn't good at the emotional. I didn't love him either, but the older I got, the more we talked and the more I liked him.

I was told he'd been appointed by the Indian government to be their trade representative in North America promoting jute and tea, something his company in Calcutta, Kettlewell Bullen, had been specialising in for decades. So, he upped sticks and left his Indian home of thirty years and, as his wife had effectively left him, went to live and work in Manhattan.

I'll tell you now how it worked out; as least as it was told to me by my mother – yes, quite! My father, who had lost a lung from mustard gas in the First World War, and smoked a hundred cigarettes a day (he opened a box of 100 Players every morning), was advised by his doctors that he had cancer in his one remaining lung which was inoperable. Loving my mother as he did, he pushed her into Darell's arms, and told her that if they got married, he would adopt her as his child. (My mother would have become my father's daughter, and therefore my sister. Really?).

Just before my second year at RADA, Darell and my mother got married (and no, my dad didn't adopt her). Darell was Irish, and with my father's financial help, they acquired a small estate in County Kildare called Piper's Hill. They planned to run a stud farm so bought three brood mares – which, when they came into season, were sent away regularly to be covered by reputable stallions.

My father had told them he was planning to live with them when he retired, so he had a suite of rooms in the house decorated for his use. He paid a third share in house, land and horses.

Money seemingly plentiful, my mother and her latest husband set about developing their business, and within a few years had tripled, then quadrupled the progeny. The youngsters remained at the farm because my sentimental mother wouldn't part with them, and eventually, they had eighteen horses of all ages, all eating their heads off, all having to be exercised – so extra stable-lads-cum-apprentice-jockeys were engaged. They funded a lot of this with Darell's savings in expectation of my mother inheriting my father's considerable wealth one day.

Then my father was hospitalised in New York. He came back to Ireland to die among friends.

I went over to Piper's Hill and slept the night before the funeral in the bedroom next to his corpse. It was the first experience I'd had of death. As one of my father's old tricks, which I'd found both exciting and frightening as a child, was to turn round suddenly looking like Frankenstein's monster and lumber towards me, I knew in the pitch black of that silent country night that the monstrous thing from next door was looming over my bed. I eventually got to sleep at about four with the light on.

The next morning, just before he was boxed, my mother urged me to kiss this shell of humanity goodbye, but with its blue lips and fingertips – a lack of oxygen at the end apparently – I just couldn't. I didn't even recognise this thing as my father. But I did help the undertakers take his coffin downstairs, and halfway down, the corpse slid and banged its head. Thud. As the song goes: memories are made of this.

He was buried in the ruined chapel grounds on the slope above the house, and it was noticed from then on that the water that we piped from our well downhill of the churchyard was sweeter.

Not long before, India had become independent of the British, and their government was loath to see this rich man's wealth leave the country, so, on a technicality (she was no longer the beloved wife of Geoffrey John Gardner but Mrs Darell Farmer) they refused to honour his will. (Why didn't he change it? Had they fallen out?). To make matters worse, it seems my dad had made enquiries as to house prices in England and had been granted immigrant status in the States, so both governments claimed him as a citizen and taxed him accordingly.

It just about makes sense to me, but that's how my mother was effectively 'disinherited'. (I was later told that my mother's solicitor had suggested that, as his son, I should be posited to the Indian authorities as his rightful heir, but that my mother had refused).

All of this resulted in Darell having to pay off some of the tax demands. In the meantime, he'd also paid to bring my grandmother over from India and house her in north London. (He once asked me dolefully if she really existed, as he'd never met her). Not long after all this, they started divorce proceedings. They sold off all the horses – one of them, Owen Sedge, to Gregory Peck. Another, Gay Trip, won the Grand National a year later. (No, that was one of the horses I didn't name). As to the National: I did go to Aintree to see Owen Sedge jumping the National course and, having once thought of being a jockey (why not?), walked the circuit when the meeting was done. The scrapings of gore on top of the jumps were horrible, and I knew there and then I could never subject horses to this cruelty. Flat racing wouldn't have been as satisfying, so there went another of my early career possibilities.

The beginnings of all the above happened at the start of my second year at drama school.

At the end of my third term at RADA (so still in my first year there), I was rather good in an American comedy-thriller, but my director, a really nice woman named Miss Catterall, told me that Mr Fernald – who'd not yet taken over the school as Principal but who had reviewed the play and praised my performance – had asked if I was a homosexual.

'What makes you think that?' she'd queried.

He'd observed I took rather small steps on that admittedly small stage of the studio theatre, but also, when I'd kissed my fiancée in the play, my hips had been angled away from her body.

Oh!

For the next six months or more, whenever I walked down the street, I took giant compensatory strides, which I hoped would evolve naturally into manly steps. I don't know when I went from mince to chunky, but I did. And from then on, I glued groins whenever I held a woman on stage – indeed off the stage too, which has got me into trouble once or twice.

This same darling director, Miss Catterall, had been contacted by a friend who ran a small seaside repertory company in Frinton, on the Essex coast. He was looking for an actor/assistant stage manager for the summer season. She wanted to recommend me. Would I be interested? Although it would be my FIRST PROFESSIONAL JOB, which was a hugely exciting prospect, I'd just started my FIRST LOVE AFFAIR, which was all-consuming. Without telling her my predicament – 'I'm afraid, Miss Catterall, Mr Fernald was right, I'm as gay as a goose. You know Paul, who was in the play with me, well . . . ?' – I dithered, to her bewilderment, but the look of disappointment on her face persuaded me: I could do the job and the man, so why not? I accepted the offer and said goodbye to the man, assuring him I'd be home every weekend of the seven-week job.

Where had the man come from?

Paul was a friend of Alan Bates. They might have gone to the same school in Nottingham, but certainly, they grew up together.

Paul was in my class, whereas Alan was finishing his final year and about to leave. But, for all sorts of reasons, it was nice to be included in their hellos.

My mother, having gone off to Ireland to live with Darell, I'd had the house in Kensington to myself for the last few weeks of the summer term. It was there, pressed against the back of a sofa, that the first tongue was put in my mouth. More of an invasion than a delicate probing, it seemed to go on forever. Was Paul trying to suffocate me? I tried to manoeuvre my head away, but he was having none of it, so I sat back and allowed myself to be stifled (little sniffs through the nose, Kerry, and you might live). I got to enjoy it eventually, but it took time before I found it sexy to push my tongue into his face. It was all right as long as things were going on elsewhere, but that first time I couldn't wait to get out of the clinch. Another person's saliva – and pints of it! Yuck. (I still don't enjoy letting people eat off my plate or offering me a spittly forkful of their food to taste).

So, thirty days after the start of my first adult 'affair', I packed my bag to go to the seaside and start my first professional acting job. Leaving my first love nest was like leaving one of the best reasons for being alive.

I'd better explain here and now the theatre's repertory system. In one way or another, it'll give you an inkling as to the pattern of my actor life. For this repertory company, I was to be involved in six plays, each play to run a week in front of a paying audience. We had a week of rehearsals, and the following Monday night, at 7.30, the curtain went up on Play One in front of the public. The next morning, Tuesday, the cast started rehearsals for Play Two. Usually, on the first day of rehearsal of a new play, the director 'blocks' it – that is, decides where the characters are going to go on stage while saying their lines. At the end of the afternoon's work, you have something to eat, return to the theatre, make-up and clothe yourself for the second public performance of Play One. Next morning, starting earlyish, you work again on Play Two, Act One, in detail, preferably having a good idea of your lines, which you've tried to din into your head the night before between the public performance and sleep. When you've stumbled through Play Two, Act One, you start blocking Act Two. At the end of rehearsals, you have a meal, you get clothed and made-up for the matinee, or third evening showing of Play One; the play starts, and the audience is entranced/amused/caught up/ appalled. After the performance, you go to your lodgings to learn your lines for Act Two of Play Two, which you rehearse the following day.

On a matinee day, usually a Wednesday or Thursday – in those days shops had a half-day closing in the middle of the week, and the matinee depended on when that was – you only get the morning to rehearse, because after an early lunch you're in the theatre, made-up and costumed for the afternoon performance of whatever play you're doing that week at 2.30. You usually play this to an elderly audience because in the evening, when you are performing the play again, the afternoon's audience is probably in bed asleep.

Speaking of matinees: at the beginning of my professional career, trays of tea and biscuits which had been ordered before the show were handed out in the intervals, and when the curtain went up on Act Two, a lot of the audience were still enjoying their refreshments. So there you were on stage, acting your socks off, and you'd hear the tinkle of spoons, the sipping and slurping, the crash of an occasionally kicked tray once it was finished with and set down on the floor under the seat, and following that the murmurs of apology to neighbours – followed by the lighting up of a cigarette. If the accident was bad enough – in other words, if there was a little scream – an usherette would wend her way through the audience to the accident blackspot, which too often seemed to be in earshot of the stage. Then the actors would hear something like: 'Never mind, dear. It happens to the best of us. Oh, just look at you. I've got a wet cloth here for your skirt. It won't show with a good sponge. Why don't you just stand up, and I can see the damage? [*Murmur*] Sorry, what was that? [*Murmur*] You don't want to be a nuisance? [*Murmur*] You're not being a nuisance, dear, but if you're sure I'll just take away your tray, shall I?' Next, the clatter as the usherette assembled the crockery. By now, we, the actors on stage, would be 'corpsing' (laughing), trying if possible to blend our mirth into our stage performances.

After the matinee, you'd do another performance of the play at 7.30, go home, go to bed, and try and learn the lines for Act Two of Play Two.

And so it goes on through the week. Friday morning, you bash through Act Two and block Act Three if there's time. After lunch, the actors scramble through a very rough performance of Act Two, trying desperately to remember everything that has been planned through the rehearsal period on how the new play is to look, sound and feel; and at 7.30, you perform Play One again to the public.

Saturday is almost always a second matinee day, so you rehearse the whole of Play Two in the morning and do Play One in the afternoon and evening.

Sunday, you spend time trying to remember everything you've learnt of Play Two: the alterations, the cuts in the dialogue, the different moves, the changes your director made the day before. Then, you catch up on your sleep, on your meals, and try to have something of a social life in the few free minutes that are left to you.

Monday morning, if all you are is an actor and not an assistant stage manager as well – as I was in that first job – you go into the theatre to find the set of Play One has disappeared (two weeks later your memorised lines will have disappeared as well) and the set of Play Two is standing in its place ready for the dress rehearsal. As you've used token chairs, tables and props the week before while rehearsing, the proper furniture on the set seems too big, the gun or the candlestick in your hand is no longer a piece of wood, you're not in your everyday clothes but in a costume that isn't your own, possibly with a wig and glued-on hair . . . Not just these strangenesses, but even as you try and remember all the lines and the director's notes from the week before, the lighting is changing around you because a technician is illuminating the set, sometimes on a ladder in the middle of the stage reaching up to the spotlights above your head, and he has to shout instructions to the electrician at the back of the hall. You don't go out at lunchtime as you're covered in make-up and costumed, so you have a sandwich and a cup of tea. Rehearsals go on in the afternoon. A cup of tea and the second half of the lunchtime sandwich at 5.30. 'Curtain up' on Play Two, in front of a paying audience, at 7.30. Voila!

With huge relief, you go to bed that night, wake up the next morning to rehearse Play Three, and the whole sequence starts again. Five more weeks to go.

This is (or was) the basis of our repertory system. Fortnightly Repertory (or 'rep' for short) means you have two weeks to prepare a play and the subsequent two weeks to perform it – so two days' rehearsal per Act. Nowadays, in the big theatre companies, or the national companies (even in some provincial reps), you get five weeks or more to get a play together. That means there's time for theatre directors to accustom the actors and their way of working with each other through games and possibly use some rehearsal time improvising. These sessions are used to break down barriers in the troupe, discussing the era the play is set, or, if it's modern, maybe physically travelling to places your characters might conceivably live. Research, debates, arguments, learning and adapting the author's lines . . . so many ingredients to a theatrical omelette.

*

In this, my first professional job, in addition to learning lines and acting in the evenings, I had to be 'on the book', which meant sitting in the rehearsal room, or at the side of the stage during performances, prompting the actors if they forgot their lines. I was doing this when I wasn't myself performing.

I also had to go around the town early in the morning and in our lunch break with a wheelbarrow, collecting any bric-a-brac, small furniture, books – whatever the theatre could cajole shops and businesses and the public to part with for a fortnight – to dress the set for the following week's play.

('No, Mrs Pritchard. Thank you, but we really do want that table in your cellar just as it is. No! Don't dust it! Please. It's perfect. No, don't get the leg fixed. Wobbly is fine. Why? Well, you'll just have to come and see the play to find out, won't you? And of course, your name will be in the programme as a donor. Oh, that's so generous of you. You'll have it back at the end of next week, I promise. Thank you').

I've never seen the like since, but the set on stage in this rep theatre was permanent. Meaning from the audience's point of view, there were three real brick walls on stage, with gaps in between. So for one play, that opening over there would be a doorway, that one a recessed bookshelf, the third a fireplace, and the fourth perhaps the bottom of a staircase, or a curtained French window, or the arched opening into a kitchen. The following week, in the gap where the week before there'd been a door, there might be a fireplace, with a window in the opposite wall where once there'd been shelves for ornaments. Every week we rang the changes, throughout the seven-week season. (Well, *I* didn't, but we'll come to that).

Another of my jobs was to help paint those walls or paper them if the play was set in a smart house. From a fashionable Regency-striped drawing-room one week (with some of the furniture and stage dressing provided by my wheelbarrow) to a broken-down hovel with a wobbly table for the next week's drama, we tried every way we could to make what was revealed when the curtains parted different from the week before.

There I was, eighteen years old, and my first professional role was that of an elderly butler in a genteel comedy called *Waiting for Gillian*. Apart from applying ageing lines to my palely made-up face, I don't know what on earth else I did to earn the rave review from the local critic in the *Gazette* five days after the opening. It was a small role, but it had some funny lines, and it was excruciatingly embarrassing to be picked out **in heavy type** and lauded over and above the half-dozen actors twice my age, playing parts ten times the size on that same stage. Still at drama school, eh? I was met by some very forced smiles the following day. Pleased as Punch but deprecating with it, I humbled myself by scurrying off to get furniture with my wheelbarrow for the next week's presentation.

The week following my debut, I was rewarded by the theatre's management with the huge – and by huge I mean, to this young novice – world-sized-gigantic role of a persistent, suspicious, interrogating police officer in his thirties, in a thriller: *Someone Waiting.*

The day before we opened *Someone Waiting*, that Sunday was my first chance to get back to London and resume my 'affair'. I tried to consolidate the learning of my lines in the train going up to town because I was sensible enough to know my mind would be in fragments once I was in bed with my first-ever lover. I planned to cement the lines into my head on the way back to the theatre on Monday.

We were in bed all of Sunday.

Monday morning on the train, I fell deeply asleep the moment my head touched the headrest. I woke up with a start when the train came to a jolting halt at a small country station. Not remembering the names of the stations on the way back to Frinton, I thought – with a shock of terror – that I'd gone past my destination. I leapt out of the train. Wrong. There were still three stops to go, and it cost me my whole week's wages to get a taxi so I could be back in time for rehearsal.

That first night I was prompted from the wings twelve times. TWELVE! I was so dazed and demoralised I spent almost my entire performance at the side of the stage nearest to the window where my lines were read out to me – the stuff of horrifying, bolt-upright nightmares.

As rehearsals for the third play started the next morning, I was given a week's notice that same night to leave the company. The director, watching my appallingly inept 'performance', was doubtless on the phone even as I was receiving my ninth or tenth prompt on stage.

My replacement arrived the following lunchtime, and with

mixed feelings, I instructed him in the art of begging furniture and props from the townsfolk, which shops and households were generous, those to avoid. And I introduced him to the wheelbarrow.

I felt rotten. I'd let down my RADA teacher, Miss Catterall, who'd recommended me for the job. My belief in myself was deeply dented. I told myself over and over that my only crime had been not spending enough time learning my lines, but what I had done was irresponsible to my fellow artists . . . on and on. I beat myself up endlessly. Still, that Sunday away had been an aperitif, and I couldn't wait to get back to London and get on with the meal.

I did my best to learn those lost lines for the rest of the week's run, but for security wrote down my entire role in my detective's notebook. I inked some of my lines on my palms and the back of my hands, I taped notes to tabletops and on the backs of furniture. But I was too insecure to know what to look at when, and the panicking detective continually gazing downwards, looking everywhere but at the possibly suspicious characters, can't have made much sense to the audience.

I was quite unused to learning by rote – apart from the chunks of poetry which were meted out as punishment at Marlborough college, and those were only ever twenty lines long, *and* we'd had a week in which to learn them. At RADA, we had an eight-week term in which to learn our roles. This longer-than-*Hamlet*, or so it seemed to me, convoluted part, with question after question, with changes of tack in reasoning and suspicion, leading a suspect on with pretended sympathy, or ice-hard with menace was at the time way beyond me. (In fact, it took me an age after leaving RADA to get the hang of learning lines quickly, and there were another couple of times in my first few years as a professional when I nearly lost jobs for the same reason. I well remember Sheila Reid, that adorable actress, lying on my bed until well after midnight trying to din lines into my head so that I wouldn't get the sack the following morning – this at Farnham rep).

The lease on the house in Kensington had come to an end, so

when I got back to town, I went to stay with Paul in his one-room flat in north London. This was the first time I'd lived unsupervised. I felt like a character in an Enid Blyton book: *Fun with Peter and Dick*, perhaps. So for the rest of the holiday when I'd been contracted to be working at Frinton, we got by on very little sleep and even less money. Paul, who was the older of us, recognised the need for a job, if only for the rent, but found himself easily persuaded by me that there just weren't enough hours in the day to be both promiscuous *and* adult.

My father, ensconced in America, had provided me with an allowance for first-year expenses but now, anticipating I would need somewhere else to live in London, added more. So when the next term began, Paul and I moved into a slightly bigger, slightly less run-down couple of rooms in Marylebone, nearer the centre of town and nearer to RADA.

On the first day of term, I tried to apologise to Miss Catterall. I hadn't got more than a few words out when she cut me short. 'Too bad,' she said and walked on past.

I felt excoriatingly ashamed of myself. I wasn't scheduled to work with Miss Catterall again, and from then on, saw very little of her about the place, thank heavens. When I did, she cut me, quite gently, dead. But she hadn't, bless her, told anyone at the Academy of the fiasco, so I continued to be given good roles.

When I'd first entered the Academy, quite a few of the female students were there because their parents found it cheaper to send their child to a drama school that taught deportment, speech, and movement, than to finishing schools in Switzerland. By now, the start of my last year, and thanks to our new Principal, Mr Fernald, the women students were altogether different to the debutantes of yore and being on stage with them was extraordinary. Remember, I'd lived predominantly with men up till leaving college a year before, so I found this new determined species daunting. I was intimidated at first to find such maturity in young females, everyone with such a commitment to acting, and to begin with, I was tentative in my reactions, then engaged, and finally exhilarated. God, what fun playing grown up grown-ups could be!

Then something else turned up towards the end of one of the terms in 1955: the students of my year were asked if they'd be interested in auditioning for a children's film. The producers needed a young man who could fence and had a convincing French accent. I got the role, natch.

The film was a swashbuckling piece of drama set in England at the time of the French Revolution. I played a stiff-necked French aristocrat, a pompous cad who'd been saved from the guillotine and brought to England. There was a duel between my character and another young French escapee of lesser birth, which was carefully rehearsed down to the last thrust and parry. It went well. However, for the end credits, my opponent, played by Robin Alalouf, and I were persuaded by the director to have an impromptu passage of arms. (That indeed was the name of the film).

'Remember, chaps, they're friends now, having a bit of fun. Just improvise, OK? Camera. Action.'

Ten seconds later we both lunged at each other at the same moment. Robin dropped his foil with a scream, clapped his hands to his eyes, and I was appalled to see blood running down his face. God, I'd blinded him!

Not quite. With my untipped foil, I'd missed his right eye by a quarter of an inch. The blade had caught him in the trench just below his bottom lashes. He was patched up with plaster, and the scene was eventually performed as a background to the credits in modern fencing masks.

Of course, I began to grow up in my personal life too. I hadn't had long-term friends since the age of twelve when I left my prep school, and now suddenly I had such a varied bunch, all as excited as I to be living this hand-to-mouth existence, all wanting to communicate their observations, their views on life. We were an eager, messy lot, but *Oh*, we had such ding-dong arguments and so much to laugh about.

You may wonder at me talking about myself as though I was

penniless. I wasn't on a grant, as most students were, as Paul was, but what my dad sent me I shared around, and so I was always broke just like everyone else.

My mother was introduced to some of my friends on a flying visit to London and took me aside after a party I'd invited her to.

'Where did you say Paul came from, darling?'

'Uh, he was born in Nottingham.'

'And Jamie? Is that a Scottish accent?'

'No, he's Irish from Liverpool. Erica's from Scotland. Why?'

'Aren't you friends with Thomas? I thought you liked him. Daphne [his mother] asked me to say hello, sends you her love . . . but he wasn't at your party, was he? Or did I miss him?'

I'd known from early on where this conversation was going, Thomas having been to Eton.

'Nah' – broadened to irritate her even further – 'Tom's OK, but I wouldn't call him a chum.'

'What a shame.'

My mother had seen me act on several occasions and had particularly liked my portrayal of Robert Browning, the poet, in *The Barretts of Wimpole Street*. In another play, acting the lead role of a cheeky Welshman who turns out to be a psychotic murderer, I gave a performance I was particularly proud of – the internal academy judges had assumed I was a native from Wales when they'd reviewed it. It elicited from her a, 'Mmm, yes, you were good but not as good as when you were playing that nice Robert Browning. You looked so romantic in that'. Robert Browning was a gentleman. A more fitting role for her son.

I invited Paul to Ireland for a short stay in one of the holidays, and her vague mistrust of him turned to outright dislike when he observed that the dahlias in our borders reminded him of gaudy cabbages. My mother didn't have to say, 'What a common remark'. I saw it in her face.

Paul and I were together until after we both left the Academy when I was seduced by quite the handsomest young man I'd met till then. Paul was distraught, but I'd let my mother's prejudices influence me, I suppose, because by then, I already disliked the overspill of saliva in his mouth and his crooked teeth. I also thought he was a tad camp. Deep I wasn't!

Tony, Mr Handsome, was working for a prominent interior designer when I met him. There was lots of face-to-face kissing and fondling of each other's nubbly bits, and what I most remember of him are his dark brown eyes with thick dark lashes and almost black hair. He had a nicely modulated middle-class voice, he was manly shaped, and he was absurdly gorgeous to look at. We'd been sharing a really pleasant top-floor flat in Chelsea for eighteen months when one day I uncovered a stash of photographs he'd had taken of himself, naked, with and without an erection, to be sent to *Pen Pals*, a dating magazine. (This was, of course, way before internet dating). I was actually more intrigued than shocked, but we talked it over and got past the recriminations. The relationship pottered on for another few months, and we had a good enough time, but we both knew we weren't the love of the other's life.

You need, in your mind, to overlay my acting career with this and subsequent relationships. I was sometimes working, more often than not away from home, only getting back at weekends. Knowing the chances I would sometimes be out of work, I had taught myself to touch-type, which was fun as it was so near to playing the piano, and now and then found myself employed by large companies in a room full of women secretaries. I was somewhat lonely not being able to contribute to the pros and cons of Peach Blossom nail varnish or where best to get your hair done, but it was preferable to emptying out piss pots in tiny rank-smelling rooms in small hotels near Victoria Station, that's for sure – another way to earn a penny.

I did a six-month stint in weekly rep – one of the places I was nearly sacked from because of my inability to learn masses of lines quickly – which in retrospect turned out to be almost the most fun I've ever had as a professional actor. We did creaky melodramas, up-to-the-minute comedies, Victorian thrillers, Oscar Wilde's four-act version of *The Importance of Being Earnest* as a musical, Ibsen, Shakespeare, Arthur Miller and Tennessee Williams, meaty modern dramas recently on the London stage, and seaside farces. (The local rag of my lead role in Miller's *All My Sons* said, and I quote: 'Kerry Gardner does not have the face for tragedy'). I played a fourteen-year-old in a Strindberg. I could be tall, fat, old, young, camp, straight and everything in between. The costumes altered weekly, as did the colour of my face, my wigs, moustaches and beards, and my eyebrows went up and down. (In desperation, anything to look different, I soaped out my own eyebrows and pencilled in false ones half an inch higher this one particular week. That was for Oscar Wilde. I looked ridiculous).

But easily my most memorable moment came when, in a Graham Greene play, *The Potting Shed*, playing the fat fifty-year-old brother of the leading character, I bustled onto the stage at the end of Act One and pronounced to the assembled cast and audience: 'Oh, God! You'll never believe it. John's hanged himself in the potting shed!'

My character had the last lines at the end of the first and last acts, and on this occasion, I'd got them the wrong way round. At the end of the first act, I delivered the play's final line when we were all waiting eagerly for 'John' to arrive. The line should have been: 'You'll never guess who's in the hall. John's here!' Buzz of excitement from the assembled company on stage. Curtain falls.

Instead of which, on that first night, I told everyone, the audience included, that the anticipated hero of the story wouldn't be appearing as he was dead and dangling in the shed - end of play. The curtain falls on shocked actors and surprised audience – especially the ones who'd seen it in London the year before. More bewilderment when the curtain rose on John centre-stage at the start of Act Two. Nothing was said about rope or shed, and the play continued as though nothing untoward had happened.

But I really bamboozled them all at the end of Act Three, the very end of the play, when John *had* killed himself, and I couldn't resist delivering my own version of the final lines: 'You're not going to believe this, but he's really done it this time. John's hanged himself in the potting shed. Again.' The audience was utterly bewildered at the actors' hysterical laughter on receiving news of John's second tragic ending. Even his fat brother seemed secretly pleased with himself.

That season was fun because of the helter-skelter of it all. And we had a social life. Some of the older members of the audience would invite us out for lovingly prepared teas between the matinees and the evening shows on Wednesdays and Saturdays. And we were the luminaries in the pub after the show at nights. Big fishes in a puddle, loving every second of our small-town fame.

All this had happened without the aid of an agent.

At the end of those six months, I was offered understudy and assistant stage manager for the first production in the West End of *The Diary of Anne Frank*. A beautiful, devastating, haunting play, which in London had an unbeatable cast.

Assistant stage managing, in this production, meant changing the props on set in the darkness in scene breaks when the curtain descended silently, and Anne's voice carried on the story; making the sound of the Nazis breaking into the house (by throwing a trash can with great force against a wooden pillar below the stage); giving the cast their beginners' calls; checking they had all the right props in their pockets before the next scene. It also meant helping the Wardrobe Mistress during the day and distributing the clothes into the various dressing rooms. A dogsbody, in fact. And once a week, usually a Saturday morning, with one or two of the original cast and the other understudies, I played Peter, the part I understudied, on stage.

The Diary of Anne Frank ran at the Phoenix for four months, and when the show finished in London, we took the production to Streatham Hill Theatre – still London, but at the southern extreme. After the very last performance, while dogsbodies and stagehands were helping dismantle the set, an insignificant stranger who'd appeared in the wings asked me if he could meet Perlita Neilsen, who played 'Anne'. I referred him to my boss, Thelma Holt, the stage manager. She was a little short with him because we were frantic to get the scenery down and out of the theatre.

'She'll be very busy packing up because this was the last performance, but . . .' (looking at his pleading face) . . . 'but if she has a moment. Who shall I say is asking?'

'My name is Otto Frank.'

Anne's father never saw the play but attended all the productions around the world, wanting to thank the actresses who'd played his daughter.

After that gem of theatre, I was flattered to be asked by Frith Banbury, the *Anne Frank* director, to understudy and assistant stage manage the next of his productions in London. I still had no agent, and my choices were made on just how much fun I thought each job would be. I had no idea if it would be good for a career – what exactly was that? – but being paid to live and love in London was a definite plus. And the stars of this show, Michael Redgrave and Diana Wynyard were Big. So, of course, I accepted.

Nothing much to report on that except . . . For the first few weeks of rehearsal, Michael Redgrave was dissatisfied with the performance he was giving. Even I realised it wasn't that much different to the performance he'd given in the film of *The Browning Version* – in which he was magnificent. Day after day the feeling of his frustration was palpable. And then suddenly one morning in a rather drab rehearsal room: a breakthrough – magic. The subtle differences were extraordinary. It was as if a wand had been waved over a work-a-day piece of theatre, transforming it into a work of art.

The play, *A Touch of the Sun*, by N. C. Hunter – a very well-established English playwright – was set in England and the South of France and graced by two quite exceptional performances by real-life father and daughter, Michael and Vanessa Redgrave, both of whom I watched keenly from the wings and from both learned how to make stagecraft invisible.

Oh, yes, and something else I learned which has stood me in

good stead throughout my life: how to iron. There were four male actors in the cast, and the Wardrobe Mistress needed help to iron all those shirts – laundered for every performance. I learned to start with the collar, then the yoke, the cuffs, the sleeves couldn't have a crease along the top edge, so that was fiddly, then the back and the front panels. She eventually trusted me to iron Michael Redgrave's shirt. Another of my claims to fame!

Towards the end of that play's run in London, I turned twenty-one. My mother and Darell had booked the party for my birthday at a restaurant in the centre of town months before. A week beforehand, my mother was rung by the manager to be reminded that we'd all have to be off the premises by eleven when the restaurant closed. Shock, horror: the play came down at 10.15, and none of the actors, including myself, could get to the premises before – well, at about their closing time.

I'd invited maybe twenty people to come and celebrate, a lot of them from outside London. Michael Redgrave came to the rescue and offered his apartment for the party. I was thrilled and gratified. Not long out of RADA and having my twenty-first at the house of a theatrical colossus! My mother and Darell wrote off hurriedly to everyone with the new address for the celebration. But then, two days before the party, Michael's youngest daughter, Lynn, contracted chickenpox, so that was that. We couldn't have it there.

My friends and I – in the new mini car, a Gogomobil I'd been given by my mother and Darell – dashed about town leaving messages at the various new venues we hoped to be at, with one definitive party address after another. In the end, not one of my out-of-town friends made it. Not that there would have been any room for them where we finished up – a small flat belonging to the actor I understudied, Dinsdale Landen. So from the grand panoply of a smart London restaurant in Knightsbridge, we finished up with London's acting elite sitting on the carpet in this basement flat being served by dinner-jacketed waiters from the posh firm of Searcys who picked their way gingerly through the tightly packed legs on the floor delivering delicious food on porcelain dishes which we ate on our laps. It was bizarre and wonderful. (It was only the other day I met someone who turned out to be a good friend of Dinsdale's, and this someone told me that not only had the caterers brought their silverware and crystal for the party, they'd swathed sections of the actor's room in material, and scrubbed some of the paintwork. Apparently, Dinsdale was astonished at the transformation. But he didn't tell me that at the time, so I took it at face value that he'd furnished his home to look like an Edwardian bordello. I thought his flat a bit camp, really – all that draped velvet).

I should have been disappointed, perhaps, but I wasn't. A few months before, my life had been delightfully complicated by a wayward young actor I'd met at a party. John was my age, dark, walked like a dancer – could have been a stevedore if it wasn't for his first-position feet – with the wickedest smile and a growl in his voice to go with it. It was rumoured he had a boyfriend, but he was tantalisingly flirtatious with me one minute, matter of fact the next.

Tony looked after my mother. She liked my flatmate – so suave and well-spoken. I flirted with John, excitedly in thrall and behaving like a boy who doesn't know which hand the sweetie's in on this my first day of adulthood. I tried reining it in as I was aware of the many grand theatrical personages surrounding us – the grandest sitting on the few chairs available, the rest of us on the floor at their feet, where we belonged. I don't know if the grandees and my mother enjoyed it, but I didn't notice. I only had eyes for John.

He didn't have anywhere to sleep that night, so with Tony's agreement, I invited him to stay at our place. Whooping with drunken glee, I drove them home in my tiny new car at five o'clock in the early dawn of summer, the car's roof open, John standing and loudly declaiming Shakespeare to the sleeping boroughs of London as we whizzed through them to Chelsea.

Tony's and my flat had two rooms, with the kitchen and bathroom below, but by now in our relationship, post naked snaps, I was sleeping on the bed-divan in the sitting room, while he had one of the two beds in the smaller room next door. No hint of a fuss was made when I offered to bring the now-spare mattress from next door for John to sleep on.

Tony wished us goodnight and left to go to bed. I stared at this comparative stranger in the shaded room, this wicked dark-haired sexual tease, as he turned away from me and appeared to settle down on the mattress to sleep. I longed for him, and he was only three feet away. How on earth could he go to sleep? It was my birthday! My heart was bursting as the world quietened. I heard Tony settling in his bed on the other side of the wall. John heard him too. He turned his head and leered.

I was knocked out of the grounds for six.

Nothing was said the next morning, and I saw John on and off for the next year, but we never lived together. He was a well-employed actor, so not always in London. I badgered him to tell me he loved me, but it was only a year later that he did. He gave me a small marquetry box, which I have to this day. Inside there was a key. The key to his heart, he told me.

I had what I wanted. Until a few months later when he went off with someone else.

I was in Ireland with my mother and Darell, laid up with jaundice when I learned of his new relationship. The letter was very matter of fact. When I was no longer throwing up, I brought my yellow-tinged eyes back to London, hoping my pleading would change things. No chance. He'd left town on a job, and I didn't see him again to talk to for another three years.

It hurt my only recently ripened heart like hell when John left me. I had no idea what to do to ease the anguish. But my heart, which I thought had been shattered forever, mended miraculously when my foot was trodden on by a French waiter. Looking back, my heart must have been broken into the tiniest inconsolable fragments for, oh, at least six months.

CHAPTER 5
Skittle

When do you suppose it is, with the *Beano* and *Dandy* behind you, that you learn to differentiate between simple comic japes and a sequence of words which make you smile or laugh with their interplay of real and imaginary ideas? Double entendres materialise from smutty school jokes, probably. But wit?

While I was still at Marlborough, when they were in England for the summer, my parents would take me to see revues, dramas, musicals and delightfully daffy comedies in the West End of London with the likes of Yvonne Arnaud, David Tomlinson and Athene Seyler starring. My parents 'did' a show in those days – always dressed up, more often than not going on to a club afterwards to dine and dance, the dancing interrupted by the late-night cabarets. Looking back on it, I can't believe my luck that I saw some of the supernovas of their day: Marlene Dietrich, Noël Coward, Leslie Hutchinson (Hutch) and, many years later, Lena Horne[1] – all favourites of those supper clubs. Sitting at a table surrounded by the chicly dressed, floating in the soft musky smell of cigars and expensive perfume, a spot would light up a piano on a raised dais, and into the creamy white light would glide The Star.

It was there in the cosy dark that the process first began for me – the difference between jokes and wit: the obviousness of the one and the subtlety of the other. I was alerted to the presence of the latter by the unexpected reaction of the grown-ups around me. Why did they just laugh? That wasn't funny, was it? Much later, the penny

---

1   To hear sexual innuendo done to a T, you must listen to Lena Horne singing 'Honeysuckle Rose'. And 'A New Fangled Tango' will have you in stitches. Both are on her Waldorf Astoria disc.

dropped, and it was only slowly the coin and my brain came into sync. Scintillating and seemingly effortless, wit wasn't 'flagged up'. Sometimes it just needed an innuendo or a pause with a well-placed inflection of the voice. Or a word. Maybe just a glance.

At RADA, my background had led me to expect a profitable career playing middle-class nitwits coming through French windows, racquet in hand, asking, 'Who's for tennis?' In those days, there was always at least a half-dozen frothy comedies on at any one time in the West End, along with the more serious plays of Rattigan, the aforementioned N.C. Hunter, William Douglas Home and Graham Greene – all middle-class writers – and I would have slotted snugly into any one of them. But six months before I left drama school, my future seemingly assured, an angry young playwright, John Osborne, consigned my easy career to the dustbin. If not for him, I might today be a well-to-do National Treasure!

Right now, one of those National Treasures is banging on about working-class actors not being given a chance: 'Only the public school lot get a look in'. She is now a Dame, a thoroughly middle-class honour, one of the hundreds of actors from my earlier days who benefitted immensely, after John Osborne's explosive entrance onto the scene, from the superb claque of British and Irish working-class dramatists who followed: Willy Russell, Shelagh Delaney, Arnold Wesker and countless more, all of them writing about the underprivileged – for stage, television and film.

During that time, as a middle-class actor from public school, I couldn't get a look in. It was only fifty years or so later (too late for me) that the public began to lose its fascination for the 'angry' – the tribulations of the hardworking, the malcontents and the suffering – and turned to posh escapism: *Downton Abbey, Victoria, The Crown,* all stuffed with superb actors from all classes.

I would love to know how many of the amazing younger actors of today – Andrew Garfield, Daniel Mays, Russell Tovey, Carey Mulligan, Olivia Colman, Hugh Skinner, Lee Ingleby, Denise Gough, Andrew Scott and Ben Wishaw – went to posh schools.

The same with the older actors: Lesley Manville, Emma Thompson, Mark Rylance, Tom Hollander, Lindsay Duncan, Hugh Grant, Penelope Wilton, Harriet Walter, Martin Shaw, Hermione Norris, Colin Firth, Sarah Lancashire, Brenda Blethyn and Eileen Atkins? (No, I lie, I don't need to know, so don't tell me). They can turn their hands to anything: rich person, poor person, beggars and thieves, all believable, all with appropriate accents. So, come off it you whingers, you need an acute ear, and nowadays, if yours isn't as fine-tuned as theirs, work on it. What goes around has come around again.

I know the price of entry into the actors' academies is prohibitively high for most, but how come the drama schools of today are turning out more actors than ever before? If acting is something you *have* to do, you'll find a way – drama schools aren't essential. And television turns out endless socially embracing drama (*Happy Valley, Broadchurch* and so forth – not to mention the Soaps). Like a hungry animal, TV needs an endless supply of fresh bourgeois meat along with the spuds and sprouts.

*

Since RADA's inception, the Final Term Showcase was (and still is) attended by agents, casting directors, theatre managers – the great and the good of our business, all those who can further students' acting careers by finding them paying work. At the end of my first year, that Finals Showcase had been at the huge Her Majesty's Theatre in the heart of the West End. There I saw Peter O'Toole, Albert Finney, Alan Bates, Richard Briers, Brian Bedford, just some of our leaving students, performing disparate scenes which showcased their brilliance, leaving the audience saucer-eyed – and me tingling with excitement. Could I do that?

Our Finals year didn't expect any less. Getting leading roles over the two years of training had become a habit for me, so it was a huge disappointment when the director of *our* Finals Showcase, the new Principal of the Academy, Mr Fernald (*Is Kerry Gardner a homosexual?*), used the occasion to show off not our talents, but his.

He chose to do a German play, Brecht's *The Caucasian Chalk*

Circle, in its entirety, in the Vanburgh, RADA's new theatre – maybe a thirtieth of the size of Her Majesty's. It was a piece that needed a cast of twenty, and there were only three showy lead roles. I was one of the seventeen finalists who didn't get one. So after two years' training, the majority of us were playing small roles and walk-ons in front of prospective employers. We were changing costumes, beards, wigs, and accents till our heads whirled. Among other roles, Paul played a Prince, and me his nephew. I tried grabbing attention in the tiny part by camping it up – thereby confirming Fernald's suspicions of me. I got some cheap laughs, but the memory makes me wince.

The set Fernald had designed for this his first production at RADA was by far the most impressive I'd ever seen on our Academy's main stage. The expensive costumes were bespoke. I'm sure the production looked wonderful. I'm sure too the new Principal of the leading drama school of the time was pleased to watch us Finalists realise the play as he saw it in his mind's eye. (He was afterwards rewarded with a directing job in the West End – *The House by The Lake*, in which his wife had a prominent role. I wish his student-actors had done as well out of it).

I'm more indignant writing about it now than I was at the time. I tried to rationalise it: fair enough, I'd had a decent crack of the whip throughout my two years at the school. The daylight robbery of our moment in the sun didn't seem too dismaying then. We'd been told getting an agent was useful but not essential so early in our careers.

Of course, that wasn't true – even then. Now the drama schools' courses last three years, and some well-known actors' agent or manager is called in to lecture the first-year pupils on how useful agents are to an actor's life. Because, as of old, at the beginning of year two, these gimlet-eyed acquisitors prowl about, snapping up talented students from their first public appearances in the two RADA theatres.

Competition is fierce – and piracy rife.

Not so long ago, I heard of an agent from one of the bigger international agencies telling students: if you're not pretty, don't bother to get in touch. What a thing! That's well over three-quarters of them dismissed because of their lack of 'looks', after three years of training. There are less greedy managers, thank heavens, for the plainer and talented, but the big supermarket agencies cream off the prettiest from the top. And they are quite ruthless about dropping clients if their looks haven't brought in the anticipated dividend within a year. Their older actors they get from those brought on by the smaller agencies and are ready to fall into their laps – ripe off the mother tree as it were – with promises and flattery. (You must read William Goldman's expose, *Adventures in the Screen Trade*, to understand exactly what I'm talking about: scandalous and very funny).

When I left RADA, the diploma given to me by the Queen Mother clutched in my hand, but without the more important agent, I believed, with the wide-eyed innocence of a nineteen-year-old ignoramus, that for me everything would turn out all right. So it did – in a very roundabout way.

Osborne's play *Look Back in Anger* was a derisive poke at the middle class, at the privileges and pretensions of the British Empire. It was a stunning piece of agitprop, of intellectually sharp cynicism. It was so shockingly different to what had gone before, it found a huge, admiring audience. Overnight it changed the face of British theatre.

But ten years later, instead of a sensible mix of the old and new, theatre managers were still producing more and more of the same explicit plays about the pain of the proletariat. It made for a long and fruitful era of creativity and produced a glut of wonderful stage and screenwriters who dissected England, laying its pretensions bare. But however entertainingly the facts are presented to them, the well-to-do don't enjoy facing the realities of the less fortunate forever. Why would people who had the money to be entertained in the theatre want to pay to be mocked – or ignored? The habit of the affluent going to the theatre died. (A few of them went to the opera instead – the wives to be seen and the men to sleep). Without wealthy theatregoers in the supper clubs, the cabarets with those highly paid exotic luminaries disappeared.

Then again, those who enjoyed the new down-to-earth drama certainly didn't have the money to pay the prices charged for seats in the larger West End theatres, so in an attempt to recoup their fortunes, the London theatre managements shelved drama, put on extravagant musicals and put up prices. At this moment of writing, there are five 'straight' plays or comedies in the West End and thirty-five musicals. In the days of my studentship, the ratio was the exact opposite.

Television, almost free to watch, became more and more diverse. That, too, had a long creative period when superb screenwriters were given their heads. The population at large was happy to put dates in its diary to watch good drama. That era is now fondly remembered as The Golden Age of British Television – the best in the world.

But, as with so many things of worth, greed put an end to that. Prime Minister Margaret Thatcher needed money – for a war to make her more popular, perhaps – and raided the television bank vaults, television being 'a license to print money' as she put it. She auctioned off all the existing television companies. The television producers, desperate to hold on to their 'money-making machines', bid ludicrously large sums to hold on to companies they already owned. The result was that although a lot of them retained their television stations, they had nothing left with which to make the worthwhile which they'd been so good at.

So accountants were called in, and they decided which projects would be profitable and which wouldn't. Innovation, observation and subtlety went out of the window – and in came the banal and the cheap: soaps, reality programmes and the cult of celebrities, with no nutritional value to the brain. That's what accountancy did for television. Those who stay at home for their entertainment these days are offered a diet of flashy junk with only the occasional gleam of the worthwhile.

The still adventurous viewer was then to be found in the cinema

– whose turn it now is to reinvent itself because 'blockbusters', the money-making, entertaining mind-mushers, have taken over.

Nowadays, if you want to see intellectually challenging work, you'll find it in the smaller theatres and in foreign and independent film – Hollywood, with its eye on profit, having copped out of any responsibility to adults. So independents were born. The best treats in the theatre outside the smaller venues are to be found in the subsidised companies, the National and the Royal Shakespeare Company. They can afford to produce the larger cast plays, the old and the new, with government aid and outside monetary help.

Sadly, the gentry haven't been attracted back in sufficient quantities to 'serious' theatre to make it profitable again because they don't understand, or can't be bothered to work out, the complexities of the big companies' repertory systems. And now, to make matters worse for them, very few theatres advertise their productions outside of London, and those that do, put on musicals.

OK, so off my hobbyhorse and back onto earlier ground.

I'd been at RADA with actors who'd been born and brought up in the regions outside London, and what was required in the new drama was the genuine. I was genuinely from India and an English public school. The rug of my new career being whipped out from under me, my fellow trainees did rather better at staying upright.

Out from the cosy fold of the Academy at nineteen plus, I found employment through exchanging news with acquaintances, reading the trade papers and dropping in on casting agents' offices. Compared to now, work was plentiful. I got a season of six plays at Eastbourne, another weekly rep where I nearly lost my job because of an inability to learn my lines quickly, but where I *did* get to play the back end of a cow in *Jack and the Beanstalk*. No lines at all, just lowering bottles of milk and cartons of cream through the udder and doing a soft-hoof shuffle. This was followed, not long after, by the six-month stint at Farnham Rep which I've already described – the potting shed, the eyebrows? After that, I climbed many a staircase looking for jobs, and at the top of one in Shaftesbury Avenue, I got my first (tiny) part in television, a musical starring Julie Andrews and John Fraser: *The Little Matchgirl*, adapted from the Hans Christian Andersen fairy tale.

I had one line of dialogue in it: 'Who is that beautiful creature who just came in?', which was meant to be whispered in awe as I stared at the transformed Julie Andrews, but which, with pent-up excitement, I addressed to a fire extinguisher on a wall nearby. All drama on television in the early days went out live, so with a limited budget and fewer cameras, the direction of my look needed to be believable when the director cut to it, particularly as my character was part of a group of party guests at the other end of the studio, miles from the action. For us, Julie Andrews was red and cylindrical.

But, to my star-struck joy, I did get to stand next to the two leads of our show in the BBC lifts the day before transmission: the beautifully aloof Andrews, and the even more beautiful John Fraser. She didn't say a word, but his merry eyes spoke volumes.

The casting agent who next helped me – not the one who chased young men around his desk, but possibly one of the many who chased young girls – got me an audition for *The Long and The Short and The Tall*, which was to be performed in rep just outside London, in Guildford. In the West End, the play had starred Peter O'Toole, early on in his meteoric rise to international fame.

I got the job. This was a *three*-weekly rep. In those days, most cities in Britain had their own theatres where the staple fare was reproductions of recent successes in London mixed with a few classics. As putting bums on seats was a priority out of town, the more old-fashioned work was rehashed for a parochial audience who weren't keen to hear four-letter words and be reminded of society's exclusion of the less fortunate. This was a well-made play *with* four-letter words. Provincial audiences were going to have to be made to learn – or do without. Of course, the bourgeoisie outside London resisted the modern gritty plays too – so the artistic directors of the theatre put them on in their tiny studio theatres created for just that fare. But that ruse wasn't financially viable for long, so now almost all of the theatres in the smaller cities around the country have closed down. Television soaps dish up make-believe angst so much more cheaply. You're comfortably sat at home and can make rude comments – or a cup of tea.

In this excellent but somewhat humbler provincial production of *The Long and The Short and The Tall*, I played the part of another Welshman: Taffy, the radio operator. Set in the jungle in Malaya during the Second World War, the story is of a platoon of British soldiers who find themselves marooned in a peasant hut behind enemy lines, cut off from their regiment by the Japanese army. The squaddies don't immediately understand just how dire their predicament is, so there are some comic moments at the start of the play, but then as the enemy closes in, it gets more fraught and exciting, until its tragic end. At midpoint in the story, the British lads go out and, by sheer chance, capture a Japanese soldier. They bring him back to the hut to interrogate him, strip him of his possessions, and finding his family photographs endure agonies as to whether they can execute this other human who is as obviously terrified as they.

One particular matinee, the five of us squaddies huddled together on stage desperately trying to contact our regiment by radio, knowing the Japanese could intercept our signal. Suddenly, we heard 'Che Sera Sera' being whistled loudly in the jungle outside. Dumbstruck, no longer soldiers but actors in a theatre in Guildford, we wondered what on earth was going on. Then we saw the face of the young Japanese guy who played the soon-to-be-captured soldier staring at us through the window of the jungle hut. He was dressed in his everyday street clothes.

'Oh, shit!' he said loudly, and disappeared.

Ken Tanaka, or Kenzaburo Tanaka to give him his full name, had forgotten there was a matinee that day, and by pure chance, had come to the theatre to see if there was any post for him at the stage door. The doorkeeper, thinking he was there for his performance, greeted him and made no further comment. He'd strolled onto the stage whistling and, thinking there might be a rehearsal in progress, peered through the window of the set to see what was going on. I don't suppose the audience knew how near they were to having the second half of the performance cancelled for lack of a Japanese hostage. What if Ken hadn't come by the theatre when he did? And did the audience recognise, in the scruffy, terrified soldier who was dragged on a few moments later, the cheerful, good-looking young man with the chunky gold chain around his neck who'd recently peeped at them through the window?

A month later, I auditioned for the BBC Radio Repertory company and failed to get in. I've always regretted this. To get to play a myriad of parts in every English regional accent in the classics, modern drama, comedy . . . who wouldn't want the challenge?

It's obvious that radio drama has to have a very different technique to visual drama. Not seeing the protagonists of a story – the way they're dressed, their looks – creates its own difficulties for the listener. There are sound effects that help set the scenes for your senses, but being truthful to your character while facing a group of other actors in their jeans and sweaters, all of you reading your lines off a page in front of a microphone, needs an extraordinary concentration of belief in your make-believe world. But for the audience, it can be just as fulfilling as any visual characterisation – or just as dull.

To put it simply: in radio drama, you use the various tones and nuances of the entire range of your voice to make-believe convincingly. In theatre, you have to remember that the people at the back of the auditorium need to hear what's said without the people in the front being blasted out of their seats – a completely different form of artifice. And on screen, you have to be aware of your facial muscles along with the normal volume of your voice. A tiny roll of the eye on camera contains the same message as a lift of the brow on stage – but on radio, the lift of an eyebrow while acting, say, a Restoration dandy, has to be put across with only the tone of voice. Meantime the guy playing opposite you, far from being bewigged and made-up with a beauty spot, may have a day's growth of beard on his face and be wearing a Yankees t-shirt.

Another way to earn a living then was in B-pictures. In the sixties and early seventies, there were these shorter feature films (or 'quota quickies', as they were called) that supported the main film, and many actors learned their screen technique from these pot-boilers. I was never fortunate enough to get one.

I'm a bit vague in my mind about the chronology of my earlier days as an earning professional because I did so many bits and pieces of work. But from now on the events of my life become more settled in my mind, mostly because the seemingly casual youthful sex became more meaningful, and I can measure my life's memories between the emotional highs and lows of more serious affairs of the heart.

Rather ungallantly I think of Paul and Tony falling into the sexual whizz-bang category of the young adolescent. Then, on my twenty-first birthday, I fell in love with John. I think that's a fair description of what happened. Certainly, my heart seemed shattered when he left me, jaundiced as it was. But it mended soon enough, so maybe he should go into the pyrotechnics compartment too.

Through John, I met a lot of his friends, who were an interestingly varied group. For instance, I remember spending an extraordinarily dull evening with John Vassall, a soon-to-be-unmasked Russian double agent, in his unimpressive cramped flat beside the Thames. Once my John pushed off, I was still feted by his 'refined' friends: a member of parliament, a doctor, a banker and an interior designer. Without scruple I accepted a gold Dupont lighter, seats at Covent Garden and Wimbledon, dinners, and photographs for my portfolio. I gave nothing in exchange, except for my charming personality, I promise. I always said no to the gifts to begin with, but they insisted, thinking one more bribe, one more treat would get me horizontal, and I eventually accepted. 'I did warn you,' I would say when they were affronted at my final refusals. Let's face it, at twenty-two, I was a non-consenting tease with no thought of anyone's feelings except my own.

At one of these smart outings, at an 'in' restaurant, my foot was stood on by a waiter. I gave out a small 'ow' which nobody noticed, then as the pressure continued, I looked up crossly, ready to complain more volubly. Taking not the slightest notice of me and serving vegetables onto my plate was a young Marlon Brando. Or his twin, dressed in the restaurant's garb. He glanced at me briefly before getting off my foot and moving on to dole out veggies to the person next to me.

Looking at physical beauty can empty the world of everything else. Perhaps even more than looking at a wonderful work of art or seeing a fabulous landscape. The waiter in this French restaurant was one such exceptional work of beauty. I stared at him quite openly as he went about his job. I wasn't staring alone. Everyone at the table was ogling him. We hadn't seen him before. Where had he come from? He wasn't the guy who'd served our food up till now.

Giving us vegetables seemed to be his only mission. Afterwards, he moved around the restaurant but never came back to us. I tried to be jolly company for the rest of the meal, but I was in a state bordering on shock. I glanced at this apparition as often as I could without being obvious, but there was no sign he even knew I existed. Never once did he catch my eye. Had I imagined his treading on my foot for so long? Perhaps he had a wooden leg. I was very het-up – just look at the gorgeousness of him!

Time to go. Hell, what to do? Nothing came to mind. I needed to go to the lavatory, which was upstairs. I hadn't been in the loo a moment before there was a pounding of feet taking the steps two at a time, and in through the door barged the beautiful waiter. He grabbed my face between his hands and kissed me hard.

'My name is Marcel.' His accent was wonderfully French. 'You are Kerry. I hear people say. Ring me, please'. He pushed a piece of paper into my hand and thundered back down the stairs again.

I was dazed, tried to pee but couldn't. My breath came back slowly. I looked at the piece of paper and realised he'd put his name on an unused restaurant invoice with its name, address and number at the top. Nothing else. Why not give me his home number? Better hurry, my friends were about to leave. I washed my face and went uncomfortably down the stairs.

They were waiting by the front door of the restaurant, dressed in their overcoats, smiling at Marcel, who was now no longer a waiter it seemed but the cloakroom attendant. The girl who had taken our coats at the beginning of the evening was standing by, looking amused. My friends thanked the gorgeous man for his services. They put some money into his hand – which he handed to the girl. I thanked him, too. He ignored me and the coin in my hand. But as he helped me on with my coat, he murmured 'you call tomorrow' in my ear. A second later, I was outside on the pavement, wondering how to survive the night without him.

I rang the restaurant the following morning to be told by a male voice that it didn't open till 6.30, and Marcel wouldn't be in before 5.30. Oo was calling?

'A friend.'

Did I want to leave a message?

'Please tell him Kerry will call later.'

What did I do with the day? I sat on my hands till six o'clock, then dialled the number again.

'Oui?'

'Is, er, Marcel there?'

'Oo is calling, please?'

From now on, in this story of Marc, you can get the flavour of the French-speak by missing out on the aitches. For instance, Heathrow (the airport) is pronounced by the French, *Eazrow*. And try a zed for 'th' (e.g. *zis* for this). I'm not going to write in pidgin English. You supply their so-attractive accent from now on if you care to.

'I'm a friend of his. My name's Kerry.'

'Ah, oui! Marc!'

'Oui?' (My new man – from a distance).

'You have a call. Kerry.'

'Merci.' And he was on the phone. 'Hello. I am happy you call.'

My mouth was dry, and my heart thumping.

'Of course, I call. How could I . . . not? After . . .'

He waited for me to say more. I couldn't.

'You are free this night? Après my work?' he asked.

I'm free for the rest of my life, I thought fiercely. What I said was: 'Yes.'

'There is a club, Domino, in Kensington High Street. You know where?'

'I think so. Yes, yes, I do.'

'You wait there, please. I finish work . . . late. I see you après minuit . . . you understand French, yes?'

'A little, yes. I'll see you at the Domino Club after midnight.'

'I must go now. I see you . . . after midnight.'

I looked at my watch, my heart still booming. Three minutes past six! How on earth could I wait another six hours?

I was in the club half an hour early. It was a 'queer' venue (this was the sixties) where you could drink late and dance on a tiny floor of amber glass lit from beneath. There was none of the pounding music amplified till your world was just noise as nowadays. This club had good sexy disco music, and, as the males gyrated, lots to look at. With their shirts on. Some of them even with neckties on after work.

Marcel was late. I'd been there an hour, drinking coke, smiling polite sorrys at the enquiring looks I got, when he slid onto the bench next to me, leant over casually and kissed me on the mouth. Our love affair had started.

'We have customers. They not leave. Henri see me mad, ay, yi, yi, he say me, go. Go see your Kerry.'

'Your Kerry is right.'

He smiled brilliantly. 'I have bath, and . . . I am here.'

In this club, I was free to kiss his handsome face. So I did. The second time I nuzzled his nose with mine before licking his tongue. 'You smell wonderful. You look wonderful.' He smiled contentedly and kissed me again.

I leant against him, listening to the music, his arm proprietorial over my shoulder, and my hand sliding up his back beneath his white t-shirt. Smooth. He smelled of my favourite perfume: Monsieur by Givenchy. This stranger already owned me.

'Do you live close to the restaurant?' By now, my arm was scooped around his unknown waist, my fingers exploring.

'Cloths?'

I laughed. 'Where do you live?'

'I live up . . .' He pointed upwards, 'restaurant.'

'Above the restaurant?' I felt a stab of jealous suspicion and tried to smile. 'That's convenient.'

He grinned happily. 'Now – *we* live a-bove restaurant – toi et moi . . . Oui?'

My worries melted. 'Yes.'

He lit a cigarette for me and put it in my mouth. Three puffs later, I took it out to ask, 'Upstairs, over the restaurant, do you think?'

I must have been frowning.

'Non? OK, we go . . . we get? . . . other place . . . uh . . . Now we dance, please.'

He took a quick pull at his cigarette, put it in the ashtray, and dragged me to the dance floor. I just about got my cigarette into the receptacle before lift-off.

Overjoyed, bemused, I watched this amazing specimen of manhood as he moved unselfconsciously in front of me, his eyes closed, smiling. This wasn't a peacock showing off. He wasn't aware of the people who bumped into him. The music and the two of us were the only things in his world.

We danced for maybe ten minutes, then he led me by the hand back to the table, scooped up his cigarettes and matches, and we were outside. He hailed a cab and started kissing me the moment he'd given the driver the address. More self-conscious than Marcel, I caught the cabby's eye in his driving mirror. He looked away quickly.

When we got back to his room, a rather sordid untidy bedroom, warm, with the smell of food from the restaurant two floors below, we were impatient to get into his narrow bed. And during that long night, those insecurities, those exhilarating moments of knockabout emotions that led nowhere; those puzzling Is This How It's Done? moments of nervous naivety of a young man from no fixed background, all those non-sequiturs of my life were soothed and led somewhere calm. Everything slotted into place.

I remember only one occasion when we talked in sentences. It was when we were about to sleep, and he was stroking my brow. He smiled tenderly at me. 'Mon *biquet*.'

'Beekay? What does that mean?'

'Is baby animal with . . . ' He mimed horns from his forehead. 'Make cheeses, climb trees.'

'Goat?'

'Goat? Peut-être. Very small, very sweet. Ma muzzer – my modher she call me that, when I was . . . a . . . children?'

'Child. Yes, young goats are kids too.' He didn't understand.

I woke in the morning in his arms, my cheek pressed against his chest. He smelled of the Sobranies, a scented Turkish cigarette he'd smoked the night before. I've loved that smell to this day. He had a job to go to, so he was out of the bed first. His bathroom was no bigger than a large cupboard, and because the door wouldn't shut as some of our clothes were hanging on it, I was able to observe him; and I marvelled at the poise of his head, his gleaming dark hair slicked back, the slash of his thick eyebrows above those dark brown eyes, his straight nose.

No, he didn't look like Marlon Brando at all. He had a longer face, a stronger jawline, and his hair was darker. This was no one but Marcel. He was mine; I had no doubt of it. I was a young invincible twenty-something.

For three weeks, we only left the bed when he had to go to work. But he had no telephone, which is an actor's lifeline. Within a month, we'd moved, renting a modern two-room apartment with a bathroom and galley kitchen. It was situated in Westminster, on Horseferry Road, not far from the Houses of Parliament – but over a mile from his work.

I didn't look for gainful employment until the rooms had been painted and decorated. Burnt Orange was a new colour on the paint charts, and being theatrical, I chose this dramatic tone for the sitting room. Marcel, who wasn't too sure of the orange-brown, wanted the bedroom a more conventional pale apple green. So that's what we had. We painted the interconnecting hallway, the kitchen and bathroom an apricot white. (Going into the sitting room from a nearly white hall was a pleasant surprise but also an assault on the senses).

We spent more money than we had, but he'd worked so hard at the restaurant without spending on any luxuries – you only needed to see where he'd lived before I met him - he was a spendthrift, investing his savings on our homemaking. I didn't have a lot, but every penny there was we used.

He was very easy going, was Marc. Very occasionally, our horns locked in battles of dominance, and as I have a quick temper, the fights could be fierce. But we made each other laugh a lot – he could be very funny with his mixture of fractured French and mime. He was an inventive cook, a tireless lover and an easy friend. I woke up every day knowing I was safe for the first time in my life.

CHAPTER 6
Her and Holidays

Six months after Marc and I had created our own love nest, my mother came to London with my tiny half-brother, Mark, to stay – ostensibly for three weeks. She didn't tell us she had initiated divorce proceedings with Darell before leaving Ireland, and my mother and her baby remained with us in our two-room flat for seven months. We gave her the bedroom as there was room for a cot in there, and Marc and I slept on the sofa-bed in the sitting room. It wasn't much wider than the first bed we'd shared – which at least had been sweaty from choice.

To begin with, their presence didn't come between us, as we really only lived for each other, but from day one, intimacy in front of her went out of the window. I hadn't told her of my homosexuality, and I became self-conscious when the three of us were together. Marc was sanguine about the deception, but as time went on, I just got angry. My mother couldn't help but treat the two of us as her servants. My darling, being a foreigner, was also patronised. I was often so enraged on his behalf I wanted to shake her. (Of course, deep down, I must have been angry at myself for my gutlessness. But 'coming out' was a dicey thing then. What we did was against the law. Certainly, against middle-class convention). To get away from her, we spent more money on outside entertainment than we could afford. We became refugees, as I thought then. Marc went to work in the late afternoon, and I'd get home (ha!) to clear up the indescribable mess my mother had made of the kitchen and hand her back their belongings which were scattered all over our flat. She'd had servants in India, servants in Ireland, and now she had us to look after her. I seethed with impotent fury, and my darling man, coming home after midnight, would try to cajole me out of my moods.

Eventually, it became impossible to remember the fun times I'd had with her on our holidays together. As a child, I remembered her as teasing, funny, gorgeously scented and glamorous. Now we began to argue angrily, as I'd heard her do with Darell. After three months, my temper snapped, and I shouted at her to get out. Either she found another flat for herself and the baby, or we'd have her evicted. (It makes my toes curl when I remember the childish scene).

She was a master at the silent treatment, and as always with her, I apologised at the end of the second day of refrigeration. She needed persuading to forgive me, but she relented: she understood my feelings, but it would take time to find somewhere else to live. 'Of course,' I told her. A month later, I shouted, 'Haven't you found somewhere, for Christ's sake?', lived through the permafrost for a couple of days and apologised again. The intervals got shorter between my outbursts until she eventually said she had found a place and would be leaving the following week.

Marc had spent more and more time at the restaurant, volunteering to work other waiters' shifts, and although he said he was doing it to build up his reserves so as to spend more on our home, by now nothing he could do or say could jolly me out of my sparkling anger. So when I told him one night on the phone that she had found somewhere else and was leaving for sure, he was so pleased for me that I realised how I must have blighted his life with my petulance.

'I will come home early if I can, *biquet*. We will make great love.' (Living with an Englishman had improved his English no end. Full sentences. Thank heavens it never changed his accent).

We had the best time in months. It was loving – but quiet. I was still too jumpy, expecting my mother to barge into the room any moment – 'and another thing!'

She left with my rather cuddly half-bro to live in a basement flat in Knightsbridge. Smart area, smart flat, too. She obviously borrowed heftily from the bank in expectation of her divorce settlement. Of course, she was angrily disappointed when it eventually came through. What did she expect? She'd helped her husband get through nearly all of it.

I neglected my wee brother for the next few years. I should have gone to see my mother if only to take her nagging pressure off him. I should have gone to play with him, read to him, and take him to the park, but I was so happy to be rid of *her* I forgot *him*.

I see much more of Mark now he's older, and he's turned out to be a friend. He is a large, boisterous, fun-loving, intelligent, funny, and fundamentally kind fellow who could probably benefit from an anger management course, as indeed could I – we shared the same mother. Being a Catholic – through his father – he married a worthy Catholic woman and has spent the past twenty-four years doing jobs he didn't particularly like to provide for his family. Right now, he and his wife are separating. As children, his son and daughter were sweet, the boy earnest, the girl with a sense of fun and musically gifted, but come the crunch . . . they became very judgemental, particularly my niece, who wants a career in music. I could have helped her, but she's not interested in my input – I'm the brother of Satan. If the time comes when she has forgiven her father, my contacts in the music business will be well retired, if not dead.

Once my mother left our home, Marc helped me wash down all the surfaces and repaint the bedroom. We bought another bed and a new cooker to replace the now crusty one. It took a long time to get the presence of my mother out of our home. But her presence never quite left our relationship.

Slowly I began to repay my partner's generosity of spirit, his extraordinary sweetness. I began to feel safe again, and the venom I'd felt toward That Woman! was soothed by his enveloping love.

The following Christmas, no mother or child, not even a manger, we gave a party for all the waifs and strays from his restaurant, the waiters and the cooks who were far from home. Marc concocted a feast for the eight of us, which we ate off trays on our laps, and with the help of a box of Christmas crackers, each with a whistle which played a single note, a conductor's wand and a score, we squeaked through carols and folk songs and tunes we composed until we were in hysterics. It was one of the happiest Christmases I can recall.

*

Through recommendation, I'd found myself a sometime-agent who would volunteer me for work every now and then. She rang me up early in the New Year and asked if I played the guitar. 'No, but I am musical', I said, 'it can't be difficult to learn.' (Ho, ho! Have you ever flown a plane, Kerry? No, but I'm an actor. No probs). 'Why the guitar', I asked? A script by one of her writers had been accepted by the Windsor Repertory Theatre, which would come into London if the play was successful at its outing. The boy in the play needed to be proficient with a guitar.

(I've played younger than I am most of my life – certainly on stage. I became well-known when I played a teenager on screen when I was thirty-five).

The Kensington Squares was a ridiculously silly farce about a young guitar-playing public-school lad who lives with his colonel father and dotty mother in Kensington and forms a skiffle group (it would be a rock band now). The group is spotted by a talent scout. The scout makes an offer: he will make the boy a popstar on condition he and his parents move from their conventional Kensington flat into a seedy house in Wapping, South London – for appearance's sake. (There weren't any 'educated' pop stars then as there are now). The entire family will have to pretend to be locals, and if, as he expects, the son is a hit, then the boy will buy his 'poor ole mum and dad' a posh flat – in Kensington Square, perhaps – as a gift. Yes, you've guessed it – they move back into their own home.

I got the role, learned to play some basic chords on the guitar, was measured for a glitzy spangled suit for the number I would play in front of the curtain between Acts 2 and 3, and started rehearsals mid-January at Windsor, thirty miles from London. An easy drive from home in my little car, I would set off in the early morning and return back from rehearsals at eight-ish every night. A doddle.

Windsor is a repertory theatre only by name, in that it doesn't have a permanent company of actors performing a series of plays. On the other hand, in those days it did have a different play every five weeks, a fair amount of them shows that started there before coming into London. Not only was it easily commutable from home, the owners of the theatre treated every one of their actors like stars. Three weeks' rehearsals, five weeks' playing – a lovely job with lovely employers.

I took my hired guitar everywhere with me, driving the cast mad as I sang and thrashed at the strings in a rough approximation of what I would perform on stage. I'd chosen a Jerry Lee Lewis song, 'I Go Ape', which would allow me to wail and scream, so covering up my very basic chord-work. *And* I was to be accompanied by a rock group on tape.

Once you'd swallowed the improbability of the story, the writer had contrived some very funny situations, and the first-night audience in Windsor adored it. With the success it had in Windsor, there was no question but we'd be transferring into town. Which we duly did two months later. Robin Ray, who had played the talent scout/fixer out of town, was replaced by Clifford Mollison, a well-loved Variety star, but most of the rest of the cast remained the same.

The Kensington Squares, our old-fashioned, well-made farcical comedy, received poor notices by the now angst-appreciative London critics. The reviews certainly weren't good enough to lure an audience to the out-of-the-way theatre right next to Buckingham Palace. The play only ran for six weeks in London. (The theatre has since been pulled down, and another put up in its place. There went my plaque!).

Windsor is very Home Counties (the Queen's castle towers above the theatre), so the fans I had there for my cockney pop idol were rather well-spoken and middle-aged. In London, I had the sort of teenagers outside the Stage Door I'd seen on film screaming for the Beatles, and I have to admit I was somewhat smug at the success of my disguise – both as an actor and a homosexual – as I signed autograph books and had my clothes plucked at by squealing girls.

You'll have guessed that my mother loved Acts One and Three, where I was the gent and was less taken by my scruffy Sarf London lad. Marc, who'd never seen me act before, loved every second of the play when I was on stage and thought I was way beyond wonderful – so proud he was fit to bust. He didn't understand much of the dialogue, but he revelled in the appreciation the audience showed me. In the eleven weeks it was on, he saw it seven times.

When I went to eat at his restaurant after the show, he'd plead to be allowed to take me around the tables and introduce me to everyone. It was cringe-making the few times I let him do it, but I was so chuffed at his pride and enthusiasm, all in his wonderful broken accent, I could only grin. He was obviously adored by the regular clientele, men and women, who delighted in his Gallic charm. Henri, his boss, was only too aware of what a draw he was for the business so, he encouraged him to show off. In his job, Marc was a star.

We'd been together about eighteen months by now. I noticed he was putting on a little weight, but we were the happiest of couples, and in those days, weight was not the fashion problem it is now. Not only was he the nicest of friends, he was still the sweetest partner in bed, still committed to Us.

I had elicited some interest from a middle-of-the-road agent, one of the many whom I'd invited to see the show in London, and the only one who'd managed to make it, and he rang me to suggest I meet a television director.

The director and I got on famously, and he offered me a smallish part in his latest television drama. It was the most interesting role I'd been offered on the small screen to date, and I was very cheered. And the piece had a very starry cast.

The director, John, was an ebullient charmer of a man and still boyishly enthusiastic about his job. He was warm-hearted, with a beautiful wife and two lovely young daughters. His delight in our business enthused all but the most piss-elegant actors – and our star was one of those. She 'didn't suffer fools gladly'. (A pompous affectation from bad-mannered people who think themselves and their time more important than others. How much closer to God do these beings think they are?). As I said, our female star thought John, with his bubbly enthusiasm, a fool, but he had a gimlet eye for the real, a cameraman's instinct to zoom in on the most telling gestures, and all but she loved working with him. When I saw the finished product on the screen, I was mighty proud to have been involved in its making. Our star, who was indeed a wonderful actress, was made to look good too. She took the praise as her due.

John was the warmest of human beings, and I loved him for it. We worked together again later in my career. In my days as a professional actor without an agent that was often how it went. People I worked with asked me back – eventually.

*

Marc and I went on holiday to visit his parents in Marseilles. From the sea, the city looks vast: a huge sprawl of houses up a wide slope. My love's parents lived in one of a group of high-rise apartment buildings in the northern suburbs, on the crown of the hill.

Marc's father was a diabetic and housebound, large and bald, hardly saying a word to either of us. I caught glimpses of his son's almond eyes through the slabs of lard that made up his face. His mother was bird-like. She adored her oldest son and was exceedingly sweet to me, his friend. She would occasionally come out with us when we went down into town to the cinema or a restaurant, but most of the time, she stayed in to look after her husband

Marc's and my favourite outing involved taking a slow train eastward along the coast, slow enough to jump off at a bend above a tiny deserted beach. After sliding down through the prickly vegetation to the cove, we'd swim with sandalled feet because of the *oursin*, the spiny sea urchins which lay on the pebbly sand below the surface of the warm water. Apparently, they're delicious. We'd jump back on the homeward-bound train when we were done.

The sun glowed that holiday, as did we. We agreed holidaying together was such fun we'd do it often.

On the return journey, the plane from Marseilles to Paris was like a cardboard box held together with string. We could see the asphalt in the gaps beneath our feet as we rolled down the runway and laboriously climbed into the air. The cabin was packed with farmers and their produce. The smell of the garlic along with underarm odour, the cloyingly sweet stink of chickens, geese and ducks, all making a hell of a din from somewhere under our feet, made for a nauseating nerve-wracking journey, and I was grateful the plane flew so close to the ground. With luck, it wouldn't make a fatal impact on crashing from that height.

Back in London, my clever partner was talent-spotted himself. Charles Brodie, a restaurateur, was opening new premises close to where Marc was already working. Someone had recommended that Charles look at my chap with a view to his being Head Waiter at these new premises. He saw Marcel in action at the restaurant where we'd first met, saw the way the diners were besotted by him, and, just like that, asked him to be the maître d' in his new place. It was to be called La Poule au Pot, and it was opening three months hence. Marc's duties would be onerous, but his salary commensurate. Highly qualified and highly flattered, he accepted. It was my turn to be over-the-moon proud. But for the first time in our lives together, I saw him stressed.

Because there was just enough of a gap after he'd worked off his notice period in the old restaurant to get away, I thought we should find a sunny beach to give us time to rally his confidence – though, of course, that wasn't how I rationalised it at the time. His father had worked most of his life as a French civil servant in Tunisia, and Marc had been born there. So it was to Tunisia that we went, to Sousse, a small seaside town where a friend of the family still lived.

To my way of thinking, the younger male Tunisians are among the most beautiful men in the world. For a start, that area of North Africa was overrun by the Romans those many centuries ago, and the combination of Italian and Arab blood produces the most astounding masculine beauty – which includes blond Arabs with blue eyes. Secondly, the country being so poor, to make a living the young men all aspire to represent their country at sport, hoping that way to change their fortunes. Their young physiques could have inspired Michelangelo. But corpulence is proof of wealth and success, so by the time they are in their mid-thirties, most of those superb bodies have been bloated by the prevailing customs. Like so many in this world with little, they are a peaceful happy people, living in harmony in the warmth of the south Mediterranean sun throughout the year. I haven't been back for a very long time, but that's how the country presented itself to me then. (Of course, politics have ravaged the country since).

In the early twilight, Tunisian men of all ages strolled along the seafront arm in arm, sometimes hand in hand, sprays of jasmine they'd bought at the street corners perched over their ears, talking animatedly in French. In the meantime, their wives were at home cooking the evening meal and putting the children to bed.

It was overwhelming to be among so many attractive males with the intoxicating smell of jasmine in the warm dusky air. And even though I had one of the most beautiful men in the world by my side, this overloading of the senses made me . . . well, maybe not hungry. Peckish?

In Sousse, we stayed with the friend of Marc's family – a homosexual who had an Arab chauffeur and a wife to take care of him, as both of his legs had been blown off below the knees, the victim of a bomb in the Algerian conflict. Eddie looked after his every need, and his wife did the cooking and cleaning.

Each day we had lunch at the same courtyard restaurant, and there was one young dark Arab waiter, Ali, who seemed particularly struck by me. I was told he'd recently been called up to go into the army. He had a good physique but was not particularly attractive, and although flattered, I paid little attention to him.

After the second lunch in that restaurant, and at the end of the siesta we were having at our friend's home, the doorbell rang. I heard our host's voice, and then he called Marc. I was propped up on an elbow reading when my lover came back into the bedroom with our waiter from the restaurant.

'Ali has come to have sex with you. You would like that, no?'

I was astounded – but Marc smiled at us brightly and left the room. So, without a word being spoken, that's what happened. Afterwards, he smiled apologetically, murmured a thank you, and left the house. Because it was so unexpected, it was one of the most sexually thrilling things that had happened to me. I didn't complain. Afterwards, Marc and I went to the beach and swam. I had thought there'd be some reference to this most outrageously casual sharing of my body with a stranger, but no. However, the longer we didn't talk about it, the more uneasy I became. I badly needed reassurance that my partner still loved me. That night he and I had the sweetest sex. No mention was made of earlier. Everything could be OK?

Ali came by the next afternoon, and this time Marc stayed. Again, he thanked us quietly before leaving.

Although I found this novel turn in my partner's and my relationship thrilling, it was also bewildering – and somewhere deep inside me, I became fearful. My romantic young soul had never in a month of Sundays imagined *sharing* physical favours. I had always imagined love with The One being Exclusive. Where was 'fidelity' in all this? Love and honour? Thou shalt not cleave unto another . . .? We'd 'cleaved' away like billy-ho. Perhaps Marc knew me better than I knew myself. But I wasn't at all sure I liked myself the better.

But this I noticed. I only had to look at any young man with favour, and my lover was onto it. His never eying anyone up for himself made no sense.

Somewhere in the middle of our holiday, we saw, on the beach, playing volleyball, the cutest, manliest young guy. Marc called him over. The boy's smile was brilliant, and he was completely natural in his greetings. His name was Nourredin. He beckoned over a couple of the other young players and, still talking noisily, they threw themselves onto the sand beside us. Nourredin flopped down and laid his sweaty blond head on my stomach. This stranger of a few moments ago quite casually annexed my body for his comfort. We'd been using the beach café of a rather posh hotel for our refreshments, and our sun-bathing spot was close to its reserved area. The disapproving looks we got from the German families made me giggle inwardly. Such depravity, young Kerry.

He and his friends hung around with us the next day (we'd moved further down the beach to get away from Germanic disapproval), and before he left to go home that evening, Nourredin invited us to share his family's Sunday lunch a few days later.

His father was wealthy enough to have rented a modest holiday house for the summer – and we shared a bowl of couscous and vegetables sitting cross-legged on a carpet in the courtyard. It was a very simple meal for such a large family group, just one small piece of meat helping flavour the gravy, but there in the centre of the bowl was a lamb's eye. As their honoured guests, we were urged to eat it. I smiled as politely as I could, my gorge lurching and my eyes pleading with Marc to take it, because there was no way on earth, I could scoop it up with my spoon. My Tunisian-born hero did just that. I had to look away because it was too big to swallow in one, so I imagine he had to chomp on it first.

It seemed the father considered it an honour that we took such an interest in his son. The Europeans had so much culture and history to impart, and please, please come and visit them in their proper home inland should we ever come back. He was utterly genuine in his sentiments, and it baffled me as we sat and listened to him. Marc told me afterwards that Arabs in northern Africa believe young men, most of whom wouldn't be able to afford marriage until later in life – if at all – must get their sexual experience from other males perforce. That way, they wouldn't father an unwanted child. (What the poor young women do, I still don't know). He told me Nourredin's father would have known well enough what his young son was doing with these two European males and would approve the 'lessons' we were giving him.

How convenient for us! But I was still self-conscious – even though nothing had happened.

Until nearly the end of our time in Sousse, Marc asked whether I'd like sex with this lad we'd grown so fond of, and when I said yes, asked him point-blank in front of me if he knew of somewhere private, we could meet where we could go to bed. Nourredin, without any self-consciousness – even though I was scarlet – was sunnily sure he could arrange it. The next day we were told where to meet him, and Marc asked if one of his beachball pals could come along too. A few hours later, I found myself trudging through a shanty town of small bright-white shacks in the brilliant moonlight to a tiny one-room place where there were two single iron bedsteads, each with a mattress not much thicker than a sheet.

It, everything, was hugely uncomfortable.

We all traipsed down to the seafront afterwards – must have been midnight – and, sipping mint tea at a café, watched the women bathing their infants in seawater to keep them cool. Now we were all completely relaxed and talkative, happy at the thought of the recent deed rather than its performance. Marc and I returned to our house, having emptied our pockets. He told me as we walked, he hadn't enjoyed his sexual partner much, and I confessed I hadn't enjoyed it at all.

My mind in a state of flux, we returned to England the next day.

Over the following months, I got more and more confused. I loved the pants off Marc and think even now I would have been content to have had no relationships outside our partnership forever and ever, amen. On the other hand, he had introduced me to experiences I'd never imagined. experiences that were surely forbidden to couples in a relationship. But, of course, they weren't forbidden in that time of flower-power and sexual liberation – they were mind-blowing – and my partner was every bit as loving as before. There I was at twenty-three or thereabouts, an innocent sap completely at sea in a welter of swirling emotions, not knowing which way was up.

(I've often thought that if there were such a thing as a virtual reality contraption, we could wear on our heads which could give us all the sexual sensation and stimulation a real-life sexual encounter can, it would be a great aid to society. Imagine all those unloved or misshapen people out there getting their dreams fulfilled by a fantasy partner of their choosing. Travelling the world, I look around me and bet inwardly that many men, with or without families, would be interested in experimenting sexually with another male if no one ever knew about it. If only once. If it was non-threatening, it might simply become part of their normal diet: 'I'll have the disc with the "J-Lo" lookalike . . . one of the "Naomi Campbell", please . . . Have you got the "Brad Pitt" back? Great . . . and the "Chris Hemsworth" . . . and a "Rufus Wainwright". That's my free government quota for the month, isn't it?' There will always be the psychopaths, but intolerance of sexual differences would become a thing of the past, no?

The same would apply to females. Shirley).

*

Along with many others, I helped Charles Brodie decorate his new restaurant, hanging baskets of grapes from the overhead light fittings and decking the walls with ancient farm equipment (saws, plough blades and wooden rakes). Marcel, who had already interviewed and picked his front-of-house restaurant staff, was training them in his way of working, telling them what sort of manners he'd expect from them, showing them where everything was to be kept, how he wanted the tables laid, what to do in this or that situation. It was a worrying task but essential. All complaints would land at his door.

The restaurant opened to great acclaim from the critics. The food 'was as good if not better than anywhere in London charging those prices', the preparation was 'beautiful', the wine menu was 'superb in its choices'.

It was my turn to be oh so very proud of him. (And, after all these years, that superb restaurant is still open for business in Ebury Street, still with that paraphernalia I helped hang on the walls. And the baskets covering the lightbulbs – I imagine someone's dusted them since).

I was offered an acting job soon after the restaurant opening and discussed with Marc whether I should do it. He was still fine-tuning himself and his staff and was probably relieved he wouldn't have to cope with me in his spare moments. So, yes, I went up to Scotland to play one of the Broker's Men, a fun part, in another production of *Jack and the Beanstalk* – this time in Aberdeen, 250 miles away.

Pantomime lasted through Christmas and well into the New Year with ten or even twelve performances a week. Most of these are matinees so young children with their families can come and enjoy themselves. For an actor, they're noisy fun, and completely unpredictable. Lots of ad-libbing is called for because children will interrupt throughout and participate as though their lives depended on it – exhausting but exhilarating. In Scotland, we worked on Christmas day, because New Year's Eve is their special holiday, so there was no chance of my getting back to London during those three months.

While I was away, there was a burglary in our Horseferry Road flat. Extraordinarily, only *my* possessions were stolen. All the long-playing records my father had sent me from New York, all those latest musical comedies, my best overcoat and a large suitcase were pinched. Marc had no suggestions as to why, no explanation as to how, except that for a short while he'd invited one of the restaurant staff to stay. The waiter had been evicted from his home, and perhaps this guy had made a copy of the key and let himself in another time when Marc had been working? This man had been sacked by Charles soon after and hadn't left a forwarding address. I was credulous, even proud of my fella who was still looking after the waifs and strays of the world, upset at my loss – my father was dead, so there was no way of duplicating my recordings – but not inconsolable. What are possessions after all?

I was young and trusting. And naive. All for one, and one for all!

Marc's new boss, Charles, lived in a house quite close to his new restaurant. There were some vacant rooms with a bathroom on the top floor which he thought might suit us. Marc could live within half a mile of his work. He could walk or bicycle there if need be.

Two and a half years after we'd met, we moved home again.

CHAPTER 7
'When I'm Cleanin' Winders'

Brian had come into Charles's house through the basement flat – not through a jemmied door or window. He'd been invited. Looking at him, you'd be forgiven if, at first sight, you weren't sure about that. He was what, in those days, you might call a bit of a geezer. The downstairs flat he'd been invited to was where Michael, a charming but occasionally waspish middle-aged actors' agent, lived.

The invitation was issued like this. On his way to his office one morning, Michael had seen this young man up a ladder lathering the window of a rather grand Edwardian house and had called up from the pavement to ask, in his clipped voice, whether the lad was available to clean windows in other areas of London. He was, and was given an appointment then and there to come and see this smoothly affable toff at his home. (The word 'basement' wasn't mentioned). As the scheduled meeting was after working hours, Brian arrived in his best suit and without his bucket and washcloth. He stayed for three years.

Charles, our now-landlord and owner of the house, occupied the ground and first floors with his long-term, younger partner Geoffrey, and by the time Marc and I moved into the top of the house, Brian had been elevated up a floor to a small bedroom under the stairs which was opposite the front door of the building. I had been told about him, but we hadn't met when Marc and I first transferred our belongings. The following day I collected the last of our things from the Westminster place and let myself into our new home – into what I'd supposed was an empty house, as it was lunchtime, so both Marc and Charles were working. I stopped dead in my tracks as I came face to face with an Athenian god. Nothing had been said to prepare me, so my defences were nowhere to be seen.

'Kerry, yeah? I'm Brian.'

The apparition smiled. My head lowered, and a bewildering twilight engulfed me. I dropped the suitcase I was holding onto my foot. He rushed to help me, and it took us three or four trips to get all the bits and pieces out of my car and up to the topmost rooms where Marc and I were now living. The move was done far too quickly – meaning all too soon I had to stop and face him again. My mouth was dry, and my heart was beating fit to bust.

Brian was probably the most unsettling youngster I'd met up to that moment in my life. He was about my age, maybe an inch shorter, slight, with dark, tight curly hair and steel-blue eyes. You might mistake him for a gypsy. Along with his openness, his warm inquisitiveness, his cockney voice, the unscented smell of him, he was my yet-to-be-realised sexual fantasy. After the first meeting, I found he wasn't tough enough for a 'bit of rough' – too cheerful. Grime-under-the-fingernails, unconsciously sexy more like it. Beside Michelangelo's David, I felt like Little Lord Fauntleroy – with buttery legs. I'm not sure if in my shyness I was even able to smile, but I thanked him formally, and he went off down the stairs, back into the empty house below.

I sat down – I had to – listening to him moving downstairs, and the disorientation eventually passed.

For 365 days a year I had only to go down two flights of stairs to see my fantasy in the flesh. He was going to be living with me in the confined space of a house. With Marc and me. Oh. Suddenly the gap between this Brian and me opened up like a telescope, and I was looking through the wrong end. I grieved at the loss of something that had never been mine.

In this, our new home, the rooms were old-fashioned conventional, and I didn't like the fact that we were no longer self-contained as in our modern flat with our own front door. I didn't immediately care for it. It was ordinary, and white – I missed our colourful walls. We were there because it was obviously more sensible for Marc to live nearer his more important new job, which was now a mere half-mile away, in the same house as his boss who could, if it was convenient, give him a lift to work in his car. To look on the bright side, we were higher up than in Horseferry Road and had a cheerful view through the treetops across a wide residential street. Three other plusses: apart from the owner and his boyfriend downstairs, there was a dog, a King Charles spaniel named Benji, and a unmitigatedly gorgeous young man named Brian. And below them a well-known actors' agent. Not my agent, but *an* agent.

Back to the everyday story of this young thespian.

Michael, the agent in the basement, told me one morning that the Old Vic, a theatre on the South Bank of the Thames, was looking for a spear-carrier, a walk-on. Would I be interested? Because if I was, I should go and meet the theatre management right away. He'd suggest me for the job if I wanted it. It seemed to be in his remit.

I had already played a lead role in the West End a year earlier, so this new job might seem a big step down. But it was in a very prestigious theatre – London's National Theatre at the time, if you wanted to put it that way. I needed the job for my C.V. Looking back at my career to date, I realised the work I'd been seen in was either frothy or insubstantial, and this ten-month season of classics added heft . . . even gravitas (two words I've always wanted to use in context).

I went along to meet the Old Vic management, got the job, and was engaged to do three Shakespeare plays, another by the Englishman Oliver Goldsmith, and the fifth by the Russian, Anton Chekov.

So it was that in 1960 I completed the trio of traditional starts to an actor's career: my first part had been a butler; soon after I played the back end of a cow in a pantomime; and my first part at the Vic was that of a spear-carrier – in the Zeffirelli production of *Romeo and Juliet* with John Stride and Judi Dench. And to underscore my progress, I also understudied the Apothecary – an ancient chemist with potions to spare. ('Something for the weekend, Mr Montague?').

I spent almost all the working hours of the first five weeks of my contract rehearsing in the theatre until the first night of the first play. We opened and read the rave reviews the next morning just moments before starting rehearsals for the second play.

Five weeks later, with the first of the plays, R and J, still performing to the public every evening (plus matinees on Wednesdays and Saturdays), the second play opened and, as before, moments after that first night, we started rehearsing the third play of the season, performing the first two in repertoire. When the third play opened, and we were rehearsing the fourth, the first play came to an end and dropped out of the season's programme. This unrelenting schedule continued for nearly seven months until the fifth play was on, during which time I only used my new home in Pimlico for the hours of sleep and all-day Sunday.

Although the workload was tiring, it was also immensely stimulating. I was part of a team of nearly a hundred people, what with the front of house staff (the box office personnel, the ushers and the cleaners) and the backstage staff (stage management, scenery shifters etc.). And along with designers, prop-makers, painters and musicians, there were about thirty performers. A fascinating mixture of new acquaintances, some of them already internationally famous – the Italian director Franco Zeffirelli and the composer Michael Tippett to name but two. As box-office draws, there were the established 'name' actors, then a couple of up-and-coming youngsters, who have since up and come. A third came and went.

And as if all that wasn't heady enough, there were the marvellous words we were working with. Some of the most beautiful and dazzling sentences in the English language danced around the dark auditorium, and a few of them were launched new-minted by me! I don't know that I've been any happier or more contented in my work since.

Towards the end of that first year, Alec McCowen, one of the leading actors that season, called the company together. The Old Vic and the Sadler's Wells Theatre companies, both of them started by Lilian Bayliss, took it in turns to host an evening's entertainment every four years or so – and this year, it was our turn. Any ideas as to what we should present? After a long silence, I found myself suggesting I write a cabaret, lampooning the plays we'd done through the year, in which the leading actors would play walk-ons, and the walk-ons take the leads. 'Good,' said Alec. 'But you have to be the Master of Ceremonies,' says I. 'Fine,' says he.

We had almost no rehearsal time. I thought what I concocted was funny, but our guests that evening seemed completely bemused by our in-jokes. Perhaps if we'd done it *en pointe*? Ah, well.

I saw very little of Marc, whose job running the now very successful La Poule au Pot had taken over every waking moment of his day and late into the evening. We met in bed for a few moments before we fell asleep and woke up together before we went our separate ways. Our relationship was for Sundays.

I was mingling with some very good-looking young people in the theatre – actors in their first flush of youth are often very attractive, let alone their second or third – so Brian's astonishing initial impact dimmed. And by now, this once chubby duckling had had it confirmed that he was pretty gorgeous himself, and my self-worth was given a further boost by the few flirtatious males and females in this new-to-me theatre company. My partner thought I was the bee's knees, but then he would, wouldn't he – he loved me.

At last, after many months, my love's job became almost routine to him, and we resumed the contented relationship we'd had before. But I was still flummoxed as to why he'd introduced other sexual partners into our idyll in Tunisia, and I was still uneasy. The first glint of gilt had come off my romantic gingerbread, but did it matter? I was living high on the hog, and the crackling was delicious. Then, with more free time from the restaurant, Marc began to bring men back in the early hours of the morning and introduce them into our bed.

By the third year of our 'marriage,' I found myself on a merry go round. It was the sixties, what I was doing was exciting, seemed almost de rigueur, but to this middle-class prude, it was still unsettling. And the longer it went on, the more I became inwardly ashamed of myself. Not that I joined the dots at the time.

*

Back at the theatre, life got better and better. One of the principals I understudied in Shakespeare's *A Midsummer Night's Dream* fell ill, and one matinee I found myself on stage playing Lysander opposite Judi Dench's Hermia. As I finished my very first speech – 'you have her father's love, Demetrius. Let me have Hermia's' – I knelt at Judi's feet, looking up at her adoringly, and there was a huge laugh from the audience. 'Heavens,' she murmured, her eyes widening, and I exulted. I went from strength to strength I was that good. So good that two coachloads of theatregoers who'd been in the theatre that afternoon wrote to the management saying they couldn't imagine the part being played any better by the leading actor I had replaced. That leading actor got well enough to return for the evening performance, so I found myself back in my much smaller role. Bastard!

Then another middle-range actor left the company. I've no idea as to the reason why and oddly enough I haven't heard of him from that day to this, but I'm sure because of those letters to the management I was promoted to his more important roles for the last months of the season. My status in the company was on the up, and life was varied and tasty.

Extraordinarily enough, one of those better parts was the same as the second role I'd had at Marlborough College: Titinius, in Shakespeare's *Julius Caesar*. But here I was playing it with grown-ups for grown-ups, directed by a Greek director, Minos Volonakis. A Greek director for a Roman story? Why not? And he had such a wonderful slant on it – it was to be played as a Greek tragedy.

The set was by Nicholas Georgiadis. A huge bronze disc hung in the centre of the blue sky cyclorama at the back, and a steep flight of stairs was a permanent feature upstage left. Material drapes were flown in for different scenes (leather drapes for the scenes in the tent), and Octavius Caesar's army was in dark brown leather with fixed jigsaw-like pieces standing out in front of their bodies – body armour, or shields, perhaps. Like the set, it was odd but effective.

In this Greek director's version, Titinius was Cassius's young lover, so in the Forum scene, the parade before the races, all the male runners came on, our mentors' arms draped over our shoulders. My lover and protector, Cassius, was played by that fine actor, Robert Eddison. Brutus was played by John Gregson – to me at that time of *Genevieve* fame.

We all got engrossed with the concept, and Minos was inspirational to work with. In the crowd scene after Antony's oration, while the crowd raced about shouting for vengeance with torches flaming, Carol MacReady tore at her hair and keened downstage. God, it was exciting to be an actor.

It was only during the first night that it dawned on us that we'd been sold a pup. Thank heavens I was downstage right with Brutus's army when Emrys James as Octavius Caesar shouted out his defiance from the top of the steps opposite. And as his army, two abreast, disdain on every face, retreated back up the steps away from us, each one of them stepped on the back of his leather cloak and fell off the stairs onto the stage like ninepins, at which the audience laughed and cheered. The critics were gleefully venomous the next day.

But we'd believed utterly in what we'd been doing every second until that first night.

On tour later, I was singled out in the Oxford *Times*: 'It comes to something when the only moving moment in this Shakespearian tragedy was provided by Kerry Gardner as Titinius mourning his dead lover on the battlefield'. I enjoyed that. Guiltily. And it reminded me of my ageing butler in that very first professional performance I'd given at Frinton. I avoided looking the leading actors in the eye that week in Oxford as well.

By mid-August, all the season's plays had opened and been reviewed, and the most successful four were still on view to the public. I was in only two of them, so I found myself employed, paid a pittance, dazed and happy, and – it came as a shock –with time on my hands. There were no rehearsals during the day, and sometimes

I had two or maybe even three weekday evenings free. Marc worked some lunchtimes and five evenings a week.

I felt like a parolee on a spree. Imagine the intoxication of Adam when he first saw the real world with all its temptations. That was me. Still young, I was being paid to live in London, the very centre of the universe in the sixties. I used public transport to get me to every corner of the city. I explored each of the boroughs on foot. I went to dance class, played tennis, smoked pot, visited the cinema regularly, met up with friends in pubs, saw more theatre, took occasional day trips to Stratford-upon-Avon to see other Shakespeare plays starring fellow performers Laurence Olivier and Vivien Leigh (didn't know them but, what the hell, they did what I did, so we were mates), and partied a lot. All these things I did with or without Marc. This was the era when drabness and conformity were old hat, and freedom became compulsory – the Beatles, skiffle groups, Mary Quant, Carnaby Street, the new fashions for men and women. I was Tommy Steele's ping-pong partner back at the theatre. So, I was the axis of the world, and the world was London-centric. Peace and free love, man. Dunked and dunking, I splashed about happily in this permissive pool.

I went to eat at a greatly reduced cost to the restaurant where Marc introduced me to his favourite clientele and where, because I was now more at ease with a small amount of success to my name in the theatre, and personable – and good to look at, did I mention? – I enjoyed myself.

'What do you do?'

'I'm an actor.'

'How fascinating. Are you famous – I mean, should we have seen you in something?'

'You can see me in London in a couple of plays at the moment.'

'Heavens, what fun, we'd love to come. Which theatre?'

'They're Shakespeare plays. At the Old Vic.'

'Ah. But at least you could join us for a drink.'

*

Back at the homestead, I'd learned some more about Brian. A year or so before, in his early twenties, I suppose, the police had cautioned him for exposing himself in public. Apparently, a young woman had stood in the window of a house across the street fingering herself. Standing at a window, perhaps even in the house I was now living in, he'd joined in the fun, and the two of them excited themselves up the Richter scale. An old biddy living opposite had seen him and rung 999, watching all the while until the police arrived. So, he was caught cock-a-hoop, and cock-in-hand.

Ah, well. It seemed Brian, who was so wonderfully easy on the eye, was basically straight. Maybe flashing at women wasn't terribly 'straight' – but it got his pecker up, and that ironed out my rumpled fantasies. But then again, what about Michael down in the basement? How did he fit into this? (And a few years later, he got married and had a kid.)

Coming from my rather proper background, I found Brian's deeds of daring wickedly attractive. He'd once asked Marc and me if he and a couple of friends could use our kitchen. Whatever they were up to, he obviously didn't want Charles knowing about it. One of his pals, who looked all of sixteen, was cheeky and very attractive, so of course we said yes. Brian told us afterwards they'd been divvying up the money from a gas meter one of the two lads had forced open. Boys can be such scamps, eh? Endearing if they're good to look at, but *villains* if they're ugly. I found it impossible not to forgive Brian anything. He was just so coltishly uncomplicated – so very sexy in his naughtiness.

There was a fashionable men's clothier in the King's Road where one week, with almost all the money I was paid, I'd bought a pair of charcoal pants. The first time I'd worn them, they'd split from below the crotch in the front to the belt at the back. I'd been very indignant when I returned them to the shop, and a sniffy assistant had asked me if I'd sat in them.

'Of course, I did!'

'Sir, these trousers aren't meant to be sat in.'

I'd laughed at the joke, but he'd been perfectly serious. Grudgingly he'd had them mended at no extra cost to myself, but as you can imagine, I was somewhat wary of sitting in them again.

I hit on what I thought was a brilliant wheeze. I asked Marc with all the innocence I could muster if he thought it would be a good deed if I gave them to Bri, who never seemed to have two pennies to rub together. 'Is nice idea,' he'd said.

Permission granted, I waited for a day when the house was empty except for Brian and myself. The scene set in the room behind me, I hovered at the top of the stairs until I heard him moving on the floor below, then ever-so-casually leaned over the bannister and called him.

'Bri, is that you, mate? Got a moment?'

'Yeah.'

'Come up, will you? I've got something to show you.'

'Sure.'

I nipped quickly back into the bedroom as he came up the stairs. Then there he was in my doorway, an enquiring smile on his face.

'Come in, come in.'

He stepped into the room. The sun outside was brilliant, and it suffused his gypsy face as in a stained-glass window. I felt nearly sick with fear and longing.

I was once told by someone that I have an irritating habit of trying to become the same social class as whoever I am talking to by the way I speak. She said it was patronising. But I think it makes people relax and accept me more easily. I swear it's unconscious. Irritating to that ex-acquaintance, it has the desired effect. So, with this gorgeous cockney, I moved my hint of an accent to the east of London.

I began: 'Listen, mate, I bought these trousers, cost me nearly twenty quid they did, must have been mad, a whole week's wages, and they bloody split, didn't they?'

I'd lifted them off the back of a chair where I'd carefully placed them and now held them up for inspection.

He looked a little confused, as well he might with the syntax and gobbledygook I was spouting. 'Yeah?'

'Well, they've been mended, you wouldn't know they'd been damaged, but I wouldn't feel safe wearing them again, would I?' An attempt at a smile, 'So as you're thinner than me, I thought they'd be safer on you.' I'd nearly finished. Was I gabbling? Why did I feel slightly ill? He was smiling, but he didn't have a clue as to what I was on about.

'Any good to you?' I asked.

'Ah ... yeah. Thanks. They look great.' I tried to look nonchalant, but inwardly I was begging for a merciful conclusion to this staged farce. I cleared my clogged throat.

'You should try them on perhaps. See if they fit.'

Was that a slight smile? Had he twigged where this was going? 'Right.'

He turned away from me, took off his shoes, undid his trousers, then stepped out of them, leaving them on the floor. I didn't even peep. Believe it or not, I was so riddled with anxiety I stared into the corner of the room. Only half turning, he put his hand out and, waking up, I gave him the pants. He stepped into them, tugged them up, tucked his shirt in and fastened them. They fitted him like a second skin but bunched a bit around his ankles. He turned around.

'What d'yer think then? Bit long?'

Tousled hair, a wrinkled shirt with a pair of form-hugging pants below, he looked like the sexiest model you could imagine.

'Nah, they'll be fine when you're in your shoes. They look great on you. I want you to keep them.'

Not a smile, a raising of the eyebrows. A 'was that it?' look. 'Er. Thanks,' he said.

He took the trousers off. I saw a flash of his pasty flank and looked away hurriedly. When I looked again, his shirttails had covered it as he straightened and tossed the charcoal pants onto a chair. He bent to retrieve his old ones, pulled them up, and smiled interrogatively. My glazed smile seemed to reassure him all was done, and he left the room, new trousers in hand.

His first attempt at seduction in tatters, Don Juan sat down, his mind in despair.

CHAPTER 8
Where's the Logic in That?

I mentioned that two-thirds of the way through that first season at the Old Vic, I'd been promoted from understudies and walk-ons to more featured roles. You've forgotten already? This is like pulling whales' teeth.

OK, so one of these roles came about like this.

I'd understudied an actor who had left the company halfway through that first season, and one of the parts I took over, though smallish, was pivotal to the story. In Shakespeare's *Twelfth Night*, Sebastian is a booby, a conceit that helps conclude the play on a happy note. I played him as the earnest young man as written, and his earnestness is such that he is often unintentionally funny. He's a hot-headed young idiot to whom one extraordinary thing happens after another, so he finds himself in a continual whirl of annoying distraction. This firebrand is, without any warning, vamped by a complete stranger, a gorgeous piece of patrician totty, who has mistaken him for his twin sister, Viola, because, unknown to him, she is pretending to be a man. He comes away from their first off-stage tête-à-tête in a daze and has a bewildered, funny speech about the extraordinary situation he finds himself in. It's only at the end of the play that the penny drops when he discovers his twin still dressed as a man. Delicious stuff. I didn't look anything like Barbara Jefford, who was playing Viola that first season when I took over the role, even though I inherited a wig the same colour as her hair and cut in the same style. But we were dressed identically, so it was *just* possible to believe we could be mistaken for each other. In the dark. From a distance. (Never mind, that's theatrical licence – and in Shakespeare, you need a lot of it).

And, by the by, what's with all this homoeroticism in

Shakespeare's plays? In the one I've just mentioned, *Twelfth Night*, Sebastian has a slavish friend, a ship's captain, who insists on financing him ('a Dupont lighter, matey?'), and the Duke Orsino has a yen for the boy Viola is pretending to be. In *The Merchant of Venice*, there's Bassanio and Antonio, his older mate, who dotes on him – in a very doting way. In *As You Like It*, Orlando is encouraged to woo Rosalind when she is successfully pretending to be a man, and so on. Being bisexual wasn't too surprising in Shakespearean times, obviously.

This *Twelfth Night* was a wonderful production by Colin Graham that looked ravishing – à la Watteau.

Towards the end of my first season at the Vic, the artistic director had advertised auditions in the trade papers for an important role in *The Tempest*, which was to be produced the following year. I asked if I could audition for it. The lead character was to be played by a comedy giant, Alastair Sim, one of our best-loved British actors, a true star in the less crowded firmament of the fifties and sixties. Well, now, this famous man was on his way with the director to the manager's office for a design meeting one afternoon, and they took a shortcut through the back of the stalls during a matinee of *Twelfth Night*. And it just so happened I was on stage doing my 'bewildered' solo speech. He stopped to watch my performance – then told the director I was to play Ariel' in *The Tempest*, the part advertised.

'But we have five people auditioning for you tomorrow!' the director expostulated.

'We'll see all of them, but – what's his name? – *that* lad is going to play it.'

Alastair Sim had the sort of clout that wasn't to be argued with. Between the shows that afternoon, I was taken into an empty dressing-room by the disgruntled director and told I'd got the advertised role without having to audition. AND my salary would be upped by a whole pound, from £17 to £18 a week! I was effectively signed up for the following season.

(The pair of charcoal grey trousers I'd bought, ripped, had

mended and given to Brian cost me £15 from that smart men's clothiers, just to give you an idea as to the worth of my salary then – and the extravagance of the purchase).

That same production of *Twelfth Night*, in which I had attracted the attention of Alastair Sim, was so successful it was recast extensively and carried on into the next season. The following year my wig was changed because my new twin had auburn hair. She and I didn't look alike either. That new 'twin', Eileen Atkins, is now a Dame of the British Empire. So, where's my title? She'd be *nowhere* without me! As for Judi . . .?

*

It was about this time that a letter was sent to me from my Littlefield House Master, Mr R.A.U. 'Jumbo' Jennings. In it, he asked if it had been me who'd put a fish into his bath?

Before leaving college, maybe six months before, I had won a goldfish at the Mop Fair, a fair that visited Marlborough town every five years or so. (You know the sort of prize I mean: a tiny fish swimming in a small plastic bag knotted at the top). I bought a foot-long glass aquarium for it with some gravel, pretend seaweed, and a little sunken castle (just as its home might have been in the ocean), and it sat on top of my desk in my study – until I was about to leave at the end of my final term. Someone suggested I flush it down the loo, but I had emptied it into my House Master's old bath outside his garden shed. Two years after my departure, he'd gone to clean his wellies in the bath when a huge – well, large – fish came up to greet him. I like to imagine – à la Jaws – first the wellies, then Mr Jennings disappearing down that goldfish gullet. *The Thwackee's Revenge* is what the film is going to be called.

*

At the end of that first season, the Old Vic company went on tour for six weeks, after which there was time for a quick holiday before we were to start rehearsals for the next season in London. So, Marc and I went to see his parents in Marseilles.

His father was now bedridden. His mother seemed frailer,

imprisoned as she now was in that small apartment as the sole carer of her husband, till death did them part. She was much cheered by her oldest son's visit, and the week we were there, we took her out gallivanting as often as her conscience would allow.

I remember we went with her to see one of Édith Piaf's last public performances, where Piaf shared the bill with her new young husband, Theophanis Lamboukas – a man half her age and twice her height. It was grotesque. In her black dress, with that extraordinary voice now at half strength, Piaf looked like an emaciated fledgling. When she wasn't hanging onto the microphone-stand in her solos, she clung onto Theo's brawny arm, looking up at him adoringly, with a tremulous smile and her eyes blinking.

In the blackout before the penultimate number of the show, there was a drum roll crescendo, a clash of cymbals and a trumpet shriek. A melody started, underlined by the rhythmic pounding of the bass drum. Suddenly the pitch black was sliced open by an amber spot, and into the light strode Theo, oiled and stripped to the waist, his magnificent torso gleaming. He sang his number powerfully – so overwhelmingly boosted you couldn't make out the tune. At its conclusion, a moment's blackout while the audience went mad applauding, before the full stage lighting blazed, stunning the eyes, and the happy couple, granny and her young matelot, were discovered centre-stage, holding hands, looking us and their future bravely in the eye. They performed the rousing finale clasped together, the gleaming hunk with his very own sparrow. In the adoring tumultuous applause which greeted the last note, she hopped into his arms, looked trustingly into his face, and he carried her off.

But even at half strength, Piaf had an extraordinary charisma. 'Non, je ne regrette rien.' Thank the high heavens. And her hunky husband changed his name to Théo Sarapo soon after, going on to record many hits after she'd died. He inherited all her debts, but that magnificent not-to-be-denied guy changed his name and his repertoire, going on to be a mega-success in France. (I looked that last bit up).

For the second week of our holiday, we crossed the Mediterranean to Sousse to stay again with the French amputee we'd lodged with before, Gerard. But this time we were there in the Tunisian winter, and although it was hot enough during the day to swim, there wasn't the stifling heat at night, so there were no families visiting the coast from inland, no mothers bathing their youngsters in the sea at midnight, no throngs of Arab men promenading hand in hand with jasmine tucked over their ears while their wives cooked their supper and put their offspring to bed, no Nourredin and his netball pals – an altogether quieter town.

One noon, I wasn't sure at the time quite why, our friend's carer, Eddie, drove us all to a quiet stretch of sandy beach tapering into the distance, empty except for a ragged man on a donkey coming towards us along the white sands. None of us were dressed to swim, so Marc and I wandered through the dunes for a short walk. When we returned, I saw our host being pronged by the donkey-man in the surf, Eddie nearby cradling the artificial legs. It was a bizarre sight that's stayed with me through the years: the sun glaring off the white sand, flashing diamonds off the sea; Eddie, a black silhouette with a pair of legs clutched to him; one man with his swaddling pulled up around his waist hunched over the truncated naked torso of another in the froth of gentle waves. Neither Marc nor I mentioned it then or later, I through fear of seeming prudish, he perhaps because he was inured to it. Whatever, he seemed unperturbed, and our host, normally a taciturn man, returned home in high spirits.

When we got back to Gerard's apartment, I looked at it with more interest. Five sizeable rooms, old-fashioned clunky furniture. I don't suppose he had money to spare, disability pensions don't go far, but then he did have Eddie and Eddie's wife as carers which must have cost a franc or two. But there again, life in Tunisia was cheaper than in France.

I was still a young prig, I'm ashamed to admit, and I'd found the episode sordid. Flying back to London, I knew I didn't want to go to Tunisia again.

*

My second season's rehearsals started, and the first production we opened to the public was the revamped twin-fest, *Twelfth Night*. Marc, who had loved my performance the first time around, and who I'm sure started the round of applause at the end of my 'dazed' scene on the first night – though he denied it – was ebullient when he fanfared me into the restaurant after the show with a public proclamation of my greatness. My darling's pride made me smile happily through my embarrassment and the following day's favourable reviews compounded my feeling of success.

*

'You can sit over here if you like. If you know what you want to eat, I'll get it for you.'
And
'You'd get a much bigger laugh if you changed those two sentences around. If you don't mind my saying.'

Two pronouncements I made that I know changed the course of my life. (Mind you, Judi Dench's reaction to: 'You have her father's love, Demetrius. Let me have Hermia's' sealed my fate).

The first was said one lunchtime in the Old Vic canteen during that first rehearsal day for *The Tempest*. (You'll remember our well-established routine: we started rehearsing the next play soon after a first night). So there was Alastair Sim – playing the leading role in the play I hadn't had to audition for – in the canteen doorway, looking a bit lost. A hush had fallen over the assembled actors at the great man's appearance, and because I'd been to public school, I knew my manners.

'You can sit over here if you like. If you know what you want to eat, I'll get it for you.'

He looked relieved, and I ushered him into the chair next to mine at a table for four, told him what there was on offer in the way of food and jumped the queue to get him his choice of meat and two veg. By the time I got back with his plate, he was engaged in chat with the others at the table. Easy. Me at my insouciant best. And my life changed forevermore – although imperceptibly over time.

Alastair was an affable man and rehearsing with him was a joy. He obviously admired my reading of Ariel. And because I knew he'd personally chosen me it helped our working relationship. After three weeks of intensive rehearsals, Ally, as he had asked me to call him, suggested I might like to come and meet his family at his country home once the production had opened.

I've said before: too often, we actors go into production so exhilarated by the concepts of the director, the designer and the composer, that we sometimes lose sight of the eventual look and common sense of the thing. This time, after all our passion and hard work, we were found wanting.

Our first night was greeted with almost unanimous disdain by the critics. Our star, universally loved for his witty performances on film, had dared to play Prospero, an iconic Shakespearian role, as darkly comic, and he was reviled for it. 'Like a much-loved uncle playing magician at a kid's tea party' was the gist of them. Except for one highly respected critic of the *Sunday Times*, the most senior of them all, who praised Ally to high heaven, insisting it was the most believable creation of Prospero he'd seen in his long theatre-going life. Perhaps because he later realised his was a lone voice and was determined his view was not to be taken lightly, he referred to Ally's performance in his newspaper column every two or three weeks.

The Sims never read notices, so they were blithely unaware of the critics' verdict of his work. And as he was such a popular actor with the public, the theatre was packed for every one of the scheduled performances, so the management couldn't have cared less.

My notices included: 'Kerry Gardner played Ariel as if he was showing that you too can have a body like mine.' And, 'For a non-singer, Kerry Gardner sang the difficult songs intelligently.' (Michael Tippett had written some of his most viscously tortured music for *Songs for Ariel*, and as I'd only ever been in a school choir, I thought I tackled them bloody well. If, and I say if, *if* I sang any of it flat – which I didn't – no one would have been any the wiser). I was damned with faint praise in some of those other reviews – the ones which deigned to notice me at all.

The outline of the play: a ruler is ousted from his kingdom by his brother, who has him cast adrift with his infant daughter in a leaky boat, which finishes up on a deserted island. Deserted of humans, though there are two 'beings' there, either or both of which could be in his imagination. When his daughter is of marriageable age, lo and behold, his usurping brother and his retinue are shipwrecked off the coast of this tiny fiefdom. With the aid of the two 'beings', our hero leads them through terrible imaginings and hardships before forgiving his sibling and blessing the union between his brother's nephew and his daughter, Miranda - played by Eileen Atkins.

So, it's a story of two men who learn about themselves through adversity, acquiring wisdom – which of necessity leads to forgiveness. In the end, the duke, Prospero, resolves to put away his playpen for a life of the intellect.

Actors do enjoy shouting and trembling with wrath, so in this particular play, when the actor playing Prospero uses histrionics, it suggests the author wrote about a deeply flawed personality whose perception of himself *after many years* is paper thin. That may be true of the brother, but it can't be true of the hero. Ally brought the hero Shakespeare conceived in this, his last play, to a believable truth – but his knowing moments of dark comedy gave with one hand what they took away with the other, and the critics complained that he robbed the play of its grandeur. (Except, of course, for the one who insisted Ally's was the only viable representation of the character that he'd ever witnessed).

For my part, I'd found the spirit I was playing huge fun to work on but extraordinarily difficult to realise. Ariel isn't supposed to be human, so nothing I'd observed in my life, no emotion I'd experienced could be used. A 'thing' without feelings – thank heavens it spoke English. Thinking about it now, it may have been better if I'd voiced it in Esperanto. *Reductio ad absurdum.*

The renowned set and costume designer, Leslie Hurry,

imagined the amorphous character I played only wearing a strip of seaweed to hide the telltale part of the actor's gender. So, my costume was basically a G-string, onto which was sewn a piece of spangly seaweed. With skin-toned ballet shoes, I was to be earth-coloured. But because I was also a spirit of the air, I had silver glitter in my hair and silvery patches on my arms and legs. 5 foot 10 inches tall, I looked like a flighty muscleman (see the review above). And because standing up I was almost as tall as my master, Prospero, on stage, I was taught by Alexander Grant of the Royal Ballet how to move swiftly at a crouch. I suspect I looked like a ricocheting brown bullet – enhanced with silver tips. (Mind you, I crashed once onto a rock, and at that matinee the children found the obviously human blood running down my legs a hoot).

If I'd been surprised at the response of youngsters to my performance when playing a pop star in my last show in London, I was amazed by the numerous letters I received from them because of my appearance in this. OK, so this time, there were one or two articles about me in the paper with photos of the nearly naked me in flight, *and* the play was a set text for exams that year, so the matinees were thronged with kids. But I was asked the most outrageous questions, some of them penned in beautiful gothic script – those were from young convent girls – wanting to know the dimensions of my penis under that seaweed and what it could get up to. And I'd be called to take phone calls at the stage door, where cultivated adults would inquire if I'd be interested in meeting for a drink, or . . . Couched so politely, their evil intentions made me grin. Except I was a serious actor, so how dare they?

I hadn't mentioned my lover by name in all my conversations with Ally but knowing that the invitation to go down to his home for the weekend was going to be repeated, I'd asked Marc how he felt about it.

'You must go, *biquet*. Is very nice for you.'

'Saturday night, coming back to London with him Monday morning, you sure?'

He was – and didn't seem to mind at all that he hadn't been included in the invitation.

'I do not know them. What would I say?'

The second weekend after we'd opened the play, Ally and I drove down to his home in Oxfordshire, Forrigan, and I met his wife, Naomi, the most adorable of women, and his daughter Merlith – less welcoming, even unfriendly. Not hostile exactly, but she often teetered on the edge of sarcasm and that both hurt and puzzled me. I was only three years older than her, so we were much of an age. What was the problem?

Their house was at the bottom of a densely wooded valley, a modest brick building in an encroaching circle of bushes and tall trees. The interior was plain and unremarkable, almost to a fault. It smelled of the cigars Alastair smoked throughout the weekend. I've always found the smell appealing.

(He once offered me one from a cedar box. It was tubed in aluminium.

'Would you like one of these? They're very good.'

I refused, said I smoked cigarettes.

'Used to smoke those, but I was told they were bad for the health, so I took to these. I don't inhale, so they won't do any harm,' he explained.

He died fourteen years later of mouth cancer. The nicotine from the cigars collected in the saliva under the tongue. And I threw away my last packet of cigarettes the day of his death).

In this Scottish household, the females were subordinate to the males, so I found myself waited on. There was absolutely no resentment to this arrangement.

A couple of years before, I'd stayed with a fellow actor, David, in his home in Bellshill just outside Glasgow on our way up to do the pantomime in Aberdeen. David's mother and sister were at home when we drove up to their council house. Warm and friendly, they showed us our room before making us something to eat. We had been chatting for some time when the backdoor opened noisily, and David's father arrived home with some mates after an evening in the pub. His wife and daughter were already on their feet when he shouted from the kitchen, 'Bring us some food, woman, we're starving,' before continuing his conversation with his friends. He cast a not unfriendly eye over me when we were introduced and sat down heavily where I'd been only a moment before. David and I excused ourselves and went to bed. The family had left the house by the time we got down the following morning, all having gone to work.

Five years or so later, I was invited by a Scots friend to dinner at another Scottish household in London. My host was a well-to-do television comedian of considerable repute, and he and his wife lived in an elegant house in north London. I was introduced to Moira when I arrived, and she gave us all a drink before retiring from the sitting room to make dinner. My friend had known our host for years, so a merry time was being had when our hostess came in to announce that the meal was ready. We trooped into the dining room, where she served us our first course – then left. It was only then I noticed there wasn't a place setting for her at the table. The two Scots men obviously found nothing odd in this, but I became more and more perplexed, particularly as she came in to check whether we were ready for the next course before bringing it in, serving us – and disappearing again. At the end of the meal, when I asked if I could take plates away and help do the washing up, my host was somewhat impatient. 'Of course not, son, Moira'll do that.' She didn't join us for coffee, and I never saw her again.

In both these examples, the women were treated kindly but not as equals.

At their house, Naomi and Merlith were an essential part of the household, but on that first visit, when I got up to put a log on the fire (and I was only a few feet away from it), Ally shook his head, 'No, don't you. Naomi will do it.' She wasn't in the room when he said it.

It went against everything I'd ever been taught – so through the years, I'd discreetly help whenever needed, taking pleasure in Naomi's silent smiles. She insisted it was unnecessary, but she was pleased, and pleasing her became one of my main aims in that family.

It was during those last days of playing *The Tempest* at the Old Vic that Ally did the 'pilot' of a possible television series called *Misleading Cases*, adapted for the screen by the BBC from an A.P. Herbert short story. (The pilot being a try-out of what might become the first episode of a series). As I wasn't in all the plays being staged at the Vic, I had enough time off to be in the pilot. I wasn't surprised to be offered it. Ally was playing the judge and, because he was the co-star alongside Roy Dotrice, the television company worked around our theatre schedule.

My role was that of a young policeman who finds a cow with I.O.U. painted on its side tethered to a lamp post. Apart from a short scene filmed on location – the scene at the lamp post – the rest of my part was to be shot in the courtroom, with me in the witness box explaining what I'd seen to the judge.

The half-hour comedy's story was simple.

Scene One: A middle-aged householder has a running dispute with the Inland Revenue. The morning the story starts, a final demand from the tax authorities to pay his dues comes through the letterbox.

Scene Two: A policeman and policewoman are pounding the beat when they come across something which has attracted a crowd of onlookers.

Scene Three: A judge tells his wife over breakfast of the court case he'll be presiding over that day. He's looking forward to it with gleeful anticipation. It seems he's met up with the litigant before.

Scene Four: The second half of the interrupted street scene with police, crowd – and now we see the cow with I.O.U. painted on its side.

Scene Five (and by far the longest): The courtroom, where Mister Everyman argues his case against the tax people in front of the sympathetic and mischievous judge.

As this was a 'live' television show to be performed in front of an audience, we shot Scene Two/Four, the only filmed segment, first.

*

If you like bacon sandwiches, or butties when the bacon comes in a bun, and mugs of sweet hot tea, breakfast on these film shoots is in never-ending supply. You can get all the trimmings, the fried eggs and sausages too, and there's always a bus furnished with tables where you can eat. But standing in the cold morning air eating salty bacon between two slabs of bread that has soaked up the juices takes a lot of beating. Earth has not anything to chow more fair!

An actress I'd not worked with before played the female constable in the filmed excerpt. We shot the scene in a small road off Fleet Street not far from the Courts of Justice. The section of the street she and I needed to stroll down was cordoned off from the public – and jam-packed with the film crew, their paraphernalia, the aforementioned canteen bus, a small group of extras, and a large cow. We got it shot within the morning. A fortnight later, we went into a rehearsal studio where the interior scenes were blocked.

Many years ago, in the BBC Rehearsal Studios in Acton, West London, there were three floors of enormous rooms, each maybe half the size of the huge studio spaces in the Television Centre where we would eventually tape the show in front of the public. We rehearsed our lines in one of these and blocked our moves. Before the cast arrived at the rehearsal room that first morning, an advance guard of technicians had marked out a floor plan of each of the rooms the story was set in (living room, breakfast room and courtroom) with white gaffer tape on the floor. From above it would have looked like a giant architect's plan: each wall, door and window in their exact place marked out on the shiny floor in white. The furniture and props provided were only approximations of the real things we would have on the set when we came to the taping – trestle table and stackable chairs standing in for a regency dining table with Chippendale chairs, for example. The same as in rep.

After two days, the actors had learnt their lines and dispensed with their scripts. In that time, we'd had the moves we were to make blocked by the director, so the next five days were spent with the actors and director changing this move, trying a different inflection on that line, working towards making the relationships between the characters so real the audience would be happy to suspend their disbelief.

On our last morning in the rehearsal room, we had an invasion of cameramen turn up for the run through. We acted out the scenes with these men standing among us, each representing his camera, while the director told them, quite loudly: 'Camera One, medium shot . . . *aaaand*, cut to Camera Two, close up.' The man who'd been Camera One now moved like a chess piece to another spot nearby, as the director said: 'Camera Three through the doorway, long shot of the entire group . . .' (we went on saying our lines as if these peculiar interruptions weren't happening) '. . . *aaand* Camera One, over the shoulder shot close up.' Camera Two and Three moved like ballet dancers to their new positions while the director choreographed them around us, we acting away as we had so carefully rehearsed, trying to pretend these burly intruders were invisible.

Sunday, the seventh day after rehearsals began, we moved into Studio 3 in the BBC Television Centre for the taping in front of a live audience.

On that Sunday, Naomi turned up at the studios to be with us and watch the final rehearsals. Studio 3 was like an airplane hangar with racks of lights, loudspeakers and monitors hanging overhead. The three sets to be used in the story had been built in a row on one side of the rectangular studio, with a tiered bank of seats for the spectators in the other half. (If you watch *Mrs Brown's Boys*, you'll see the set up. As you will in *The Graham Norton Show*).

Roy Dotrice was playing the part of Albert, the man being hounded by the Revenue. Roy was a very popular character actor, known by the television public for his endearing rogues and loveable eccentrics. He was also a superb performer in more serious roles, both in theatre and film.

Naomi, Ally and I had lunch together in the restaurant. Neither of my companions at the table appeared the slightest bit nervous, but I had butterflies in my stomach. Feeling slightly queasy, I picked at my food. The vast canteen we were in was a hubbub of noise with the clatter of plates and cutlery and the animated chat of a huge crowd of announcers, weathermen, actors, directors, cameramen, sparks, dressers, you name it – the essential personnel for making hours of programmes for that screen in the corner of the room.

At three o'clock, we had our last dress rehearsal and afterwards retired to our dressing rooms while the audience was admitted into the studio. Over the tannoy, I heard the mutter of conversation turn into a quiet roar as the seats filled up.

The part of this policeman didn't feature heavily in the story, and I had just the two scenes: the finding of the cow tethered to the lamp post in the road and answering the judge and counsel's questions in the witness box. My second professional performance at Frinton, while still at drama school, had been the part of a policeman, and I was rather hoping it wouldn't turn out quite as disastrously. But I'd enjoyed myself thoroughly throughout these rehearsals, so I wasn't concerned. However, it was my first real 'part' on television – that *was* a bit concerning.

And then, over the tannoy in the dressing room, I heard Ted Austin, the warm-up man, greet the audience and, literally, warm them up with jokes and anecdotes to get them into the mood for what was to come. Ted appeared regularly as a comic on television variety shows, and this audience had seen him often enough to welcome him fondly. Five minutes of chat, and then the stars, Ally and Roy, were introduced to the spectators, to much applause. The first actors to appear were called over the tannoy, the lights dimmed on the audience, came up on the first set – the living room – and we were off.

It started with Roy, playing our anti-hero Albert, coming into his sitting room, opening a letter he had just received from the Inland Revenue. He swore amusingly (this was a family show) and complained to his heedless children of the situation he found himself in. The authorities were demanding yet more tax from him, a debt he hotly disputed. His children had heard it all before and were not listening. He told his rowdy group of offspring that he had anticipated this further demand, and for their future education, he would demonstrate how, legally, it was possible to satisfy one's debtors in many interesting and, if possible, awkward ways. Money wasn't always necessary. One of his brood asked if anyone had heard the noises during the night seemingly coming from their garage. Their father smiled.

The next scene was the first half of the filmed excerpt of the police couple walking the pavement and coming up behind a small crowd at the curbside. The audience had to look upwards at the monitor screens to see this piece of the story on film, and as they did this, the technicians, at ground level, were wheeling four monster cameras from the set of the first scene through the yards of coiled cable to the judge's dining room, the third scene in the story – the two rooms built side by side, only a few yards apart. The somewhat puzzled laughter from the audience at the filmed excerpt which followed, with the crowd at the kerbside surrounding the cow with I.O.U. payable to the Inland Revenue painted on its side, was not surprising with all the distracting activity going on below their level of vision.

Listening to the gently amused reaction of the audience to both these first two scenes, it seemed disappointingly different to the usual level of raucous response to other 'live' shows I'd seen on the television at home. But then there was so much movement going on with the cameras and the sound-booms it was easier for the audience to look up and watch the show on the monitors, rather than crane their heads to get a glimpse of the actors through the bustle on the studio floor. What they could see on the monitors would be what they would eventually see in their living rooms. On their way home, they'd be wondering why they'd bothered to come so far to attend a studio recording. My first live comedy television show, and it was going to be a tepid failure.

I had been called to the set from the dressing room before my film sequence was shown, and I waited, jaws clenching, in the dark behind the mock-up of the courtroom, while Ally's scene in the breakfast room with his wife sailed serenely on only a few yards away on my right. Again, the audience seemed only politely amused. I was despondent – and I didn't remember being that nervous before in my life. After the controlled temperature of the dressing room, the heat of the lighting and the breathing presence of four hundred invisible spectators made me more and more claustrophobic – like a caveman waiting in the dark for a sabre-toothed tiger to pass by outside. Why on earth had I ever thought being an actor would be fun?

Relief from my near panic came in the form of a break in the action. Ally got a line wrong, so Ted Austin came in front of the audience again. He told everyone the director had decided there would have to be some reshooting of the two studio scenes that had just played. (He was connected by an earpiece to the director's glass booth way up at the back). Apparently, there'd been some boom shadow on one of the walls during the scene in Roy's home with his children. (Booms are microphones on the end of long telescopic poles. These are extended by a sound man above the actors' heads while a scene progresses to pick up and amplify the everyday tones used for screen dialogue. Should a light catch them and cast a shadow on a wall or on a face . . . a retake). Also, one of the children had fluffed her lines, so that had to be reshot too. As for Mr Alastair Sim . . .

It was only after this break that the whole process made sense to me.

When the taping starts, the audience – who have travelled miles – have been expecting something especially funny, and the actors, hoping to deliver it, are tense. After a week spent rehearsing their characters till every word is real to them, the actors are suddenly surrounded by a herd of dinosaurs (the cameras). They're in a vast new cavern in what seems like real rooms with real furniture, and on the other side of these swooping monsters with cameramen on their backs there are serried ranks of spectators wanting to be convinced that what can't be seen properly is as funny as they'd been led to expect. It isn't. It can't be. And then, suddenly, there's a halt. Foof. The tension is broken – and the actors revert to being themselves. Relaxed. Which inevitably results in their joking and fooling about – which the audience loves. It makes them feel as one with the actors and an essential part of the mix. (I've never got a director to admit to it, but I suspect that even if a comedy show with audience participation has gone perfectly, he will still manufacture an excuse to go back on a scene or two so as to doubly involve the spectators in this way).

Ally had fluffed a speech in the breakfast scene, so while he waited to be told what the director needed to reshoot, Ted made a joke at Ally's expense, Ally had a quick comeback, and the two off-the-cuff remarks produced guffaws of laughter from the audience. If they hadn't been before, they were now hooked. The punters felt the actors were their personal friends, and the atmosphere became that of a huge party. All the gizmos hanging overhead, the cameras and crew, the unseen director issuing orders from on high like Big Brother, made this particular studio a very extraordinary and special place for us all to be.

Taking advantage of this bonhomie, Ted told the audience they were a miserable lot, their laughter at the jokes in the first three scenes had been pathetic (they loved that), and as the BBC needed a *good* laugh track to go out with the show when it was aired, they were going to be made to sit through the first three scenes again. 'And try to do better this time! You laugh loud enough, and you can tell your friends at home – "that was me!"'

The now newly perfected two scenes were gone through again, and this time, with Ted windmilling his arms, urging them on, the spectators were deafening in their appreciation. For instance, their sighting of the cow provoked such hilarity that when I saw it a few months later at home, it sounded hysterical.

Of course, none of these contrivances were seen by the public in their homes when the show was eventually aired. But it was then I appreciated why busloads of audiences, hundreds of people, travelled many miles across the country to attend these live studio recordings. They were going to get to know their favourite actors personally and maybe spot a star in the making. They were there when things went wrong, so they were in on a secret that the rest of the public hadn't been party to.

The courtroom, which had been curtained off from audience view for the surprise effect, was unveiled for the screening, and although they could see it was made out of canvas flats like the other two rooms they'd already seen, it looked so realistic they applauded loudly. Ally, as the judge, had a few things to say from his podium, there was some verbal fencing between opposing counsels – all found mighty funny – and I was called into court as the first witness. I marched in, my heart in my throat, my helmet in the crook of my elbow. I rested it on the rim of the witness box as I was sworn in, and . . . yes, my live appearance went well. The audience found it funny, and I went off into the dark area behind the set again, job over, unless there was a retake – which there wasn't.

The rest of the scene went with a swing, and the applause and cheers of approval as the actors bowed and the end credits rolled was joyful.

The show was so successful with the general public when it aired three months later that the BBC decided to make six more episodes. Ally and Roy, playing the same characters, starred in the slightly remodified series: the judge's wife became a bit scattier, I seem to remember, and a rather pompous son was magicked out of thin air to be part of their family. Roy lost one of his children – where the girl went, we were never told – and gained a wife, but what made it so successful was that the writing was even stronger. However, my character had no more to do in the story.

*

I became a regular visitor to Forrigan at weekends, maybe once or twice a month, relieved that Marc was happy not to be included in the invitations. I was a fish out of water in these new surroundings of family life, my presence in their home taken for granted, an accepted cog in their world. These two existences of mine were so far apart. Marc and I were happy with our matter-of-fact relationship. He was the rock from which I dived and came back to for sunshine and safety. The intellectual sea I was swimming in with this new family was always bracing, but the water was choppy, and I was often way out of my depth. Never mind the tennis, the card games, the chess, the cryptic crosswords and the backgammon we all played, the weekend groupings were there for the conversation – and young minds were encouraged to contribute but weren't given quarter.

Ally and Naomi's country house was reserved solely for their loved ones. They had a flat in London where they could entertain acquaintances.

Naomi lived at Forrigan, their house in the wood, where Ally stayed three days – Friday lunchtime or evening to Monday noon – spending the rest of the week in London, in Hampstead. This was when he wasn't working. Naomi would come up to London on Tuesday night or Wednesday early with a new supply of pre-cooked food and go back to Oxfordshire on Thursday or Friday. And I've never in my life met two more contented married people. They both read voraciously and would discuss books, newspaper articles, television drama, thoughts that had come to them while reading or observing, and I believe, because of their weekly spells alone, each found the other constantly new and stimulating. And how they made each other laugh!

Sometimes the Frys were there at weekends, the author and his wife. Then, among other things, the talk would be of religion – Christopher and Phyl being devout Christians, the Sims devout atheists. Terry, another add-on son like me but considerably older, was a professor of linguistics at Cambridge University and, with his wife, the conversation was often about language and its uses – the first time I'd heard of 'semantics'. The artist Edward Wesson (there was an Arab market scene of his over the fireplace, he designed the sets for one of Ally's commissioned plays, and painted Ally's portrait for the Garrick Club); or the Sims' married doctor friends, John and Joan, who lived across the valley in their self-designed home, Ossicles. When they dropped in for tea, we'd hear about their lives as lecturers, menders of bodies, hospital politics . . . One time when I was there, so was William Golding (*Lord of the Flies*); another, the author William Trevor. All the conversations were leavened with a great deal of laughter. Jokes as such were non-existent. Originality of observation was the norm. Although I was often flailing, I had a facility with words so I could make people laugh (nowadays, words dance about just out of reach), so I was accepted in these clever folks' company, even though my intellectual contribution was non-existent.

Then there was Peter, another surrogate son even younger than me, once an actor, now a trainee teacher, who would sometimes bring his bee-hived girlfriend with him. He was reserved, bespectacled, and a bit scruffy, was Pete, and she was smartly turned out in the short skirts of the day, with lots of eyeliner and a mound of blonde bouffant hair. My young, uninformed mind didn't expect their relationship to last, but even as I write this, they've been married for forty-three plus years. Pete knew what he was doing, and his wife Norma was and is every bit as astute and clever as him. And still much prettier.

So I left Marc at home these weekends. He never complained or seemed to mind. He would ask, with a limited amount of interest, what I'd done over the two days, and I'd say informatively, 'the usual', but, as I said before, apart from playing games inside and outside the house, the weekends consisted of talk. I didn't tell him much about that because, on the whole, I didn't understand more than the gist of what had been verbally laid out and dissected. I was curious to know what he had done the time I was away. 'The usual,' he would say – and shrug. He had so many responsibilities to the restaurant I supposed he was busy.

He was always solicitous of my love, of my well-being, was as proud of me as it was possible to be, and I accepted it all as my due.

And I loved him, but I have to suppose now, mainly because of what he so unsparingly gave me, I was the beloved – and that's what you give the object of your adoration. Yes, I was that callow.

But through the years, as my intellect began to be challenged, I found my lover wanting in curiosity, and my perception of him began, oh so slowly and subtly, to change. I asked him sometimes about his views of ideas that I'd recently been introduced to, but he'd get bored and change the subject as fast as he decently could without yawning.

It only occurred to me, *many* years later, to wonder what he'd done on the Sunday of those weekends, his free day, because although he told me he'd been here or there with friends, most of whom I knew and could, I suppose, have checked up on, I was self-centred enough to assume I was enough for him. Certainly, his ardour never flagged. He was my standby. And doesn't that say it all? I was without proper care of him, but he was always sunnily mine, so I assumed he was happy. We were happy together, so it must be as I thought. I'm inclined to do that!

PHOTO GALLERY

Child and Mother c.'39

Me dungareed

Sankence'45 -'54

Jodphured with Petey

Mother and Podge

Mr Daddy and child

Dorothy Wilding Studio portrait of my mother

Littlefield Platoon Cup

Me on Belmore   Belmore over hot coals

Girlfriend Jo with ankles

Tony Mr. Handsome (right) at the Cafe de Paris

Me and Sheila Reid in Easter, Farnham

Che Sera Sera

Alastair's slaves - Ariel (above)

Number 10 - PA to the PPS to the PM

Naomi

Martin

The brothers, Martin and Dorian, and bum

Martin and Bosky

Martin and Pajero

Early days

Forrigan 50th Birthday, **Who's who?**

Flying Nephew

Brother Mark and Biscuit

Martin's Bouncy Castle on his 60th

Barging on the Canal du Midi

Discarded costume design for Nausius

Jessie

Vignaux de Bas

First Spotlight picture c. '57

Last Spotlight picture c. '73

Our Civil Partnership, '06

Georgie

CHAPTER 9
Bolshoi Spasibo

Touring can be fun, but where you stay is a lottery. Mrs Grimmond in Leeds can be very comfortable; Nick and George in Liverpool with their black nylon sheets can be dicey. Before you go on tour with a play, you are offered pages of 'digs' by the theatre management: landlords and landladies around Britain who welcome performers on their way around the provinces. The leading actors can choose to stay in hotels if they wish, but the rabble can only afford digs – unless you're well-heeled or very precious. If you do a lot of touring, you get to know the goodies.

Playing Ariel in *The Tempest* – covered in body make-up, with gold and silver spangles in my hair – I needed to have a bath or a shower every night after the performance, and in most of the touring theatres in those days there weren't showers for everyone, only the lead actors had a bathroom and loo attached to their dressing rooms. In Newcastle, autumn as I remember, I had to soap off that make-up in four inches of tepid water in a small bathroom with a pane missing in the window and only an overhead bulb. The husband of the couple in whose house I was renting a room worked in the mines, and they took in lodgers to supplement his wages. It was in these same digs that I could hear the mice scuttling in the cabinet next to my bed.

We were performing *Twelfth Night* around the provinces for the first half of the week and *The Tempest* in the second half – Thursday, Friday and Saturday matinee and evening. Naomi came on tour with us when Ally joined the company on the Thursday, and I mentioned to her that I had had to change my digs that week because of the sheer misery of soaping off at midnight in a freezing bathroom – and the cavorting mice that kept me awake. 'No, no, dearest, that won't do!'; so then I was in digs from Monday to Wednesday of each week, and a room in their hotel was booked for me for the second half when Ally was performing. And then that wouldn't do either, so I was booked a room in whichever hotel they were staying in from the first day of each touring date, which they paid for, and I gave them the comparative pittance I would have paid had I been in digs – the comforts of stardom on eighteen pounds a week!

It was during the last weeks at the Vic playing *The Tempest* that Ally told me there was a play he'd commissioned which was being picked up by a West End Producer with an eye to bring it into London – and there was a part in it for me if I'd like to be in it. The play was called *Windfall,* and it would go on tour before coming into town. Would I be interested? This was how success came about, I thought; this was the big time, having another acting job offered while I was still working on something quite else, and of course, I said yes, script unread.

Alastair had commissioned theatrical pieces all his working life. He'd been in London with several of James Bridie's plays that he'd previously worked on with the author (their country house, Forrigan, was named after one of them – *The Forrigan Reel*); he'd asked William Golding to write him a play, and the result was *The Brass Butterfly* (about a Roman who discovers nuclear fusion and decides fissionable material has only limited domestic use), which he directed in London co-starring George Cole, his protégé, with sets by Edward. And the author of *Windfall,* Michael Gilbert, had written for him before. Being such avid readers, the Sims would, every now and then, come across novelists who wrote dialogue that read well for the theatre, so Ally would arrange to meet with them and persuade them to write something for the stage. The extraordinary William Trevor was one such, and he wrote a witty and haunting piece, *The Elephant's Foot,* which Ally directed with two big stars of the day performing alongside him, but which couldn't be got right despite all the re-writes on tour, and so never came into London. (Essentially, Ally played the wrong part – to my way of thinking). It cries out to be revived.

In the New Year, I started rehearsing with Alastair on *Windfall*. In the cast were some of his old chums, plus three youngsters: Merlith, his daughter who had never trained as an actress but had been in another of his productions; Peter Furnell, a really fine actor and another of Ally and Naomi's 'boys' (married to the beehive, yes?), who had worked with him on stage before; and then me, another of their lads.

I can't remember ever being so at sea in my working life as an actor. Ally had chosen me to play alongside him in *The Tempest* because of something he'd admired watching me do on stage at the Vic, had been happy with my performance as Ariel, and now, suddenly, I couldn't get anything right. He came to the first rehearsal with his lines learnt. His chums in the cast knew that was what he wanted, so they had a good idea of their lines that first day, as did Merlith and Peter – they too had worked with him before, so knew the ropes. I stepped into that rehearsal room expecting to work on the role I'd been given as we rehearsed, but no, not a single inflection, not a line I had only just learned was delivered to his satisfaction (did I mention he was the director as well as the leading man?). There was absolutely no chance I could develop this rather wishy-washy role in the way I might have wanted had I been given the opportunity. It could have been interesting, even quirky – everything I'd done up to then had been – but we'll never know. What I brought to rehearsal didn't measure up to his concept of the part from day one, so his vision of my character was bullied out of me. It wasn't mine; it was his. He dulled my senses with his constant harping, which made me as the character dull. And through those tortured rehearsal weeks, my love for him turned to despair and, sometimes, hatred.

A middle-aged actress, Margaret W – another member of the cast who wasn't used to his ways – would come off the stage into the wings during those last days of rehearsal in tears because of his unkind comments. As she stood beside me in the dark, I would grit my teeth, willing myself not to show emotion. Naomi would try and ameliorate my humiliation during those ghastly weeks, telling me it was his reputation (and some of their money, I realised later) which depended on the venture being a success, so please forgive his impatience. Heavens, did I want to believe her. This demi-god I had come to love had been in The Business for thirty or more years than me. I respected him, of course, I did, even though he was suddenly this tyrant, so eventually, I thought the problem must be with me. I couldn't be any good.

I had been Ally's driver most weekends I went to Forrigan – and when they'd driven up to the various venues during the *Tempest* tour, I would drive them for the rest of the week, including taking us all home on the Saturday night or Sunday, so on this tour around the UK, I was usually the chauffeur. It was taken for granted by the Sims that I'd want to stick to the arrangement we'd had before – I'd stay with them in their hotels rather than in some grotty bed and breakfast. It was wonderfully generous because what I gave them barely covered a quarter of the cost of the well-appointed rooms I found myself in week after week. But almost immediately we went on tour, I knew it was a mistake. Rehearsals in London had gone horrendously for me, and it was only a few days before the tour began that my slavish performance started to elicit faint praise from him, which I resented. *I've lost sleep and cried blood for this miserable cardboard cutout of yours.*

But I didn't have the gumption to leave such a comfy set-up. Saying 'no, thank you' would have been a statement too far and altered our relationship – which I was trying hard to pretend was on course. So, I accepted the gift and resented the givers. But in that period of having my belief in myself eroded, I had no sense of what was up or down. I clung to the luxury as a comforter, even while I envied the other cast members who, after the show, could get away from their dissatisfied leading actor/director and spend some self-time out of range – never mind that they were doubtless in less attractive surroundings.

I learned more from that humiliating experience than at almost any time since, but I wasn't aware of it then. I remember once, in a lounge in Gleneagles Hotel, saying that I thought a landscape above the fireplace was spoilt by the wooden post in the middle of the picture.

'Oh,' says my once-friend and now stage-director-from-hell, 'I didn't realise you were an art critic. What's wrong with it?'

My twenty-four-year-old stomach did a despairing somersault. 'It's a pity,' I said eventually, 'because it's made it a picture about a post.'

'The management of this hotel thought it was good enough to display, but you beg to differ. You should tell them.' My spirits were already crushed enough, so I said nothing more that tea-time.

And again:

'Why do you wear that signet ring?' he asked.

'My father gave it to me. Well, I inherited it after he died.'

'Was that the man who changed your name . . . but didn't really want you?'

'Er . . . yes, if you put it like that.'

'There's an anchor on it. I thought you said he was in the Indian army.'

'It was my mother who made it up for him, it was her present to him, and he wore it ... as long as I can remember.'

'So, when someone remarks on it – is that gold, it looks solid, and what's that on it – you tell them it belonged to your father who was in the army. Do you also tell them he didn't care for you?'

I dreaded what I would hear next. 'No.'

'So, it's a conversation piece.'

I was silent.

He and Naomi believed we should go out in the world, poor naked forked creatures that we are, without special pleading, without remarkable trinkets, noticeable clothes, look-at-me talismans – just do the best we could with what we had in our heads, with whatever wits that had been given us. Without pretensions. But without those things, Kerry was nothing. I was twenty-four, barely aware there was a scheme to things. It meant shedding all my traits, my tutored middle-class personality, my charm (and God was 'charm' a sin in their eyes), and at that age, I wasn't capable of getting by on my wits. Grow up and think like us was how it sounded. And I was barely out of the cocoon.

After the tour, the production came into the Lyric Theatre in Shaftesbury Avenue, was damned with lukewarm reviews, and died soon after. Another victim of the Kitchen Sink Theatre.

Come the end of *Windfall* in London, I absented myself from their country home. My confidence as an actor deeply dented, I made life with Marc my solace. Sex could always be relied on as a balm, and now, perhaps, to jolly me out of my mood, Marc made sure there were other playmates in our bed to dull the senses.

I found out later where most of these lads came from. There was a hostel for sailors by Waterloo Station where bargain hunters could go and get their pick of men – for a price. As I never paid the money, I never did find out the price. But the sailors were between leave and returning to their ship, or just off the ships spending the night at the hostel before catching the train home in the morning, and if money was on offer . . .

The Horse Guards were also easy. They were good for a ride.

So sex was easy to come by, although in those days, homosexuality was against the law, consensual or not.

(If you expected a meaningful chapter or two of the difficulties and danger of being 'queer' in the seventies and eighties, then I can't supply them. People in the arts have a tolerance and acceptance of the strange, which they use for their work, so deviance is a welcome slant on the everyday and banal. Artists don't have to *indulge*, just use their imagination. But nor do they condemn).

I don't want you to think I had no other friends all this time just because I've told you only of the sexual specifics of some. The rather effete older gentlemen I'd been introduced to by John, who'd offered golden gifts and expected golden returns, were no longer around. Marc and I had a group of gossipy and fun restaurant acquaintances, most of whom we invited home every now and then and to whose homes we were invited for social intercourse. For Marc, there was also his ex, Roelof, a South African – about my height, a little older, nice enough looking but a tad waspish, and sometimes outrageous. Socialising with him could be fun.

I never brought home my younger acquaintances from the theatre. I'm talking about my time at the Old Vic here. (*Windfall* was full of older people, most of them golfers and members of the Garrick Club: Whisky-and-Sodas). We were competitors, us youngsters, so the nearest we got to a relationship was a skin-deep actors' flirtatiousness. I'd had one in my bed the first time we went out on an Old Vic tour, but the moment we returned to London, our sexual friendship stopped by agreement – and he went back home to his wife.

It wasn't as though I didn't pretend the Sims mattered to me. I went to Forrigan occasionally for the weekend, mostly out of duty. Certainly to see Naomi, but she seemed somewhat remote. In retrospect, it was, of course to be expected, but at the time, it didn't make it any more welcoming or understandable.

It came to a head the following Christmas. Ally was playing Captain Hook in *Peter Pan* at the Scala, a theatre in north Soho since demolished. I went to see the production with the presents I'd bought for all the Sim family, but I had no intention of going to their home over that festive period. Ally was enjoyably himself in the piece – and was it Margaret Lockwood or her daughter playing Peter? – but I only remember going backstage after the show to see him in his dressing room with the family presents in hand.

My smile fixed on my face; I went on up to his dressing room. He was at the mirror, unwigged, but still with his make-up on. (I had seen a matinee, and he had an evening performance ahead).

I went through my banal speech of congratulations, and he listened in silence. Eventually, I held up the bag of presents I had in my hand. 'And these are for under the tree at Forrigan. I'm really sorry not to be with you this year, but . . .' He interrupted me: 'So these are from your guilty conscience, are they? We haven't seen anything of you for months, and you think these make up for your absence? If you can't be there to give them to us, you should take them away, Kerry. We won't want them.'

I stumbled down the stairs into the street, tears running down my face, and I dumped them all in various waste bins along the way to the Tube.

I cut myself off from the Sims completely.

As to my acting career, I can't remember what happened to it then, so immersed was I in my alternating anger and self-pity. I did get work, but I was taking time getting back my self-confidence on stage and although some of it was well paid, most of it was pretty ordinary. I thought I wasn't much good, so what I did wasn't important.

No, that's not true. I was asked by the director, Frank Hauser, to do a Molière triple bill for the Oxford Playhouse Company, which was to open their revamped Oxford theatre before touring. (Another classic – educated accents were acceptable in those). In the first play, *The School for Wives*, I played the young gallant, a boisterous youth with lots to say for himself. I wasn't in the next piece, *School for Wives Criticised*, but in the final play, *Impromptu of Versailles*, I was given the small role of an old roué – which I loved playing. Lecherous and slimy, bewigged and undoubtedly with bad breath, I had the time of my life in the role, and I think made it very funny. The best compliment came in some Stratford-on-Avon paper which said how much the critic had enjoyed my young lover, Horace, in the first play, had hugely enjoyed the roué I'd played in the third, and it wasn't until later he'd realised the two parts had been played by the one actor. It was a lovely company of some very fine, well-known actors. And I was among them!

Back in London, Marc had been told by an elderly restaurant regular that she wouldn't be seeing much more of him, sadly, as she was leaving town. She was finding her maisonette in Belgravia too much of a responsibility, and her children were urging her to come and live with them in the country, where they could take care of her more easily 'now Daddy's dead.' She was about to put the flat on the market and wondered if he knew of anyone who might be interested? She remembered Marc had always enthused about the prettiness of the particular area where she lived, so before she contacted an estate agent, would he, perhaps, be interested in taking a look at it? What could be nicer than having someone she was fond of living in her home of forty happy years.

Marc was surprised at my excitement when he told me. 'Find out when we can look at it. I mean, if we like it, we could . . . I dunno. It's even nearer to your restaurant than where we're living now. How much will she be asking for it? She didn't tell you? I mean, if we really like it, you could ask her to hold on before putting it on the market. I think I met her and her husband, but does she "know" about Us? Perhaps you should go and look at it on your own first.'

I was in a fever of hope. I had become really jaded with the small two-room flat in the shared house we lived in with Charles, with its shared front door and staircase, and this seemed an escape – if we could possibly afford it.

He went to see it and rang back. For a man who had no interest in homes as such, he was enthusiastic.

It got even better. The residents of the house had use of a tennis court in the private gardens outside. The only drawback was that this larger flat would be left completely empty of furniture – so we'd have to buy the lot. I've never been extravagant with clothes, but the prospect of doing up another home excited the hell out of me; it still does, even after all this time.

How much was it? He still didn't know. He'd wanted me to see it first before asking.

I was bowled over when we were invited to visit. It was the most elegant space I could ever have dreamt of living in – a maisonette on the third and fourth floor. The sitting room had high moulded ceilings and a working fireplace; there was enough room on the landing to fit half a tennis court, with light pouring onto it from the cupola above, two large bedrooms, a kitchen and a sizeable bathroom. The stairs leading up from the lift to that first landing and then on up another floor gave it great individuality. And, at the top, the smaller room that looked out over London was under the roof's eaves. A garret with sloping ceilings – we could put on a performance of *La Bohème* up there!

Mrs Elphick, the owner, was in her early seventies, I suppose. She was obviously sweet on Marc. We'd met before at the restaurant, but showing us around the rooms, she only had eyes for the good-looking maître d' with the adorable French accent.

I tried to keep my voice from squeaking when I whispered to Marc how I would beg, borrow, or steal to live there, and with a smile only he could produce, he confirmed to Mrs Elphick we were very interested. If he'd told her he was in love with her, she couldn't have been more thrilled. 'Well, dear, if you like it that much, I'll give you time to arrange your finances.'

This flat had a leasehold of another 43 years. I'd be over 70 when it came to an end. By that time, Marc and I would be in need of a geriatrics' home without so many stairs.

I went to see my bank manager, who I liked because he was obviously a bit stage-struck, and somehow convinced him I was good for a loan. He knew I had worked twice with Alastair Sim, whom he adored, and he thought the price of the flat was a bargain for the area it was in, and the bank would be only too happy to finance my half of the mortgage. And he would be grateful if I could get him first night tickets when I next worked on stage in London. He would insist on paying for the tickets, of course. Oh no, says I, it would be my pleasure. He positively burbled.

We moved in. As Charles's place had been ready furnished, we had to borrow two camp beds for the first six weeks until the new double bed we'd ordered arrived, and we spaced out the three or four pieces of our furniture around the otherwise empty rooms. Mrs Elphick had left her Regency-stripe-with-little-floral-bouquet curtains and her Persian-style carpets. Those carpets had been very good quality once but were now worn. OK, so we'd sand the floorboards, varnish them a light colour, lacquer them, and use that as a base for new carpets – but those could come later. Right now, we had a home of our own with a front door of our own with which we could lock out the world – a maisonette in Cadogan Square, no less.

With so much room, the place was OURS.

*

One day another restaurant regular offered Marc the use of his Eaton Square flat. The man was going to be putting his Mediterranean yacht to bed in preparation for the next summer season. He and I had met. Would we like to have a sort of home-away-from-home holiday at his place? As sort of house-sitters, I supposed. (It has only occurred to me while writing this to wonder, seriously, what Marc had done to earn this man's extreme trust and generosity. How green around the edges was I?).

Since I'd harshly ejected my mother and my wee brother from our flat, I had seen as little of her as possible. We'd made up, but I still felt guilty. I persuaded Marc, against his better judgement, that it would be kind ('Wouldn't it, sweetheart?') if we had a party to celebrate his and my mother's birthdays which were only a few days apart. *And*, although we'd refused the flat owner's offer to stay there, would he object if we used his flat for a party? Marc asked, and I bet he hoped the answer would be no, but there was no objection.

The flat was on two floors, the ground floor and basement, but it was in one of the most exclusive squares in London. It chimed perfectly with my mother's snobbishness (and probably mine). We took her to see it, and she was obviously thrilled to have such a grand setting to entertain her ex-pat friends. (Quite a few of the Calcutta British had returned to England after India's Independence Day). That the flat was bristling with marble statues of nude men elicited no comment. Nor was reference made to the number of charcoal drawings of unadorned males on the walls. Most of those were in the bedrooms and lavatories. Maybe she thought it was à la mode that smart society in London had tired of the female form and had taken to displaying men in all their sometimes obscenely gifted glory instead. Do you think?

My mother had never come out verbally with any suspicions she may have had about my relationship with Marc (a *foreign waiter*, for heaven's sake) or the suitability of my *living* with him. Perhaps it's my turn to be naive, but I think she probably knew in her heart of hearts what we got up to, but she liked my partner as much as she was able (after all, he'd given up his bed so that she could stay in our flat with her child); he was solicitous each time we met and charming as only he could be. And after our disagreeable parting, when I could at last face taking her out again, she was only too happy to be seen with me in his restaurant – one of the most socially 'in' places in London. The meals at La Poule cost me nothing, there were plenty of famous people eating there to murmur about, and she was always our guest. She gave every appearance of liking him. Not me always, but him, yes.

We had the party on a Sunday so our working friends could attend.

Before you read any further, here are my excuses for what followed. I'd never given such a sophisticated party – ever. Not in a month of Sundays did I imagine the difficulties there'd be in giving such disparate social groups a good time together. I thought you just named a venue, made sure there was enough food and drink, and invited friendly people around to enjoy it.

The evening was much like a long trail of fuse leading to an arsenal of dynamite. I've given better parties since, but then that double-birthday disaster was the nadir from which one couldn't help but do better.

We'd invited our friends and acquaintances for any time after 6.30, and they wandered in throughout the evening. Her society friends had been invited for 7.30. 'You can't invite people to drinks and dinner at any old time – it's just not done. We'll serve the food at eight.' What she meant, of course, was that Marc and I would serve the food at eight – which we were too lazy to do. Marc waited on people all week, the food we were offering hadn't been cooked by us but came beautifully presented in bowls and platters from the restaurant, so all we did was lay it out as a buffet, with smart borrowed cutlery on the side.

Our friends didn't mix. It was a bit like inviting a group of down-and-outs to a Buckingham Palace tea party. My mother held court on the ground floor, and our lot gravitated to the basement – where the food was. By the time she led her contingent downstairs, there wasn't much left on the table. I don't blame her now, but then? She made a scene, and I got angrier and angrier. Eventually, when the party had broken up, when the last of the wine had been drunk, and I was taking the food receptacles to my car to return them the next day to the restaurant, I saw from the pavement, in dumb show, my mother and my lover arguing inside the front room. And then, suddenly, she slapped his face. The briefest of pauses, and he slapped her back. The savage hatred of my mother the exchange produced in me was shocking. I cheered. Loudly. At midnight – there in Eaton Square.

I'd come a long way from when, as a child, I'd thought she was the most beautiful, fun mother there ever was, who made me glow with pride when she turned up at my first English school for the sports day in her summery dress – although I'd wished she hadn't worn that hat! We found it easy to make each other laugh.

As I re-entered the house, this woman, my once-adored mother, swept past me and out.

'What happened, sweetheart?'

'Your mother, she call me a guttersnipe. She slap me.'

I rushed to him and hugged him, lifting him into the air as if he'd won a title fight. 'I'm so sorry,' I said as I swung him around delightedly.

The breach between her and Marcel was never healed, although they later got to a state of polite pretence where manners plastered over the cracks.

*

Thanks to my teacher at my first school, Mr Lousada, I'd grown up in love with classical music. When all my discs were stolen that time from Marc's and my flat in Horseferry Road (all my Sinatra, Ella Fitzgerald, Peggy Lee, Sarah Vaughan, and those musicals from Broadway), I'd decided not to replicate them but to go on collecting the classics which I knew would satisfy me more. (Except for *My Fair Lady* – who could live without that?).

The only recording of mine that hadn't been swiped was Tchaikovsky's First Piano Concerto – which had been on the turntable – and that started my new collection.

We'd made friends with a man who ran a tiny specialist record shop in South Kensington, and he introduced us to Mahler – a bolt from the beautiful blue for this rather conventional collector. I remember the Bruno Walter Columbia label covers to this day. Our collection, my new collection, had started when I hadn't too many spare pennies to rub together, and we rationed ourselves to only one long-playing vinyl recording a month. And up in our room under the roof, we'd lie on the floor, our eyes closed, and listen to each disc – until the month was over and we could buy the next. So through our knowledgeable friend, I learned of Richard Strauss, Elgar, Schoenberg and Shostakovich – the first two bowled me over, and the last two I found difficult to decipher. And we discovered for ourselves Dvořák, Saint-Saëns, Sibelius, Haydn – all the tuneful masters who, for satisfaction, rank alongside Brahms, Beethoven and Schubert as far as I'm concerned. Later still, when we could afford it, we spent serious money on concerts at the Festival Hall.

I realise that, up to now, I've recalled Marc through our various sexual shenanigans, but I need you to believe we always had a deep friendship too. His understanding of my hurt after my rejection by Ally made him all the more caring and loving. And lying side by side on the floor in the room at the top of the house, holding hands, sharing that music, was wonderfully healing.

I played tennis, I swam, I enjoyed marijuana with friends, and I got better. We'd been living in that lovely flat for eighteen months when one day I was walking in central London and saw Ally's car pull out of a side street onto the main thoroughfare. I ran after it down the middle of the road, a good hundred yards or more, until it had to stop at the lights. I opened the passenger door and sat down heavily in the seat beside him.

Still panting: 'You're a shit, you know that don't you?'

There was a moment's silence. 'That's more like it,' he said.

*

I had in happier times done his secretarial work, which hadn't amounted to much: answering the letters he received from the public at stage doors or sent on by his agent. For the autograph hunters, he had a cyclostyled reply along the lines of: 'Mr Alastair Sim has not signed autographs for many years as a matter of principle, and I'm sure you'll understand he can't make any exceptions.' I would enclose this short, polite (unsigned) note in the stamped addressed envelope – if it had been supplied, if not, the letter was binned – and post it on my way home later. (Ally found signing his name on a piece of paper just because he was an actor nonsensical – why not ask the supplicant for an autograph? Their job was probably more useful to the world than his. I remember being beside him at a stage door one day when he refused to sign autographs for a group waiting outside. He was very polite, but I heard a woman say, sourly: 'Who does he think he is?' But that was his point. He didn't think what he did merited that sort of meaningless hero worship). But the letters appreciative of his work, those that didn't ask for a signature, got it at the bottom of the letter he'd dictate to me, and I'd type up. We would then eat the food supplied by Naomi and do the crossword – or play backgammon or watch television. I only went up to Hampstead to see him once a week, and if it was a Wednesday, Naomi would be with us – the best evenings of all.

He put his principles into practice when he turned down a knighthood. I saw the letter from the Powers that Be; those people authorised to offer such things, ('if it should be offered, would you accept . . . etc.') and his dignified letter of refusal. He told me that after he and Naomi composed the reply, she'd suggested they cross off his PS: 'I can still hear my wife laughing from where I sit.'

Some evenings I would take him through the lines of a part he was about to play. That was real fun. Every now and then, he'd ask as we were going through them: 'You didn't laugh, didn't you find that amusing?' and I would say, 'Oh, no, was it meant to be?' And he'd roll his eyes and explain. 'No', I'd say, 'that's not how it came over to me.' He'd sigh and try delivering the line another way, and without exception, it worked.

The most uproarious time I had was when he was preparing his role for *The Magistrate*. (He was beyond-belief wonderful in that). Of course, he and Naomi worked assiduously on learning his lines all the time, and indeed she was present at most of his performances in every play he did on stage, going through a post-mortem at the end of each show. But quite often, I could help.

Derek Fowlds once told me something he'd found wryly amusing, and it demonstrated perfectly how Ally approached the business of acting. Apparently, at the end of a scene (this was in a comedy at the Vaudeville theatre, *The Jockey Club Stakes*), Derek came off stage and apologised to Ally for not getting the expected laugh on one of his lines. 'Are you playing it for laughs, Derek?' He'd been serious.

When, later in life, it came to me to advise young actors on the art of acting, I remembered very well Ally telling me his approach to a role, every role, that is, not just comic ones – and by heavens, he was very fine indeed in serious drama. Just think of *An Inspector Calls*.

Here's what I told them (à la Sim):

First: when you get a new script, erase all the author's stage or screen directions (like *laughs* or *shouts* or *angrily*). That way, it's up to you to make complete sense of your dialogue without preconceptions.

Second: listen to what's being said to you.

Third: when answering another character, discard the obvious riposte until you've tried to justify more than that obvious way of replying. For instance, if a character in the piece asks you something as simple as 'Are you comfortable?' and the answer is 'yes', try and find three or four surprising ways of saying it. So, it might be a qualified 'yes', a fearful 'yes', a sarcastic 'yes', a suspicious 'yes', an insulted 'yes', a distracted 'yes' . . . and so on. Then try and justify the most unusual. Unless that can be used truthfully in context, you must discard it. Then try and justify the next most unusual. When you can, *if* you can with complete honesty to your character, justify an unconventional 'yes', then go for it. By choosing the least expected throughout the script (and it *must* be truthful), you tilt the perception the audience has of your character a fraction. It also helps if you, the actor, develop your character along lines that aren't merely conventional. It makes the recipient of your answer, if he or she is listening, change course, maybe only slightly. Thus the tennis match of a conversation will, or can be, really intriguing, with subtle undertones that can only be guessed at. Yours, by the elimination of the obvious, becomes the most interesting character to watch. Unless, of course, you're with actors of equal daring – in which case the audience is in for a magical time.

The above applies to every dramatist from ancient times through Chekov to Agatha Christie.

On stage, Ally would subtly alter his characterisation night after night. He'd first learn his character through its thought processes. Although by the first public performance, he'd know every line by heart, his interpretation of the character was never static. Because he listened carefully to everyone on stage with him, his response would take account of the slightest alteration in mood. He loved more than anything to be surrounded by spontaneity.

I appeared with him again on stage a few years later (I knew all about his working methods by then – I came to rehearsals with my role part-baked, even though he wasn't directing the piece) and watched him on stage from the wings while waiting to come on, noticing that the laughter he surprised from the audience could be in different places from one performance to the next and that some nights he'd play his role more inwardly, so there would be fewer laughs in the play. The particular play I'm telling you about, *Number*

10, was a comedy-drama, but because of him, on the nights when it wasn't a suspenseful comedy, the story acquired a more dangerous edge. It drove one of the actors with him on stage into a fury – but we'll come to that in a moment.

When I returned to Forrigan after the long sabbatical away, Naomi hugged me to her. 'I thought we'd lost you, darling boy.' We held onto each other fiercely for quite some time. God, it was good to be with her again. Merlith was well married by then, so there was no more sniping; Ally was careful with me, so no more cruelty; and, anyway, I was unafraid. With one bound, I was free to be my altered self.

*

In early 1964 I was asked by the Windsor Repertory Company to return to the theatre there and do a Ray Cooney farce, *Chase Me, Comrade*. I was asked to play a quasi-Nureyev, a Russian ballet dancer who is smuggled by some well-to-do young activists from the airport, where he defected, to a country house belonging to an Admiral and his wife. I learned some Russian, which I spoke atrociously, and spent a lot of the play flying in and out of the living room doors dancing, striking poses, being haughty and causing consternation among the unsuspecting household. The production was a try-out for Brian Rix and his company, and at Windsor, the part intended for him was played by the author, Ray Cooney. It worked like a dream, and Denis Ramsden and I from that original cast went into town with it to the Whitehall Theatre just off Trafalgar Square. Without an agent and happy to go into the West End, I signed myself to a Run of the Play contract. And the play ran for one year, eleven months, and two weeks! (If I'd had representation, I would not have been so stupid).

I can't tell you how hard it is to concentrate on a performance for that length of time that isn't just a run-through of the lines each night. Trying for spontaneity and believability, I'd occasionally find myself acting in front of a paying audience wondering what I was going to have for dinner that evening after the show. And the twice in those two years I had a fortnight's holiday, I came back to the play wondering what on earth I thought I'd been doing with some of the inflections and movements I'd added to the role in my effort to try and keep my performance fresh. Lordy, it became boring. One night, waiting in the wings to go on, I noticed the theatre cat wandering close by, so I carried it to behind the pretend fireplace and urged it onto the stage. The audience found it very funny that a cat had loped into the room over the glowing coals, and afterwards, I looked as innocent as a saint when asked if I knew how it had happened. Apparently, the cat had never done such a thing before.

The play was a load of piffle, but heavens how the audience loved it, and it is very satisfying to find yourself at the receiving end of a gale of laughter. But once it becomes the norm, it's a struggle not to become complacent.

And then, one evening, I came into the theatre to find that Nureyev was going to be in the audience. It's all very well blithely sending up an icon – until that icon turns up to judge whether what you're doing is not funny but cruel. And even in those early days after his defection, we'd all read how temperamental Nureyev could be. So, I was full of anxiety as I came onto the stage for my first entrance in full *Swan Lake* gear (which was never explained), my tights gleaming white and without a wrinkle – even though I'd been smuggled to the house in the boot of a car.

The audience was aware that the great man was sitting with them – how could they not be, he was very noticeable – so their reaction to my appearance was somewhat muted for a change (did they think he might cause a scandal?). And then my head was bent over my hostess's hand, kissing it as though she was Princess Odile, my legs in first position, expressing my thanks in sexily murmured rubbish-Russian, followed by a grand tour around the drawing room as though I was examining it while readying myself for my solo. I was in dancing pumps, for heaven's sake. What had I been doing at the airport?

And I had an out-of-body experience, watching this grotesquerie through the venerated Russian's eyes, a very recent and welcome stranger to these shores being parodied in his adopted country. Oh God, what if he was offended?

And then slowly, the audience warmed up, returned to their normal delighted reactions, and we skated on through the play until their usual cheers at the end. (Nobody whooped in those days. When did that start?).

I was summoned by the star, Brian Rix, to his Number One dressing room after the show. It seemed the Great Russian wanted to meet me. I got there in my everyday clothes. He was smiling at me through his lowered lids. I didn't understand, nor do I remember what he said to me, but it was brusquely complimentary, I think. But I did hear: 'I take you to eat with us. You would like?' and it was only then I clocked that the dressing room was full of his entourage. 'No, no,' said Brian, 'you must come with us to dinner.' And then, in this out-of-body experience, I saw Brian's wife, Elspeth, was there looking resplendent – she'd obviously been summoned from across town. 'Thank you, no, thank you,' said The Man, and he led me out of the room with his arm about my shoulder.

I had never been so hated and envied before.

I don't know how it was that I found myself, still with my tiny Gogomobil, driving Rudolf Nureyev up The Mall, around past Buckingham Palace, his hand on my knee, but I do remember thinking, 'God almighty, I'm responsible for this Great Man's safety.' But it was only a passing thought because soon we were at the Hungry Horse restaurant in Fulham. His posse was following behind in taxis, so we entered the place alone. The diners applauded as he came in, and before he would sit at the table that had been reserved for him, he took me around the bemused diners, from table to table, introducing me as his brother. Grappled to his side I squirmed around the restaurant, a fixed grin on my face. I've never been that ostentatious in real life, so this nonsense parading was cringingly embarrassing. Everyone was beaming as we sat, and his group joined us.

I found it difficult to eat as Rudi – that's what they all called him, and who was I to disagree – pressed against me, his thigh so hard against mine that I was inched along the banquette, and I don't remember a thing about the conversation. I only learned later his current 'friend' was in the party, and his wannabe lover too, along with his female manager. But the owner of the restaurant invited himself to sit with us, and after Rudi-ing obsequiously a lot implied that a current British male ballet dancer was as good – if not better – than him. No, no, he wasn't saying *better*, but . . .

Rudi was frosty. The man left. Only to return later, even more drunk, to continue in the same vein. So Nureyev stood, pushing the table away, 'I did not ask you to be with us,' and taking money out of his wallet, threw the contents at the man and stormed out of the restaurant. I was appalled. My evening seemed over.

But I was also British, from public school, so I began to pick up the banknotes. 'Don't do that,' I was told by Joan, Rudi's manager. 'He can't be allowed to get away with it,' I muttered, 'that's bloody childish.' So with a fistful of notes, I went to find the diva. He was outside in the courtyard of the restaurant, standing imperiously in front of the restaurant owner, who was now writhing in knots of apologies. 'Behave yourself,' I said, handing him the money. It only took a moment before he tore the notes up and flung the pieces in the grovelling owner's face. 'You are paid.' He grabbed me by the arm and pulled me out onto the road.

And so it came to pass that I found myself under a streetlamp in the middle of leafy Fulham, past midnight, being kissed by a very famous man. And then I drove him to his place.

It was early morning and light when he told me in the bath that we had the same type of hair and that I must wash it every day, otherwise I'd lose it. (I had spent real money at a trichologist in Harley Street to be told that I would have very little hair by the time I was thirty, not to brush it, only comb it if I must, 'and that's a hundred guineas, thank you.' I followed the Russian's advice, and I have enough of it even now).

The front garden was in full daylight when he led me to the gate, me fully dressed, him in a kimono.

'I go to South of France in two days. You come with me.'

'No, I can't. I, er, have a Run of the Play contract.'

'I buy contract. You come with me. Yes.'

It had been amazing, unbelievable, but not something I wanted to continue.

'No, they won't let me off. Look, I'm supposed to be . . . I have to . . . No, I can't. I'm so sorry.' I left him nonplussed at the gate as I hurried away. It was a bright dawn, and I was very aware of the houses on either side.

I saw him five years later in London as I was walking down the King's Road one sunny afternoon. He was certainly one of the most famous men in the world by then, and there he was cruising past me in a top-down sports car. He drove a little way further before stopping and turned in his seat to look back at me. I was flattered he'd recognised me. I drew up to him, smiling.

'You are busy now?' he asked matter-of-factly.

He didn't know me from Adam.

'We've met before,' I said. 'I'm Kerry. Uh, Kerry Gardner. We had dinner . . . Hungry Horse?'

'Kerry? No.' Then a big wolfish grin. 'Kerry! Yes. Yes. Is my birthday, Kerry. You come to have tea with me.'

I got into his car, and he drove us to a mews house nearby.

His drawing room was gloomy, and at first, all I could see was a grand piano in the low-ceilinged room with a vase full of what looked like roses on top.

As my eyes became accustomed to the darkness, I saw that on his sofa was a Russian scimitar and a shield. I could see they were the genuine appalling things, with the leather bindings on the hide shield and brass chasing on the sword hilt. Lying there on a damask cushion, the contrast was almost shocking. He picked up the scimitar.

'Birthday present from Princess . . .' (I didn't recognise the name). 'Is very sharp – very dangerous.'

Like a grown-up kid, he swung the scimitar around his head once or twice then, striding towards the piano, sliced the heads off all the roses with one sweep.

I was outraged at the destruction but said nothing. I didn't want this man. I suddenly remembered I had to be somewhere else and left five minutes after walking in.

*

Through the fifties and sixties, the Whitehall Theatre Company led by Brian Rix was compared in the same admiring breath to the famous team who were lauded for their farces, most of them written by Ben Travers, which ran for twenty years at the Aldwych Theatre in the 1920s and 30s. Brian was at the Whitehall for sixteen years, presenting one huge success after another with the same basic team of actors: himself, Basil Lord and Leo Franklyn.

Basil was a dear, but Leo was a hoot. A middle-sized man with an elderly baby's face, his favourite welcoming trick for guests to his dressing room was his 'impersonations': Leo the Lion and the Flying Swan. For both of these, he had to be trouserless – if you entered his room once he was dressed, you missed the fun – so there he stood, naked from the waist down, and pulled his flaccid penis forwards at the same time stretching his scrotum sideways to form wings and waggled them up and down on either side. That was the Flying Swan. For Leo the Lion, he'd push that same flaccid penis between his legs, turn around and bend down so all you could see was the orbs of his bum and a little 'tongue' poking out at the bottom of the lion's face. He never tired of exposing himself, particularly to strangers, as he always got a shocked laugh out of them. His friends told him to 'just put it away'.

One of Brian Rix's replacements, when he went on holiday, was the amazing Stanley Baxter. A great lovable man, I'm lucky to have worked with for two whole weeks.

Brian put on some short farces on television, and I was involved in two of them. It was through them that I met a witty, gentle actor, a man who I consider to be one of the best friends I've ever had, Moray Watson. (He died only the other day). Around that time, Moray was directing a play for the theatre and asked me to be his assistant. So, I got to sit in while this clever light-comedy actor directed a group of well-known comedy performers. The mechanics of making a new play work, the handling of actors' egos, the plotting of sightlines so no actor obscured another when the other had something of importance to say, the placement of furniture in relation to the exits and entrances, the diplomacy needed with stage crews and management . . . and so much more, was fascinating and educative to watch from the other side of the lights. I don't remember the title of the play, but it went on tour around England before not making it into Town.

It was Moray's mother, many years later, who told mine that I was a homosexual. My mother thought I was being my usual bloody-minded self when I refused to take the pill she'd been told could cure me.

*

It was only in the last two or three years of my relationship with Marc that it slowly wound down. He seemed to think, *we* thought perhaps, that sex would be the balm that healed. But, imperceptibly, through all that sexual sharing with others, our relationship was tarnished. For me, anyway. Pretty obvious really, but while we'd been the best of friends and lovers, I hadn't noticed how sleazy I was beginning to find this sharing – while also enjoying it. Although I loved him, he became more and more *that* person there the other side of *this* stranger's body – men he'd brought back at night after his work in the restaurant, not every night, but maybe one or two a month.

I'm not a hoarder of personal belongings, but I also got riled at the number of small pilferings that went on, objects without great value but often mementoes: like the tortoiseshell fountain pen my father had given me, a table lighter, a Jacques Fath tie, an onyx ashtray I'd bought in Aberdeen when performing panto up there. Just things, but . . .

Because my darling was becoming fat and losing his hair, I suddenly twigged that the same people turned up on a more regular basis, so not so many strangers but a gang of the same hangers-on – sometimes goodish in bed, but to talk to? Was it a coincidence? It occurred to me shamefully that I had become the display in a shop window to attract passersby.

My night with Rudi was accepted as a matter of course by my partner, and when, later in the run of *Chase Me, Comrade*, one of the most beautiful men in British film came to visit a member of the cast, he came into my dressing room to ask whether I'd like to come to dinner with them. I was both knocked sideways by the invitation and the beauty of this man but didn't hesitate for a moment to accept. I could see from his merry inviting look that dinner was unlikely to be the only thing on the menu – and at that point in my relationship, I was available.

And so it turned out that John and I met secretly for over a year, and Marc seemed unperturbed once he got to know of the affair. Resigned, perhaps, is a better word, but he had his own hangers-on. I was not proud of myself. The whole period was exhilarating and painful. Somewhere in the back of my mind, I had always thought monogamy was the right way of the world. I felt like shit – when I wasn't feeling ecstatic.

Then John's long-time partner found out – and that was very, *very* sadly that.

*

I used this story later when I was an agent to impress on actors that making a fool of yourself is not career-destroying – we all did it, and not to be afraid to be yourself. It happened not long after I met John. He was in a West End play with Dennis Price and Moira Lister, and we arranged to meet after his curtain came down in the pub behind his theatre. The full cast assembled, and I was asked by Denis what I wanted to drink, old boy? Knowing his tipple was Guinness, I asked for it; not a drink I particularly liked, but I was doing my creepy best to look comfortable with these august personages. Moira, married to an Italian prince, was being picked up by her chauffeur to go on to a party. She looked amazing in her primrose shot-silk dress, matching toque hat with a little veil, matching primrose shoes and bag – and this chic vision stood opposite me. 'Time gentlemen, please,' was called out, and seeing as I hadn't even started on the pint of the inky black Guinness in my fist, I took a big swallow – and choked. I tried to keep the liquid in my mouth by pressing my lips together. I looked up to heaven as I started spraying the beer, finishing with my head jerking downwards. As I looked up again, I saw the small brown spots of Guinness spreading slowly and steadily over Moira's primrose silk suit, the hat on her head to the points of her shoes, not sparing her matching handbag.

Everyone was appalled, not least me, knowing John would never talk to me again, and she was furious – but too well-mannered to show it for more than a second. I suppose the chauffeur who picked her up had to drive her home to change before her party. The next day I visited Fortnum and Mason and ordered flowers to be delivered to her dressing-room. John told me she was very forgiving: 'He didn't need to do that, the dear boy, really. Such an unfortunate accident.' Wasn't it just.

*

Some years later, I had no qualms about accepting a job working with Ally again, this time in a play by Ronald Millar (also famous as a speechwriter for Thatcher, providing her with her oft-quoted phrase: 'This lady's not for turning'. Come on, you thought she was that original in her uncultured thinking? It was the title of Christopher Fry's play, *The Lady's Not for Burning*, tweaked by Millar. She wouldn't have known that, but Millar would). *Number 10* was another middle-class piece produced in the theatre by Peter Bridge. There were still theatre producers like him and Binkie Beaumont who had through the years made their living from the Well-Made-Plays of Terence Rattigan, Noël Coward, Graham Greene and the likes, who later struggled to lure those moneyed punters back to the theatre. Eventually giving up the uphill struggle, they retired from the game, leaving the field to the more acutely class-antennaed Michael Codron.

As I had only ever had agents helping me on a piecemeal basis, this job came to me thanks to Ally.

Number 10 was a political play set in Downing Street during a national crisis, and I played the PA to the PPS to the PM (Personal Assistant to the Parliamentary Private Secretary to the Prime Minister – who was Ally). I tell you, my career was a hodgepodge of unconnected roles of different sizes.

Because of Alastair Sim, two well-loved names from the past, the married couple Michael Denison and Dulcie Gray, and the more modern attraction, John Gregson (with whom I'd already worked at the Old Vic) were in it. The play had a respectable run of six months in London.

If you think of a play, or a performed piece of writing, like a tennis match with each character positioning him or herself on the court ready to receive a verbal shot across the net, there were actors in those days who could only really feel comfortable if they knew exactly how and where the return speech would bounce. So, well-positioned, they could send back their reply to the exact spot on the court, the other side, where the recipient was expecting it – and comfortably placed to shoot it back. Acting by rote. If it is done skilfully, the audience doesn't know they are getting exactly the same performance as the night before and the night before that.

Ally drove Dulcie Gray mad. As the Prime Minister's dutiful wife, she had a droll scene where she came on stage, as light relief in a rather dramatic point in the play, inquiring about his well-being and offering him a glass of water with an Alka Seltzer. Well, he committed the cardinal sin of not putting the tablets into the water when she expected it in a speech she had – because that night this PM had other things to think about – so in high dudgeon, Dulcie flounced off the stage with half the scene still to be played out.

I was in the wings waiting to come on next, so that's what I did, early, and paraphrased Dulcie's lines for her (something about his suit having come back from the cleaners, and, by the way, their charlady was about to give notice). I was the PM's PA, so it wasn't too surprising I knew the state of his wardrobe and had noticed the impossible cleaner's rancour as well. And then we went on with the scene I'd been employed to give.

In the interval soon after, back in our dressing rooms, the cast could hear the raised voices of Dulcie and our director, David Scase – and then a loud bang. An assassination?

'Act Two beginners, please,' was called over the tannoy and those of us who started the scene assembled in place on stage . . . and no Dulcie. We waited. Surely she wasn't going to hold the audience to ransom by leaving the theatre halfway through the show? The stage manager went to fetch her. Then we heard screams (the curtain was still down, so it was unlikely the audience heard them), then thuds and crashing. Five minutes later, Dulcie appeared, sweating with fury, fit to be tied. It turned out that when she'd banged the door shut on David's departure earlier, it had jammed, and nothing but an axe could set her free to go on with the show.

An icy letter was delivered to the management the next day, demanding apologies from Alastair, which of course, he delivered. But the easy-going atmosphere, the rapport between Michael Denison, Dulcie's husband, and Ally never returned (he enjoyed improvising on stage with his co-star), and the building wasn't as much fun to return to for each performance after that bit of melodrama – and excitement, it must be said.

One of the most attractive features of *Number 10*, though, was the tour prior to its opening in London: it whizzed around England's provincial theatres before doing a fortnight at the O'Keefe Centre in Toronto. It was there in Canada that I met David, a young Welsh actor playing Charlie Brown in an American tour of the musical *You're a Good Man, Charlie Brown*, and it was from there I could go to the Niagara Falls. Both were momentous events for me.

I fell crazily in lust with David, and once we'd met, we spent the rest of that fortnight in bed – dragging ourselves out only to make a visit to the Falls and, of course, to our separate performances in our different theatres. Two stupendous events in my life, both momentous in every way.

You gets what you pays for, angel.

CHAPTER 10
I, Nausius

I had fallen for an actor in Canada. I told Marc, and the gaggle of hangers-on in our flat of this when I returned from the *Number 10* tour (I moved into a separate bedroom to prove my intent), and I pined for David, sending him letters telling him how much I missed him, how life was dreary without him, and as he was British born why couldn't he come to England to be with me after his *Charlie Brown* tour?

He was persuaded. David finished his tour, gave up his apartment in New York, and parceled everything he wanted to keep to his mother in Wales.

I have to confess now to certainly the most shameful treatment I've ever meted out to another human being – to my knowledge.

Number 10 was still playing at the Strand theatre when I went to meet him one morning off the plane. As I looked out for him disembarking in the observation lounge at the airport, I wondered why I wasn't excited. Why was the world monochrome? Why was I feeling slightly queasy?

David taking me at my word and selling up in the States to return to Britain was the response of one romantic to another. After three months of being on different sides of the Atlantic, with me airmailing love letters to him, the small stocky person who stepped out of the aircraft, instead of gladdening my heart, left me with the deadening suspicion that I had made the mistake of my life. I waved at him from the observation platform at Heathrow Airport, and he, looking around anxiously before seeing me, waved back with the biggest smile of relief. Oh, dear lord.

Waiting for him to pass through Customs, I quelled my misgivings as best I could, telling myself this was a huge step for both of us and hadn't we loved being together in Canada? So why wouldn't we now? By the time he trolleyed through the final exit after Customs, I'd boosted my courage and my smile. I had a few more seconds to evaluate him at closer quarters before he saw me. He really was adorable, wasn't he? My welcoming grin percolated up through my dread and was believable by the time he caught it on my face.

Perhaps I've re-imagined this through the years with the benefit of hindsight. I do remember feeling afraid – of wanting to run away. Perhaps the full realisation of the magnitude of the mistake came only slowly. Please God, I hope so. Because, if I'd known straight away it was a dreadful error, that all it had been was juvenile wishful thinking, I should have told him there and then. The pain for both of us – for him in particular – would have been horrendous and immediate, but would have saved us from that slow, slow death. But at the time, did I know for certain? I really don't think so. If I did, I was an abject coward.

Dwelling on that near five-year period of my life with David won't make for pretty reading and will show me up for the shit I am. Was? So, because I can, dear reader, I'll cut out the bad bits.

Marc was polite when I brought David back to our flat, to the room I'd prepared for the two of us. One of the fly-by-night strangers had alighted and was now sleeping most nights with Marc in what had once been our bed. We circled around each other with strained smiles.

David was an actor, so there was lots for us to share now he was back in his native lands after only six years away. He wrote barrow-loads of letters to agents and was eventually taken on by one. She wasn't one of the best, but she did put him up for a role in the West End – which he got. Sadly, the play *Romanoff and Juliet* was not Peter Ustinov's wittiest and closed after only a few months at the New London. He went up for other things, got a few, but fewer and fewer. The problem seemed to be that although he'd been born in Wales, he'd acquired an American accent during his time in the

States which he couldn't seem to shake off, and in those days, there wasn't much call for Americans in our Eurocentric theatre and film. The New Wave hadn't spent itself.

My new lover got dispirited, and I turned down one or two, admittedly unimportant, jobs so as not to exacerbate the prickly situation while regularly ringing my acting acquaintances to see if they were involved in a project in which there might be a part for him. Within eighteen months, his work situation soured to a standstill, and I became frantic in my efforts to find him something to raise his morale. For instance, the second Christmas he was here (1969 I think it was), we did a pantomime together in East Grinstead. We played a couple of inept robbers with silly names. The producers were shysters, it was badly paid, the cast was kitted out in costumes that hadn't been cleaned, and the sets were laughable (one scene was set in a forest, and the backdrop they provided was of the Arizona desert. Every third or fourth performance day, we'd come onto the stage to find another tree had been painted over a cactus on the backcloth. By the last performance, our 'forest' was still dangerously prickly).

The only good thing to come out of all that was that we met a lovely family whose daughter played the lead. Melanie, our Snow White, is a friend of mine to this day.

I had the most fun trying to make her laugh on stage. I found a storefront dummy backstage which I dressed up in men's clothes: a doublet and hose, a pair of breeches and a feathered hat on its head. Standing in the wings while her Prince was singing to Snow White, I hid behind the dummy – I'd removed the arms – and pretending my arms were the dummies, would undress it. My hands would slowly undo the buttons of the dummy's breeches, slowly, slowly, push the breeches down to its knees, pull the hose down suggestively, as in a striptease, eventually sitting the thing down on my lap as if it was on the loo. Melanie, as Snow White, would be transfixed at what was happening in the wings behind her Prince's back, the Principal Boy moving vainly up and down the stage to prevent her seeing me while he tried to woo her with a love song. Melanie (or 'Blossom' as we called her) got her own back: in the picnic scene in the cactified forest where the two robbers went to kill Snow White, she would serve us little tartlets she'd made at home, the pastry cases filled with goats' droppings from the farm – or other things. 'Eat, eat,' she would urge, handing us each a tart. 'Go on, I dare you,' she'd whisper, then loudly, 'they're delicious. I made them myself.'

Between the shows, we were invited by her lovely parents to a meal at their farmhouse – which made the job bearable and even fun.

David had taken to drinking more and more Rusty Nails. A good name for a porn star, you might think. No, these were cocktails that were made from a combination of Drambuie and Whisky. It had been in the Toronto theatre bar after one of his performances when I first saw him drinking this concoction. David had told me he only drank after the show – never during the day. He had also told me that he'd accompanied his American ex-lover to rehab a couple of years before. Why hadn't I heard any alarm bells? In my desire to rush him to the nearest bed, I obviously wasn't attentive, I thought vaguely that it meant he'd been to rehab as his lover's carer.

But once our relationship was up and running down, he needed the ease of drink more and more.

*

I've always loved American musicals: *Oklahoma, Guys and Dolls, South Pacific, Kiss Me Kate, My Fair Lady, Show Boat* – so many, many jewels – and through the years, I've replaced all the recordings that were stolen and collected many more. The day the American musical graduated from Vaudeville and took on narrative, it became an art form (which now the world copies to great effect – *Les Misérables, Mamma Mia, Phantom of the Opera*, et al). English musicals in those days could be tuneful and jolly fun but were more often than not twee and insular. Consider the titles: *The Water Gypsies, Twenty Minutes South, The Boy Friend, Salad Days*, great tunes but downright daft. Imagine rushing through the parks of London looking for a magic

P.I.A.N.O. Does that give you the idea? Fifty years on, and it's all change. Don't bother to ask *how come?* Andrew Lloyd Webber is the answer. He's a Gift to the Universe, to be rated with the greatest.

Fifteen years before this treasure wrote *Phantom of the Opera*, I adapted *Eldorado*, one of the Scarlet Pimpernel stories by Baroness Orczy, as a musical. I wrote the libretto but couldn't make any headway with the lyrics. When one of David's friends was over for a short visit from the States – a lyricist who'd written for some impressive performers back home – he asked to read my adaptation, which I now called *Pimpernel!*, and next morning had come up with two very clever sets of lyrics – a ballad and a point number. Hugely impressed, I asked him to work with me. We'd been writing back and forth for about six months when we came to the obvious conclusion, we'd get on faster talking face to face. I should get over to the States.

This coincided with David's wish to return to America. It was soon after we started our third dismal year together, and he made me a bargain: he'd give up the booze if I would go back with him to the US of A, where he was sure he could find acting work. He'd rung his ex-agents in New York, and they seemed certain they could get him jobs. Without doubt, he would be happier if he could fulfil his dreams as an actor so, even though I'd been praying inwardly to end the relationship, I was so crushed by guilt (you made your bed, matey, and you must lie on it), I agreed for his sake to give it a try. I told myself that once he was relaunched in the States, I could leave him. That's if I still wanted to. Perhaps if he was happier, we'd be happier, and I wouldn't.

'The self-deception that believes the lie.' [2]

In 1970 we bought two one-way tickets to New York. David had an American acquaintance who was willing to rent us his studio apartment for a year on 853 7th Avenue, a five-minute stroll from Times Square.

The studio was on the ground floor of an old high-rise building

---

2   A lyric from 'I Wish I Were in Love Again' from *Babes in Arms*, Rogers & Hart (1937)

directly opposite the most famous deli in New York: a largish room with one large window, two sofa beds, a tiny kitchen with free cockroaches, and an even smaller loo and shower.

We spent the pitiful amount of money we'd been allowed to bring over with us, £50, in two days. In England, we'd just had Black Monday, or was it Terrible Tuesday . . . and that was all the currency we were allowed to take out of the country. It covered one show on Broadway and a meal.

Without a Green Card, I couldn't get a proper job, so I worked at anything David's acquaintances could find me – and got paid out of petty cash boxes at half the going rate. I worked as a secretary for Joe Hardy, a Broadway director, out of his brownstone; as a typist/assistant for an antiques dealer; and for The American Society for Psychical Research.

After some months of David's badgering, his agents asked him to leave – they couldn't find him work, and they could do without him on the phone or at their door every five minutes.

I've never been so lonely in my life. All my friends in England had told me what a fool I was being, so I was damned if I was going to contact them for money or support. We lived on a shoestring. I got podgy with depression and booze. And instead of cigarettes, I smoked the cheaper cigarillos – which ate at my stomach lining. I couldn't afford to go to a doctor. The only relief from the ulcer pain was to eat more.

At the American Society for Psychical Research, I typed most of the day and had time to read some of their scientific research journals during the lunch break. These publications were as much about debunking psychic phenomena as verifying them. But . . . I read about a researcher who had tried to manufacture a noise by imagining it. He sat with his dog in his study ostensibly reading a newspaper and had been concentrating hard on creating this effect in the silence of his room for a half-hour or more – and the instant he gave up his efforts there was a huge bang, and the dog leapt to its feet barking.

More niggling to my mind was the report by a scientist who had returned home from his office, gone into his study where he'd been working with a Geiger counter on an experiment, and found the machine fluctuating madly without apparent cause. Then he noticed one of the pots of geraniums on his windowsill had been blown over onto the floor, the pot smashed and the plant lying with its roots exposed. Repotting it and putting it back in place seemed to mollify the machine. Some days later, a neighbour dropped by after he'd been mowing his lawn, and once again, the Geiger counter went frantic when the man entered the room. And then the clincher: the scientist set up a platform of eggs around a boiling saucepan of water, and when he tipped in the first one, the Geiger counter went ballistic, the second one had the same result, but by the time he got to the fourth egg, it seemed the eggs had given up hope of reprieve and the needle didn't move. So much for being a vegetarian. So much for walking on torn grass.

I was working on *Pimpernel!* one afternoon alone in the studio flat when I heard a scream. Along with all the noises you get used to in the heart of Manhattan – the clank and clatter of those metal manhole plates on the roads, the sirens, the drone of traffic – I hadn't heard a scream before. I listened. Nothing. Then another scream. It sounded nearby. It seemed so desperate I hoped I was imagining things . . . and returned to work. Another scream – even louder, this time with words attached. It was so close by I thought it sort of sounded like *Help Me*. I went to the door and listened. Nothing. I was about to turn back when another shriek of someone in real distress stopped me. I was really frightened now. I opened the door into the hallway, saw the janitor sweeping near the door by the entrance, looked to him for confirmation of what I'd heard, when it happened again. The screams were coming from behind the door opposite our apartment. Bloody hell!

My heart racing, I screwed up enough courage to knock. The janitor was nearby. He surely had heard the screams and would prevent my being hurt. I knocked again, louder this time – and looked behind me for my backup. The janitor had disappeared – and even as I looked, the door opened, and a half-dressed young woman screeched into my arms. Behind her was a giant of a man (I'm probably exaggerating) who came barrelling after her trying to get a hold. She squirmed around to get behind me, screaming: 'Don't let him touch me! Don't let him touch me!' He seemed oblivious to my body, which stood between them: 'Come back here, you stupid bitch!' Poking me in the chest with his finger, driving me backwards.

The woman yelling behind me, I was dragged towards the entrance of the building, only thirty feet away. What with his jabbing and her pulling, the woman and I eventually backed to the door and out onto the pavement where I was free of her – but not of his finger. 'Stupid cunt!' he shouted after her as I saw her get into a cab at the kerb. He turned back into the building, still muttering, and disappeared.

He was my opposite neighbour, and it crossed my mind that I would be on his hit list after this little fracas. But I don't think he saw me. I'd just been the wall between him and his desires. He may have been disgruntled, but sweetheart, my gruntles were well and truly shaken. I had never seen him before, and I never saw him again. I did see the janitor, who looked past me from that morning onwards.

I went back to working on *Pimpernel!* Liam, the American lyricist, and I had met a few times to unravel our differences, but the more he gave me what I asked for, the more dissatisfied I became with the outline we were working on. And then it came to me in a flash: what I'd written was four-square old-fashioned and conventional. I mean, the story was exciting, with plenty of surprises, but . . . The first half of the piece had our hero in a feverish state because he was being deprived of sleep by his captors. So why not tell the story of how he came to be in prison in a hallucinatory way in Act One, as if in his fever, and let the audience put the pieces of the jigsaw we showed them together as it went along. That way, the music could be modern, even discordant. In the second act, when he was lucid again and preparing his escape from the guillotine, the music could return to the 'romantic' period the story was set (1795), so be more conventional. As could the action. I worked over the whole of one night to rewrite the libretto, and with great excitement, took it to Liam for his approval the next day.

He hated it.

I lost interest in my original conception, and Liam tried to move it on with others but failed. The book is now out of copyright, chaps. There, in that drawer over there, lies the book of a thrilling musical ready to go. It needs music and lyrics. It's big and bold and will need a lot of money to realise its grandeur and excitement. Yes, anybody?

(I have often wondered since, because I do idolise Ivor Novello's music, whether I couldn't get his estate to authorise my using some of his marvellous tunes without Christopher Hassall's lyrics – which were fine for the time but now seem laughably overwrought. With Novello's music, new lyrics and maybe some new composition – fragmented variations on some of Ivor's melodies, for the first half, letting the audience piece them together – *Pimpernel!* will run for centuries!).

To keep us from going crazy, I thought I'd direct something with David and Lynn Milgrim, an actress friend of his who lived nearby and hit upon the idea of our staging *The Promise*, a remarkable three-hander by Aleksei Arbuzov. It was a play I'd seen in London. To stage it in Lynn's small apartment would be a challenge but, I imagined, just about possible.

I put up a notice in American Equity asking for an actor to play the uncast of the three characters needed. I auditioned three or four young men and chose one who was playing a small role on Broadway at the time in *The Man in the Glass Booth*, a young guy who throughout our rehearsal period couldn't decide if he should call himself Paul Glaser or Michael Glaser. (When he played Starsky on television a few years later he used both his Christian names – still does). He was intense and disturbingly sexy to be around but often annoyingly frustrating in rehearsals. He would bring moments of startling revelation to his character, I would remark on them during the notes sessions afterwards, but I seldom saw those 'moments' again. As British actors at drama school, we'd been taught how to remember those insights through rehearsing and meld them together to build our characters. That was our technique, but in the States in those days, immediacy was the vogue, so day after day, Paul would improvise, often brilliantly, but those special revelations came only fitfully and were never strung together to make the whole. He was remarkably good as 'Marat' but no better than either of the other two – when he could have been outstanding.

The play starring Judi Dench, Ian McKellen, and Ian McShane was originally put on in London by Peter Bridge. He brought it to Broadway later – and he was in New York when I asked his permission to do it. (He was the producer of *The Man in the Glass Booth*, and I knew him as he'd been the producer of *Number 10*). His only stipulation was that he be asked to our first night.

A quick précis of the play. It's set in Leningrad during the Nazi siege in the Second World War. The first act takes place in an almost empty room with just a bed in it. The second is set a few years later when the young woman who lives there has furnished it sparsely, and in the third, set in the present day, that same room is fully furnished.

If you haven't seen it you should read it, it's a very touching and funny piece. It was a huge success in London and Broadway. But right now, I'm telling you the story to give you an idea of how we staged it.

After all the proper theatres in New York had called it a night, we invited useful people – useful to the actors that is, and I prayed, to David in particular – to trudge up two floors to Lynn's apartment near the West River and watch Act One (the empty room with just a bed in the centre). We then invited them to troop down the two flights to the deli below for refreshment before returning for Act Two – by which time we'd removed the bed, returned it to her bedroom next door, and brought half of her sitting room furniture back into the performing space.

The second interval the same, but this time every piece of her sitting room furniture had been restored to its proper place when the eight people returned. (Oh, I didn't tell you, did I? There was only space for eight chairs along one wall, so that constituted our entire audience).

The performance was such a success we did it a second night the following week with another eight useful people in the audience. Then Peter Bridge demanded to see it – he'd not been free to come with the sixteen we'd invited before – so one midnight, the actors started performing the piece for a third time just for him.

I heard his snores before the actors did. I nudged him, he snorted himself awake, and a minute later, he was snoring again. I felt terrible; these lovely people had put themselves out for my sake – yes, *and* his, a Broadway producer – but still . . . We brought all the furniture back into the room while he lolled on the chair. When he woke again, we were all standing looking at him. He applauded. 'Well done, well done,' he said. 'I thoroughly enjoyed that. Thank you. I do have a few notes though . . .' I interrupted him. 'Everybody's very tired, Peter. Perhaps you'd write them down, and I'll give them to the actors tomorrow.' There were no notes; there wasn't a tomorrow, and I was bloody furious. I didn't tell him he'd only seen the first ten minutes of the play as I led him down the narrow stairs.

New York may be the most exciting city on earth. Walking the streets is a bit like being an insect crawling along the bottom of a ditch, the sky a bright blue shard above your head. The buildings are immense, and the noise bouncing off the dizzying sides of their canyon walls makes an all-pervading cacophony – not least the blaring of impatient car horns, each driver insistently claiming the street as his own, he's being impertinently blocked from using it freely, dammit. And when the lights change and the blockage melts, the car hurtles a hundred yards – only to come screeching up to another set of lights – and he pounds his horn again. As a pedestrian, you cross the wider avenues at your peril. Cars unleashed at each of the traffic lights rush terrifyingly towards you, booming, bouncing, and clattering over the huge metal plates which cover the countless road works. I don't remember where I stayed it ever being completely quiet, even at night. (Except once). The din of midtown was such a constant you sublimated it. But it kept you high on adrenaline.

There are wonderful things to do and see, but with no money in New York you really are invisible. No one showed the slightest curiosity as to my life in England. Whenever I got hold of a newspaper, I'd scour it for news of home. Every Sunday, we bought the one-foot-high pile of the *New York Times*: the American news, the sports section, the ads, the funnies, with, maybe, a page of news covering the rest of the world. England seldom featured. Maybe an inch of print at best. But we mustn't forget the Special Relationship.

*

Two marvels of beauty:

I remember one morning waking up to complete silence. It was unnerving, it was so quiet. It was no use looking out of our window to see what the reason might be, the view was of a wall. So we dressed and went out to find that it had snowed heavily overnight. Wandering down the centre of 5th Avenue on that brilliant morning, every ledge covered in snow, every car parked by the pavements a mound of white, the narrowing canyon of glinting skyscrapers stretching away as far as the eye could see, icicles hurtling down from on high and shattering quietly on the pavements, it was a hushed wonderland with only us and a few other human beings in it. A white Christmas on 5th Avenue without an Easter bonnet.

And sitting on the grass in Central Park with crowds of people listening to *La Traviata* issuing from a small conch shell of a stage a hundred yards away, from where the lead singers of The Metropolitan Opera and a small orchestra performed. Free. As evening fell, the lights in the towering buildings surrounding the park added a modern glitter, so when Alfredo sang of his love to the dying Violetta, the office lights and stars spangled above and around us fracturing our tears. Despite distorted sound from tinny speakers, the otherworld magic of it!

Then a miracle. A script from England came for me, sent by James Sharkey, an agent within the Al Parker Organisation, who had offered me representation the year before I'd left for the States. Michael Mills, the producer of *Misleading Cases*, thought I would be right to play a character named Nausius in a television comedy pilot to be called *Up Pompeii*. It was to star a comedian named Frankie Howerd. In London, I'd seen him in a really funny musical by Sondheim, Shevelove and Gelbart, *A Funny Thing Happened on the Way to the Forum*, and the television script I'd been sent seemed a direct rip-off from that – the same characters with different names. But that's all I knew of Frankie Howerd.

I was thirty-two at the time, and Nausius, the role I'd been offered, was supposed to be in his late teens – it was never specified, but somewhere near that. A youth anyway. Michael Mills had seen me play a young policeman on the beat discovering a cow in the street quite a few years before. That character had one speaking scene in a witness box. What on earth had made him think of me for this role? My new agent? Or the way I'd walked down that street with the parked cow? Ally? I didn't care. The fee for the job was almost exactly what I needed for a ticket back to England. I got on the next plane.

David came with me. His career hadn't taken off in America, so what had he to lose coming back to England?

Everything that I owned in the Cadogan Square flat I shared with Marc had been sold: the furniture I'd picked out, the objets, the trinkets. In my room, there remained the bed and bed linen. Marc was quite right: I'd not sent any money back from the States for my half of the mortgage, so he needed to recoup what he could. The flat seemed to be a hostel for rent-boys, and it looked shabby. Nearly a year away, and Marc did too.

I'd trampled the last of what he and I had had into the ground with my fanciful idiocy.

I found a small two-room home for David and myself in a row of squat terraced houses in Fulham. We bought two terriers, a Dandie Dinmont and a Jack Russell, to keep us company, Chekov and Ally. But I had a job and was earning.

185

When I met David Croft, who was to direct the pilot (to remind you, the trial episode to see if the characters and story have a further life), I told him I wasn't going to play Nausius camp – that he'd got the wrong actor if that's how he saw it. (I was being forceful, but I could afford to be, I was back on my own turf). He said that that was an aspect that had been discussed at meetings but been discarded. The boy was to be lovelorn, ardent and naive. That I wasn't effeminate was the reason they'd chosen me to play the part, he said.

I wanted to believe him, so I did.

On the first day in the rehearsal room, I was shown the costume design for Nausius, and it was so outrageously camp I laughed with disbelief. (You can see for yourself). I took it to David and asked him if he'd okayed it. He went over to the designer, and I saw them in quiet argument. The designer looked cross – it had obviously been approved. Nevertheless, it was stripped of all its furbelows and lace, but I very much wanted to keep the curly blond wig so I would be less recognisable in the outside world away from the character, so we were agreed on that, at least.

Frankie Howerd was tall, lanky and nervous. His flickering smile and fruity voice tried to cover up his shyness. That was my first impression. He had a small mouth and a toupee, second impression. Also, his arms seemed to have a life of their own, they dangled and had huge hands at the end. He was nice to everyone at that first read-through – although that changed the more sure he got of himself.

Actors' first-day read-throughs are very strange. As actors, we all want to be loved, to be admired, but hide our needs in different ways. Saunter is a good word for how we enter the first rehearsal room with a line of tables down the centre; some of us with newspapers, and of course The Script, others with satchels or briefcases from which we produce that well-thumbed bible of words with our lines highlighted. If one knows anyone else, the greetings can be excessively noisy or studiously charming – all this to hide the feeling of nakedness. We take our places at the table and look immensely relaxed, some of us already filling in the *Telegraph* crossword. Then we begin: we read the piece through, some *sotto voce* (we're saving our performance for the real thing), others at full throttle. At last, thank God, it's done – so then we can be modest and show our vulnerability. ('Why are you looking so dejected – you were wonderful!'). Or look defiant: I'll do better than that when the time comes – but today wasn't the day to show off.

Frankie had worked with a lot of the cast before, so the merriment was genuine those early days. He was particularly nice to Max Adrian and myself because, I think, we had both been in classical theatre. Not that he knew of me or any reputation I might have, but Max was a renowned actor. Why, he was on the cover of my LP of Bernstein's *Candide!* The world rated him highly. More highly than Frankie Howerd, that's for sure! (I was still arrogant at thirty-two, even though I knew a small-b bugger all).

Willie Rushton was fun to be with. He played a god from on high, making caustic comments to the camera about the stupidities of mere mortals. There were scores of good-looking females with nothing to say and almost nothing on (that came later in the performance, not in that rehearsal room), and I had a sister in the story, Erotica, a nymphette, played by Georgina Moon. (I suppose that made me a nymph).

I certainly didn't look like a teenager, but I still looked young in those days. Elizabeth Larner, who played my mother, was pretty cross to learn I was only four years younger than her, 'You'd better look a baby on that screen!'

Talbot (Tolly) Rothwell of the *Carry On* films wrote the script, and it was exhilarating to work on. (Lots of tits and bum jokes – the British love those).

However, I did notice in rehearsals – but I only mentioned it on the last day before our technical rehearsal for the camera crew – that Frankie had a couple of funny lines in a scene we had together, one immediately after the other, both getting laughs, but I was sure the one that followed the other would be more effective if said first. So, at the end of day five, before we broke, I told him:

'You'd get a much bigger laugh if you changed those two sentences around. If you don't mind my saying.'

He stared at me without expression and clenched his jaw a few times before walking away. Ah well, I'd tried – and he hadn't slapped me down.

The next day, at the camera rehearsal, he said the lines as before and got his laughs from the cameramen. But on the day of performance, in front of the studio audience, he reversed them as I'd suggested, got a huge laugh on the first line, and a roar on the second, which turned into applause – and my career took off on a different trajectory.

I had only once before seen that same look of astonishment in an actor's eyes (Judi's in *A Midsummer Night's Dream*), and I felt smug as I saw it again in Frankie's face at the audience reaction. If the punters had had any doubts as to whether they were enjoying themselves before, they didn't hold back now. They loved it. And at the end, when we all took our bows, the cheers and stamping were thunderous.

My David had been in the audience, and we went to the bar afterwards with the cast and crew. There was a lot of congratulation and back-slapping, and we got raucous with the headiness of the audience's appreciation. Frankie was modest, but our adrenaline nearly got him paraded around the room on our shoulders. The only person absent was the author, Tolly.

I've never understood why writers aren't hosanna'd. The success of our show was in the greatest part due to him. Actors, the go-betweens, get the fame. Possibly because we are the upfront, touchable, and sexiest, we get the lion's share of attention. Directors have pushed themselves into public notice over the past thirty years with Conceptions: changing the settings, the sex and/or colour of the characters (I won't ever forget the time I was in the audience watching a Shakespeare play, and I heard a loud voice from two seats on my right: 'But why is the girl's twin brother bleck?') and the overemphasis of lights, sets and costumes – 'A David Lynch Film', etc. But surely, it's the writer who is the most important part of the triumvirate. Without him, the rest of us, including the actors, would have nothing to work on, no springboards from which to leap and twist and do our perfect dives, no words to show off with, no reason to be there.

Normally the pilot of a possible series is discussed later in the higher echelons of the television company, and then it can take weeks before decisions are made as to its further life. We were told, before that evening was over, that *Up Pompeii!* was getting the go-ahead for a full series, no question. And it would start filming in the next month or so.

However . . . my agent James reminded me soon after that the whole idea of the family having a son *and* daughter was that in the six episodes to be made, Georgina and I would only appear in three each. Aaah . . . I'd forgotten, and that was a sudden deflation. But the week after the commissioning, James rang to say Frankie Howerd had insisted our scene where I showed him my poem, an Ode to my latest beloved, which he read out to great comic effect, had to be in every episode. So Nausius appeared throughout the series, and my sister, Erotica, had much less to do. (I suspect it was because Frankie needed a safety net in case there were any more comic moments that got away that he hadn't noticed. But I was never needed – in quite that way – again).

When we received the scripts for the first six episodes, some changes had been made. The author, Tolly, remained the same, but Plautus, the Roman writer/god on high commenting on the antics of the characters below, had been replaced by a soothsayer, a sort of Cassandra figure of doom and gloom. The bevy of girls was smaller except for the one my character craved who was more prominent – in at least two ways. Sorry. I had some of the pin-ups of the time playing my inamoratas, Barbara Windsor and Valerie Leon, to name but two, but all the girls were really scrumptious – it was only a few years ago at a party that Lindsay Duncan reminded me she'd played Scrubba to whom Nausius had dedicated an Ode. That name will give you an idea of how subtle the comedy was. In fact, we had some other notable actors in *Up Pompeii!* (Jean Kent, George Baker, Fabia Drake, the young Lindsay, and . . . and . . .) along with clever television comedians, so rehearsals were a hoot. Everyone had heard reports of the pilot, they'd read the scripts, they knew they were going to be in a success. I really loved working in this different milieu with this extraordinary mix of performers, all gossiping, all vying to tell the funniest jokes, all letting their hair down. The atmosphere in rehearsals was jubilant.

So what soured it for me?

After we'd finished the final camera rehearsal on that first episode of the first six episodes, perhaps an hour before the public was let into the studio, Frankie approached me and asked me to come to his dressing room in half an hour – he had something he wanted to tell me. I was agog: was this a new venture he wanted me to be a part of, another job, perhaps –what? The smile was wiped off my face when I knocked on his door and entered a darkened dressing room with just one mirror light on.

'Come and sit here,' he said in a throaty voice.

It took time for my eyes to become adjusted to the gloom, but eventually, I worked out that he was on his divan, propped up with cushions, and he was patting the space next to him. I suppose these were the days of Jimmy Savile, but I really didn't know then how to cope with this lewd come-on. I went in as far as the table in the centre of his room, 'No, I . . . er, I can't. Er, no, thank you, I'm, I'm, I'm not like . . . er, that. I have to go and er . . .' 'Come on, don't be shy, come on, there's a good chap.' He got up, and I backed around the table, keeping it between us as he advanced. As I say, it was very dark in there, and with me *err*ing and *aah*ing and him cajoling, we went around that table maybe a couple of times before there was a knock on the door, and I rushed to open it. Our director, David Croft, had come to give Frankie some notes, and I bolted past him and out of the room, my heart thudding with revulsion.

Two days later, we started rehearsing the next episode with a new cast of characters, all in the same jolly mood, and I waited for something to be acknowledged by Frankie – an apology perhaps. Yes, I was that silly. Although the mood of the other actors was infectious, I was somewhat removed from them, seeing our leading man in a completely different light. It was as though nothing had happened, and I slowly relaxed and thought myself lucky. Until on that last day before taping Episode 2, in our costumes as before, waiting for the audience to arrive, he asked me again to come to his dressing room. I said I would, and the moment his back was turned rushed off to find David, to ask him, please, please, to come to Frankie's dressing room at 6.31, on the dot, because . . . and I told him what had happened the week before. I couldn't read his expression: he looked annoyed, disbelieving, what? But he did as I asked, and a minute after I'd slowly entered the darkened dressing room and moved tentatively forwards, David knocked on the door, Frankie called for him to come in, and I walked out.

Believe it or not, he tried one more time the following week. The three of us went through the same rigmarole – and then he knew that it wasn't going to happen. But his friendly attitude to me didn't change a jot despite the rebuff, and the last three episodes were once again enjoyable to do.

If you've seen *Up Pompeii!* you'll have to decide whether what we did was fun or not, but after the first series was shown and was a huge success, I was asked to do a further six episodes and said no. I'd enjoyed the people I'd worked with, but there really were only so many times my cardboard character could look aghast, upset, bewildered or tearful, and I felt I'd rung all the changes. Downright stupid is only fun to play for a short time.

I learned later in my working life that saying no is an effective ploy if one's to get what one wants. I had really set my mind to not doing a second series when James, my agent, came back with a much better financial offer from the BBC. I still didn't want to do it, so I said no again. And then, of course, they made an offer I couldn't afford to refuse.

Back home, my relationship with David had deteriorated further. My being paid and enjoying going into work demoralised him and made his unsuccessful career in Britain seem all the more galling. That was one of the reasons I'd said no to a second series of *Pompeii*, but once there was proper money being offered, I did think that at least we could move to somewhere nicer to live. And maybe things between us would get better?

I found out only later that Max Adrian, who played my father, Ludicrus Sextus, wasn't well, and had pulled out of the series, so another actor, Wallas Eaton, was going to replace him. If the son Nausius was also going to be different, it would have been one change too many – perhaps that's what the BBC hierarchy thought – hence the vastly improved salary they offered me to stay.

But it was a mistake on both fronts. In the gap between series one and two, Frankie had changed – from a cheerful star to a paranoid one. Apparently, this had happened before in his career: he'd become so difficult in the last comedy show he'd done for the BBC, many years before, that they'd told him he would have to audition the next time he wanted to work for them; this to a man who was then at the pinnacle of success. So his career had plummeted from the heights to his having to go back to the Variety circuit where he could always get paid to do his routine. Eventually, he'd been picked up by the television satirists, he'd appeared at the Comedy Club with great success, had had a resounding triumph on stage in *A Funny Thing Happened on the Way to the Forum*, and now *Up Pompeii!* He was back in the game! What on earth in his psyche turned him from an amiable, funny giant – and don't let's talk about him being a sexual predator, the public didn't know this – to this brooding, unsmiling, suited man who turned up at the rehearsal room on day one of series two with his partner Dennis, introducing him as his manager. If there was anything we wanted to say to Mister Howerd, it would have to go through Dennis. What the hell was all that about? Was Dennis going to be giving us notes as to our performances?

AND they'd changed writers, AND David Croft wasn't going to

be directing – Sydney Lotterby was.

Frankie treated Sydney appallingly, so I saw him more than once leaving the rehearsal room in tears. Elizabeth Larner, the darling woman who played my mother, had worked with Frankie before and did her best to lighten the mood. Actors who came in having accepted their parts because their mates who had been in series one had told them what fun they'd have, arrived cheerful, and within a day had been reduced to just doing their jobs. He was particularly unkind to the women in the cast, reducing Fabia Drake, that formidable woman and wonderful actress, to tears so that she left the cast in the middle of her very first rehearsal. (It was no good her offering to *act* fat. Frankie to Fabia: 'You're proud you've lost weight, so you *aren't* fat. You're no longer right for the part! Are you?')

The sets of *Pompeii* were less imaginative and reduced in number, and the costumes were less sumptuous.

Once the cameras were on us in the scenes I had with Frankie, I found him frightening: his eyes swivelled with panic, he forgot his lines, and *ooh eer*-ed twice as much to cover the holes in his memory. I had been told he took pills: uppers to give him courage and downers to make his panic manageable. Standing a few feet away from him, I watched those drugs battling each other on his face. I was lucky to be on screen at all, sometimes, as he hadn't given me the cue to enter. When to say my next line? I just had to barge in when I thought best – not that I was sure he'd know how to cover my now unexpected entrance. Series two was an effing nightmare.

I hadn't watched series one because I was an Actor – a RADA prig, so slightly ashamed of my part in this tosh – and I certainly couldn't, and haven't, watched series two because I know I must have been awful. (I eventually watched two episodes of series one the other day, and I was quite right, I was terrible).

Yet through all this, Frankie wasn't ever rude to me, so I feel bad disclosing *my* truth about that publicly loved frightened man.

Series two came out later that year and was, it seems, just as popular as the first. In the gap between the two showings of *Up*

Pompeii! that summer, I'd been offered a role in a comedy, *The Mating Game*, which was to be performed on Bournemouth Pier. It had five lead roles, all played by well-known television performers. So, James *Dad's Army* Beck, Kerry *Up Pompeii* Gardner, Nerys *Liver Birds* Hughes, Jill *Emergency-Ward 10* Browne, and Avril *Coronation Street* Angers.

The money offered was excellent. The punters on holiday were expected to fill the theatre, it was sexy and funny, and I suggested to David he come down with the dogs to Dorset for the summer. The whole enterprise could, and should be, fun.

CHAPTER 11
Treading the Boards

To begin with, we rehearsed *The Mating Game* at the Savoy Theatre in the Strand. The stage level is deep underground, so it was always a relief to get out into the fresh air after work. Going home to David and the dogs, I soon stopped sharing what had happened during the day, the funny things that had been said, as it made him sad and envious. Trying to keep everything light-hearted was hard work. And by then, sex was non-existent. Our dogs Chekov and Ally were his only companions.

Right from the beginning of rehearsals, I noticed a couple of the cast pouring something into their tea or coffee at the 11 o'clock break. They were two of the nicest people: Jimmy was mischievous and wry, Jill warm and touchy-feely – sweethearts both. But after the lunch break, their speech delivery was slower, Jill got more tactile, and Jimmy looked at you with a cocked enquiring gaze and lazy smile when he'd finished saying his line. A sort of 'over to you' challenge. You would try and keep your delivery crisp, and you would get a return, their lines mostly correct but placed somewhere over your shoulder as if trying to escape. There they go. Over there. Sorry, what was that you said?

(Once I'd got to know Jill better, I asked her what it was she put in her coffee in the mornings. 'Cinzano, darling.' 'Alcohol?' 'No, no, darling, it's an aperitif!').

Rex Garner, the director, was very good at his job, but he too enjoyed a liquid lunch with Jill and Jimmy, so the afternoon's rehearsal was not as rigorous as the morning's.

Avril was an adorable aunty figure, acerbic and bright, and Nerys was, and probably still is, a what-you-see-is-what-you-get intelligent Welsh girl, with a great sense of fun. As time went on, the three of us began to stick together, so became a separate grouping.

Funnily enough, mine was the only character in the play to get drunk. The story, which was light-hearted piffle, was set in my bedroom. The guy I played was a flash disc jockey, so my clothes were wonderfully loud and expensive. The costume lady and I went to Cecil Gee's, a well-known men's fashion boutique, and found a black dinner suit with a woven silver stripe, a lace-fronted dinner shirt which was to show off my made-up suntanned chest, and a floppy red bow tie. That was for Act Two. Act One found me in a form-fitting pair of black pants with a brilliantly garish striped shirt. As look-at-me character get-ups, these clothes couldn't have been bettered.

My Received Pronunciation in the role was received – and returned on stage with a fashionably slight London accent.

As in touring, we were given a digs list before we left home, so we could find ourselves accommodation in Bournemouth before we went down there for the summer season – mid-June to the second week of September, the holidays plus. Because Bournemouth is a very popular seaside resort, the list of what remained free to rent during that entire period was short.

What I chose, sight unseen, was pretty dire. I booked into this top-floor flat in the outskirts of the town and hoped for the best. It certainly wasn't. I planned to move out just as soon as I could, but once installed, there hadn't been the time to go looking, what with our work schedule.

One night not long after I'd arrived in Bournemouth, soon after the first performance of the play, I went upstairs to the flat after I'd returned from the theatre and was making a cup of tea in my cupboard-kitchen, when I heard the most appalling racket. It was pop music being played at a dance-club level. At first, I thought the noise was out in the street, but it wasn't moving away, so I went onto the landing to try and locate where it came from. It was inside the house! Looking down the staircase into the dim front hall below, I could just make out a small portable radio in the middle of the floor, the distorted music blaring out of it.

Heavens! My heart thumping with fear, I inched my way down towards it. I had just about reached the bottom step when my landlady, in her dressing gown, swooped out of the dark and clamped my wrist fiercely.

'Now you know,' she shrieked, 'what I have to put up with day and night.'

'Who from?' I asked, startled out of my wits.

'You. You, you, you, you, you!' she yelled.

'But I'm never here,' I stuttered.

'You bloody people, never any consideration for others, think you're God's gift, well I've had enough. I want you gone in the morning.' And she scooped up the radio, which was still blaring, and disappeared into the dark. I returned upstairs to pack, my heartbeat still erratic.

As you can imagine, I didn't sleep much that night. I went over and over the disagreeable scene in my mind. I had only been in Bournemouth ten days, in the house only in the early mornings and late evenings, had been away at the weekend, hadn't had anyone round, didn't even have a telephone. I did play the radio, but I thought I'd been careful not to make much noise. Obviously, my idea of noise and hers was very different.

The next day, as I didn't trust the banshee with my luggage, I took it into the theatre with me. I went to the company manager's office and reported her. 'Lordy lordy, she's getting battier. We'd best take her off the digs list.'

Oh, she was a well-known weirdo, was she? Now you tell me!

'Can you find me somewhere else, please? I have a car, so it could be outside Bournemouth.'

He gave me the address and telephone number of a couple who had a house for rent about ten miles out of town. I rang them straight away, got in my car, and drove there.

Their house was lovely: a low white thatched cottage, beautifully appointed inside – their sitting room could have come straight out of a Noël Coward play: faded Eau de Nil walls, darker green velvet curtains in the low-ceilinged room; a grand piano covered in silver-framed photos in front of the bow window; upstairs mullioned windows under the eaves of the thatch, and a large double bed. Light green, fawn and cream predominated throughout the house. Very middle-class English rural.

Outside, the considerable garden was surrounded by an eight-foot-high old brick wall. In the centre of the lawn was a well. Yes, please!

The owners weren't going on holiday for another week, so I couldn't have it before then. The rent was rather more than I should afford but living there would seem like being close to heaven after being in hell. I signed an agreement to rent it for the rest of the summer and drove back to Bournemouth for the matinee.

Staying at that house in Slepe was the start of my love affair with Dorset. The county is enchanted. It has some of the most gently feminine hills and vales in England, with Iron Age and Roman remains studded higgledy-piggledy all over it. The sculpted fortress of Hambledon Hill, with the corrugated earthworks near its top, rises majestically out of the Blackmore Vale, only five miles away from where I reside now. I've lived in these parts for the past twenty-five years of my life. When I want to surprise visiting friends, I take them to Cerne Abbas to show them the giant, his outline with its enormous erection cut out of the chalk hill. If they want to conceive, they need only to make love on that impressive phallus. Or so I'm told. I've not needed to check it out.

Back then, I stayed in an expensive Bournemouth hotel for the interim. It was worth it for the normality. I'm still wary of walking downstairs into darkened areas. That screeching landlady flapped her way into my dreams quite often that summer. Once I'd moved into Slepe Cottage, although I loved the homeliness of it, driving back to it in the dark of an evening and letting myself into an unlit house in the dead quiet did sometimes spook me. But after David had been and stayed, and I'd invited the cast and stage management there for Sunday lunch, it became a welcoming sanctuary.

Bournemouth has two huge Variety theatres. Every year in those days, they were headlined by renowned comics, singers, magicians and dancers; the smaller 'straight' theatre in town doing a season of comedies and thrillers, and our Pier Theatre with just the one play, which that year was *The Mating Game*, a farce.

Before we opened the Variety shows and the plays to a paying public, before the Bournemouth Summer Season was officially declared open by the Mayor, the lead performers in the theatres were invited by him to a Rotary Club lunch at the Bournemouth Pavilion where we were welcomed to the town. The five of us actors from the Pier found ourselves sharing a meal with maybe ten Variety topliners. We sat on the long side of tables set like a comb with only four teeth, the Rotaries assembled in ranks before us on the tines.

We'd been told that someone from the Rotary would welcome us at the start of lunch, then later, after we'd eaten, the leading members of each company in the four theatres would respond, followed by a speech by the Mayor at the end. The popular Jimmy Beck was to be our representative.

The food was good, as was the wine. I got happily fuzzed during the meal. I'd just worked with a comedy headliner on television, and here I was surrounded by at least a half-dozen more, but this lot were very outgoing and easy. All of them seemed to be jokers. I sipped, and laughed, and quaffed some more.

The 'thank you for having us' speeches at the end of the meal started with the two brothers of the double act who were the stars in the Variety theatre behind us on the promenade: Mike and Bernie Winters – lots of mirth. Then the crooning headliner, Dickie Henderson, from the other big Variety theatre had the handheld radio mic passed to him – slick, cheerful and good looking he was. Then it was our Jimmy's turn – you had to admire him, he could hold his liquor superbly – and he made a cheeky, funny speech . . . then the bloody microphone was given to each of us for our comments.

Mounting panic because I hadn't prepared anything. Who were

these extraordinary people who'd invited us to lunch? A Rotary Club
– well, it was spinning now. I'd been enjoying myself, maybe rather
too much, up to the moment I realised that I was going to have to
say something. Was it fair to punish me for my lack of preparation?
Oh God!

And then the handheld thingie was there in my sweaty grip.
Expectant smiling faces in front of me, buzzing in my ears, I stood.

'Thank you for inviting me,' I heard someone boom from far away.
I was the only one standing, so it must be me. 'We have a problem
here. I'm just an actor. Actors don't make speeches unless they have
a script . . . and someone's stolen mine. Umm . . . Think of me as a
tape recorder on legs. Put a script in, I work on it, and then out it
comes, maybe a bit funnier . . . or sadder . . . That's all I do. I can only
translate other people's words . . . and I don't suppose for a moment
you know who this malfunctioning tape recorder is.' Was that a small
laugh? I grinned inanely at the empty air above my hosts' heads.

'Um . . .' I looked helplessly down the side of the long table for
inspiration and saw that much-loved dancer, Lionel Blair, leaning
forward with an encouraging smile. How friendly. I don't know you,
Mr Dancer, but thanks. I stumbled into speech again, all the faces in
the room a blur. 'Anyway, this everyday actor, me, surrounded by all
my Variety heroes (I thought even at the time: *you creep!*) can only
say thank you for a delicious meal . . . and, I'm sure you noticed, I
enjoyed the wine too.'

Happy to hear some laughter for my first impromptu public
speech, I sat down clumsily and gave the damned microphone to the
bearer, a man dressed in a tailcoat with a purple sash, who carried it
triumphantly away to some other unfortunate.

After lunch, Lionel congratulated me on my speech: 'Very funny,
very different.' Our paths crossed quite often that summer. We shared
a car park.

(Apropos off-the-cuff interviews: I was once asked to go on Pete
Murray's morning radio programme with my *Up Pompeii!* mummy,
Elizabeth Larner. Thank heavens for her chatter – without prior

alcohol, this tape recorder had absolutely nothing to contribute, not a single original thought. I seem to remember I made some fatuous remark about a piece of music he played).

*

Once you start a summer season at any of our seaside resorts, you are worked into the ground. Or, in our case, into the boardings of a pier. (There was a moment in one scene where I'd been knocked unconscious when I was lying ear on the carpet listening to the shingle being shuffled by the English Channel twenty feet below. Weird and wonderful: the sssh of the shingle, the high-pitched sibilance of the sea – like putting a stethoscope to the surface of the ocean). Mondays, we didn't perform, and Tuesday was the only other weekday we didn't have a matinee, so we were doing nine shows a week. But walking to work across the promenade and along the pier, you were surrounded by holiday folk intent on having a good time, and the town atmosphere that fine summer was festive.

The punters came to see us in their hundreds all through that season, and the play was huge fun to do because their happiness was infectious.

I went swimming early on just once – I was surrounded by bathers, but the water was freezing, and I didn't go in again.

One day I was contacted at our theatre by a representative from a large department store. They had added a new food hall and hoped I would come and speak at the Grand Opening. Why me? Lionel Blair was going to do it and had asked for my help, apparently. Oh, OK.

Lionel had obviously primed the bigwigs at the emporium as to who I was because they were effusive in their welcome. I'd dressed in my best Afternoon Opening of a Food Hall clothes – light fawn suit, blue shirt, striped green and white tie (but I wouldn't have been surprised if coming dressed as a parsnip wouldn't have been more appropriate. I'd had no idea what to wear). Lionel was a vision: he was in a navy blue and white striped summer blazer with white linen trousers and blue shoes – but then, I assumed, he'd done this sort of thing many times before and had the wardrobe. He looked terrific.

We were lined up together with the store's biggest bigwig for photographs – and Lionel grinned at the cameras with his arm draped over my shoulders. I struggled to look like a happy young father who would only buy the best for his kids. (A father being manhandled by his father? His oldest best mate?). Then we were shown around the new department – and very impressive the freezer containers and chilled shelves were, the ones we examined minutely as the cameras clicked. I made appropriate remarks, 'Gosh!' being one of them. All the while, Lionel made it look as if he was trying to charm me into buying something on display: what about this beautiful apple, just look at those boxes of mouth-watering chocolates over there, why not enjoy this extraordinary frozen cod for dinner – possibly with this scrumptious jar of pickled onions to go with it, do you think? – and I started giggling inwardly when my eyes weren't crossed in disbelief at what I was up to.

We were given tea in the staff canteen, where the personnel smiled and nudged each other, excited as they were to be sitting with Someone Famous, and Lionel gesticulated and laughed as if the cameras were still on us. Thank heavens I had prepared my excuse to leave early, so after a while said my thank yous and waved goodbye to the staff – who smiled uncertainly at me: 'Who's he, then?' I should have gone with my curly blond wig on.

One afternoon I went to see Lionel's show. He was marvellous, and the audience loved him, particularly his innuendoes between dizzying bouts of tap dancing, Fred Astaire ballroom routines and jive. His line: 'My wife's happy with the way I am,' got delighted laughter. He made reference to his children (in those days, you could be camp, but not queer). He'd obviously told the comedy duo that I was in the audience watching the show because during their act, when they were celebrating various members of the audience's birthdays and anniversaries, my name came up. 'We know for a fact that the famous Kerry Gardner is somewhere among you. Get up, Kerry, let's get a good look at you.' I stood up, the spotlight found me wilting with a stage grin, and the audience was urged to sing, 'For

He's a Jolly Good Fellow'. Bloody hell!

(I hate conjurers too. 'You, sir, in the third row, would you be so kind as to come up on stage and help me with this trick. A round of applause for the kind gentleman, please.' I'm only a tape-recorder, mate. And *my* tricks are of a completely different sort).

And then there were the headliners of the other shows' parties to which we were invited. All the Variety headliners we met were staying in large villas, usually next to golf courses, but although they were very generous with their food and wine – I only remember those parties as being outside around a swimming pool, and inside, a couple of them, some of the furniture cordoned off with tasselled ropes – the endless talk about money, and property prices, and money, and gossip, and money, became bone-crushingly dull. After a few of these parties, we relatively impecunious Actors decided none of us spoke Variety (I almost never knew of whom they were speaking), so the three of us sobersides stopped going.

Lionel did become a summer friend, and I was touched when he found me at one of these poolside parties to tell me how pleased he was I'd done the second series of *Up Pompeii!* with his mate Frankie.

The two members of the cast who drank never brought our evening performance to a standstill – although once or twice there had to be some frantic ad-libbing to cover up missed cues, missed entrances, blurry eyes glazed in silent incomprehension. (That last was usually Jimmy). Jill, who played my good-time floozie, never forgot her lines. But some evenings she just got slower and slower in her speech, her aperitif-soaked breath puffing into my face, so that by the end of the play she'd . . . talked . . . herself . . . to a . . . standstill. Which isn't the best way to make an audience laugh. But she was such a sweet woman one could forgive her anything, (certainly the audience did), and both she and Jimmy were huge fun to be with whenever we were free and could get together to socialise. We all did a bit of ten-pin bowling, for instance – but never after midday.

I remember that summer season as sun-drenched. Mind you, I was at work every evening except Sunday and Monday and doing matinees as well on Wednesdays, Thursdays, Fridays, and Saturdays, so I spent a lot of time on the pier. But coming out of the stage door into the last of the evening sun, the laughter from the performance still thrumming through you, and walking on boards above the tangy sea for a hundred yards to the promenade was lovely.

I would sometimes drive up to London after the show on Saturday to be with David, and he'd come down to Bournemouth when he could. We had an all right fortnight when he came to stay at Slepe with the dogs. When I'd go into work, he occasionally came with me to see some of the other shows after which I'd drive him back, or he'd warm up something at the cottage for our evening supper. I arranged a Sunday lunch so he could meet the cast. We got along as best we could, he and I, but despite the glorious weather, there were no longer highlights in our relationship.

As is usual with most in our business, we actors bade each other farewell at the end of that summer, swearing eternal friendship, swapping addresses and telephone numbers, and promising to meet soon. Well, I did meet up three or four times with Avril, the endearing oldest member of the cast who was also an interesting woman; we discussed serious things seriously, we listened to serious music, we swapped intellectual books. Sadly, she and the two topers died within ten years of that wonderful summer. I met Nerys at one of these award ceremonies much later. We reminisced fondly for a short while – I reminded her that 'Stoney End' by Barbra Streisand, which she'd introduced me to, was my record of choice throughout those months – but we were older and sensible enough not to pretend we must keep up the acquaintanceship. If we meet up again, that'll be nice.

David and I were living outside Richmond by then because the small flat in Fulham in that small terraced house had become very claustrophobic. He was drinking a hell of a lot, and it didn't help that I seemed to be constantly in work. *Up Pompeii!* was shown to great acclaim – wouldn't you know – and I was asked to go down to Southampton to do a television pilot for Southern TV. The script was no great shakes, but it did have the adorable Richard Beckinsale in the cast. I never got to know him well because the rehearsal period and filming was short, and the pilot wasn't good enough to prompt a series.

To make matters worse between David and myself, I was then asked to take part in a Command Performance for Her Majesty the Queen at the BBC Theatre in Shepherd's Bush. I heard later that the poor soul had only suggested coming to the BBC buildings to look at how television was made, and the Corporation decided what she must have meant was that she wanted a Command Performance. Even if she didn't enjoy herself, my C.V. benefited.

A sketch had been written for the occasion to do with the people of Pompeii awaiting a visit from a royal personage who was expected to arrive in the city at any moment. It was a tepid little piece written with most of the cast in mind, but it was not helped much by being so short in duration and not at all by Frankie's nerves. During the dress rehearsal run-through in the afternoon, there was cheerful laughter from all the entertainers who were taking part in the show but come the evening . . .! The Queen sitting comfortably, we were standing in the dark beside our *Up Pompeii!* set ready to start our sketch when Frankie gripped my arms and told me to say his lines in our scene should he forget any of them. I was thunderstruck but said, of course I would. He was the star for heaven's sake! *Me* say his lines? He'd done Specials for years, and this was my first! What?

He didn't forget his lines per se, and nor did I, but he was so nervous and *ooh*-ed and *aah*-ed so much that what he did say didn't make much sense. The little sketch fell flat on its face.

I'm not a monarchist, but I have to admit my heart started beating faster as Her Majesty and Prince Philip came down the line of the performers for a few words afterwards. Her words to me as I shook her gloved hand were very few, 'I really enjoyed that,' then a pause before she moved on. (By then, I was used to people looking for inspiration over my shoulder). Philip's were: 'Must have been fun with all those girls, eh?' – then to us all, 'Good show.'

The best thing about that 'good show' was the company I kept before the evening performance: Morecambe and Wise, two endlessly jokey fellows, said something complimentary to me in a jocular way – mind you they never stopped joking whenever they were in public. And I shared a dressing room with my favourite comedian, Dave Allen. He was very polite, very quiet, as was I, so the best I could do by way of communicating my admiration in that silent room before the show started was to cast covert glances at him while he stared intently at a fixed spot above his dressing-room mirror. His mouth occasionally pursed as he thought. That was good enough. I was sharing the same air.

Apropos the monarchy: I love my country, and the Queen does a good job, but I've never understood our national anthem. It's like school kids pleading with God to look after the headmistress. Never mind us, look after her! This worship of idols must stop. (It says so in the bible). Holst wrote the marvellous 'I Vow to Thee, My Country', and the words and great tune in Elgar's Pomp and Circumstance Marches – 'Land of Hope and Glory' – would do perfectly as it stands. 'Jerusalem' would be OK – but maybe 'the dark satanic mills' disqualifies it. Whatever. I dislike singing our national anthem – so I don't.

Come to think of it, it's probably why I find Early music from the Baroque period and before so bloody doleful. Hoot and Moan music. We are all miserable sinners, we don't deserve the munificent love we get from God, our ladies don't love us, whinge, whinge, whinge. Get off your knees and do something about it, for heaven's sake. Haven't you heard about those that help themselves?

*

David was a lovely, sweet guy. Our relationship staggered on a little longer until we were both defeated. He went back to Wales to live with his mother. I kept the dogs. And, as I said to start with, I absolutely own the blame.

CHAPTER 12
Never Knowing My Right Foot from My Left

My relationship with David ran its course over nearly five years, which meant that as I hadn't taken him to Forrigan, I didn't see much of Ally and Naomi over that period. I told them little about this new man in my life, so when they heard he and I were moving to America, they were astounded. I didn't tell them I was going for good because I knew in my heart of hearts that it wouldn't be forever. But I wasn't brave enough to admit to my cowardice, so off I went without a full explanation. I was growing up very slowly – if at all. Ashamed as I was, in my weaselly way, I hoped Naomi would have known I wouldn't have done anything quite so drastic as leaving for good without telling her why. She had come with David and me to Niagara on our *Number 10* visit to Toronto, she'd have worked out what might have happened between us, but I didn't spell it out. I might well have said in the three-month gap before David got to England and while we were still doing the play at the Strand that the young man she'd met on the coach had come to mean a lot to me. Conveniently I don't remember.

When I'd been visiting the Sims regularly during those first eight years after I'd met them, they had been aware of Marc – they'd known he was my partner and respected that he hadn't wanted to socialise with them. They were probably as relieved as me because had Marc accompanied me, after that first meeting, we'd have all realised that he wasn't really enjoying himself – so there would have been far fewer visits from me because I would then have felt honour-bound to spend my weekends with him.

I knew that David wouldn't be their cup of tea – and I didn't give them the chance to find out. They didn't probe and became resigned that I had become an infrequent visitor again. But what made matters worse was I was aware throughout that period I was making a pig's ear of my private life, and sanity lived only a stone's throw away in their company. (I've wondered through the years why it's taking me so long to grow up. It's as though, early days, I was like a ball of wool – soft, squidgy and amorphous. And it wasn't until I met the Sims that the knitting started).

As soon as David and I split up, I went back to them, my own-goal defeat difficult to acknowledge. And they didn't ask. I was welcomed back to Forrigan a second time, but there was no hint of a fatted calf.

I never let them go again.

But I had let go of my mother and young brother, only seeing them with effort. I never got over my dislike of my mother after the slapping. I'd come to see her as selfish, self-centred and snobbish – in those days, I didn't really understand what the word racist meant, but that's what she was. My mother, who knew of the Sims, of course, was quietly resentful of them and only met one member of the family, Naomi, the once.

I was in St George's Hospital having had an operation on a ruptured appendix when, by sheer coincidence, the two women arrived at my bedside one morning. I watched my mother's bright 'owning' of her darling son on the right-hand side of the bed, and Naomi's polite deference on the left – no, you couldn't call it that, Naomi was never deferential, but she was wise enough to let my mother be proprietorial. After half an hour of making sure that Naomi knew I was hers and hers alone, my mother left. I looked at Naomi in the silence, then laughed. 'That was fun, wasn't it?' She said nothing, just put her hand on mine. I have never loved a woman more.

The Sims didn't watch *Up Pompeii!* I don't think – they may have but were too polite to bring it up, and instinctively I didn't ask. And Ally did some work while I was away, most of which I didn't get to see. But I did see him in *The General's Day*, a macabre television play by William Trevor in which Ally starred with Dandy Nichols (directed by my future friend, John Gorrie). I made the trip to the

Chichester Theatre to see *The Clandestine Marriage* and saw it again when it transferred eventually to London. It was directed by John Clements in its first incarnation and by Ian McKellen at the Savoy – but Ally was visibly ill by the time of the revival.

*

Would I be interested in meeting Gillian Lynne to audition for a musical? What? I knew she'd been a classical dancer and a choreographer, so . . . why? Apparently, I had been recommended to her by Bob West, who was to be Company Manager. Oh, good old Bob – we'd worked together before. The music and lyrics were by Roger Webb and Norman Newell (who had written many international hits for Shirley Bassey, Petula Clarke, Adam Faith and such), the sets by Tony Walton (who had designed a roster of successful Broadway shows), and David Frost was producing it. It was for children. That's all I was told prior to meeting Gillian.

I went to audition for this elfin woman with her strong, inquisitive face and thin smile. I may have been recommended, but why did she think I was right for the job? – 'Apart from singing in the school choir and in the shower. . .,' I said disingenuously. 'All right, so let's hear you sing. Did you bring something?' I pulled out my sheet music, my Go-To song from *Irma la Douce*, 'Our Language of Love', and warbled with a pianist accompanying me. Mmm. (I was probably nerveless, as I was sure I wasn't going to get this job). Had I danced on stage before, she asked? Gavotte-type things in films, yes. And in discos, but that was all. 'All right. Try this.' She showed me a few angular modern steps, and I copied her. So she danced the same steps, but this time syncopated, and so did I. Now put them together. I tried.

Could she tell me, please, what the story was about? What character she thought I could be right for? Well, it was for young children, so it would perform in the mornings at the Duke of York's theatre in St Martin's Lane. The lead character was a clown who was to tumble out of an alphabet block at the start of the show, and each of the scenes – about characters in nursery rhymes – would be introduced by this clown, who would feature throughout. Oh, and there was no script to speak of, so would I be any good at writing the dialogue for the scenes he was in? That's if I was to get the job – she had others to see. I don't see why not, says I – I wrote a revue many years ago, so I think I could.

She looked away. That seemed to be that.

Me: 'How much singing and dancing would this clown need to do? I mean, it is the clown you think I might be right for, yes?' Yep, there were twelve songs, the clown would be singing in six of them – one of them a solo – there would be plenty of dancing, and the clown would be included in most of the routines. 'But Bob told me you would be right for it, so I'm taking him at his word,' she said.

I laughed in disbelief. I didn't say that of course, it would be huge fun to try, but I really wasn't qualified. I said something like 'Great', grinned at Gillian, she smiled back, her mind already elsewhere, and I left her to audition a group of youngsters in leotards who were waiting in the hallway.

Before the end of the week, I was told I'd got it. Apparently, the wait had been because the management and Gillian couldn't make up their minds between me and someone I'd never heard of, a Tim Curry. I went into rehearsals to meet the cast: Joyce Grant, Tony Robinson (soon to be Baldrick and then a television presenter), Tim Curry (who was going to be my understudy – and not long after the sensational star of *The Rocky Horror Show*), Patsy Rowlands, David Delve, Michael Feast, and a group of dancers Gillian had worked with before. Bob had been the one to ring and tell me I'd got the role. I imagined he'd argued my case, and he was in the rehearsal room that first day looking on and smiling benignly.

From day one, I was completely overwhelmed. With all the dancing I had to do, I lost twelve pounds in weight; I had all those words that went with the songs to learn, *and* some evenings I was writing dialogue for the next day's storyline when I got home. For instance, there was to be a scene where Little Bo Peep had been taken to court for losing her sheep. The Clown was the Judge – a bonus of this role was that I had a chance with each of the scenes to try out different characters. At the end of each scene, when I told the children – surprise, surprise – I'd been the Judge, or the Scarecrow, or whatever, as though they couldn't have guessed, they were raucous in their scorn. The fact that I wore the same black clown's costume throughout, with letters of the alphabet all over, and just used a beard or a hat with straw for my disguises, didn't seem to be any sort of giveaway. Anyway, the morning I brought a longish speech of exposition I'd written for the Judge on his rostrum, all Gillian had to say was: 'Fine, fine, but cut it in half – doesn't matter where.'

Came the morning I had to sing my solo in front of the cast in the rehearsal room, a sweet song sung by a scarecrow, I was really nervous. These were all hoofers and adept musical comedy performers. I finished . . . and the cast applauded. I had only a few seconds to feel gratified before Gillian cut across the applause – 'Again'. Of course, I mangled it the second time.

And in the end, that was really why I didn't enjoy rehearsals as much as I could have. The show was always going to be about her. It was very dispiriting for an actor who sang a bit and who danced a bit, with umpteen routines to master alongside professional dancers, five songs to participate in plus a solo, struggling to get things exact, to be always found wanting. Once we'd got the piece on the stage, and audiences seemed to have a good time, from the moment at the start where I tumbled out of the box to the end, *Once Upon a Time* was hugely enjoyable to do – but not until the director's dissatisfaction had been left behind in the rehearsal room. Thank heavens, unlike Ally in *Windfall*, she wasn't with me on stage throughout.

The show opened at the Duke of York's on the morning of 21 December 1972.

In her first morning gift, a book called *Shakespeare on Youth* with hippy photographs to go with each quote, she wrote: 'I've enjoyed working with you, Kerry, but with just an ounce more confidence you will have given me a fabulous Special performance.' It wouldn't have been beyond her to give me that ounce. As it was, I got it from the audience after she left. Gillian went on to give me love and thanks – and soon after to choreograph *Phantom of the Opera* and *Cats* and so much more, so it was nice to have her name on my C.V., but dance was her passion, and this actor got in the way of her extraordinary gift.

There was a recording made of the show with professional singers, and it's all the better for my not being on it. (The same can be said of my *Songs for Ariel* by Michael Tippett sung by Ian Bostridge. But at least in the booklet with that CD, there are photos of me as Ariel with Ally. Actually, it's just the one photo, but four times, to go alongside each language the information is written in).

I had a short and batty relationship with someone in *Once Upon a Time* that lasted a year or so. Maybe more, maybe less. It doesn't matter.

(What is it with so many creative people that they have to play the leading role in all scenarios – whether it's about themselves or someone else? I know we are each of us the centre of our universe, how could it be otherwise? But for heaven's sake, consider other people and at least make pretend they matter. Antony Gormley, the sculptor, is a perfect example of creator's self-absorption. You can trip over life-size and larger replicas of his body throughout the world, marring landscapes, buildings and beaches. Can't he ever get enough of himself? Yeah, yeah, yeah, he's Everyman – but Every*where*? As the saying goes: enjoyed the joke the first time but fuck a pantomime!

For ego trips, you might think this book is a perfect example. But writing this is also an act of gratitude to others, as well as the story of a *happy* homo. It is also because now I'm much older, no one seems interested in my past, just my present fooling. My history is so much dust in the wind. Never mind Ozymandias, King of Kings – I really don't want anyone despairing over my work, which is easy to do, but it's galling to be airbrushed out of existence while still existing!).

This actor from *Once Upon a Time*, only the third actor I had had a relationship with, was abject: I didn't love him, why didn't I love him when *he* loved *me*? So eventually, I capitulated and said that I did. Once he was centre stage, he strolled off – with a youngster who arrived off the night train from Scotland at six o'clock one morning to take my place in our bed. Sitting on a bench by the Regent's Canal just after dawn, with my warm bed being plundered in the building behind me was something I won't forget. To add insult to injury, it was going to be a lovely sunny day.

That actor remains a good friend, but I gave up on any meaningful attachments for quite a while after that salutary lesson: don't be bludgeoned into telling people what they want to hear unless you sincerely mean it. After John, my first 'true love', who *I* nagged, it took two more actors to teach me that.

*

Ally had cancer. The tumour under his tongue was spreading downwards into his throat and upwards into his brain. There was a new treatment I'd not heard of before with a machine called a Cyclotron, and the one in England was situated in London's Hammersmith Hospital. The medical profession had great hopes that it would be a spearhead in the battle against the disease. Maybe it still is. After treatment, the cancer abated for a while, so Ally was able to go on working. He was quite wonderful in the film *The Ruling Class* with Peter O'Toole. Ally played a demented bishop and gave a masterclass of thrillingly brave comic acting, and he appeared in London in the Garrick play I've already mentioned. But his face had changed: it was redder and rounder, which was not so noticeable in the theatre but obvious on screen. The day he died, I threw my cigarettes out of my car window and haven't smoked since.

He left his body to science, but science turned it down. Merlith gave a small celebration of his life for his loved ones in the family's London flat, where she produced a Punch cartoon: in it, a dustman is wheeling a dustcart with two legs sticking out of it. One dustman to the other: 'He wanted science to have it.' We howled with laughter. He would have enjoyed it – but by then, he'd been cremated in the hospital.

I've read part of a biography of Ally, and the précis of the whole, in which someone who was obviously conjecturing like mad for the sake of sales suggests that Alastair perhaps had a sexual predilection for young boys and girls. The Sims had wanted children, but nature hadn't provided them with more than the one precious daughter. Our youthful presence in the houses which he shared with Naomi and their loved ones was proof of their need. To them, communication was of utmost importance, and that included young minds. To think was to live.

As he said of himself, 'I wasn't a good enough teacher, so the only other thing I could do was be an actor.' Naomi told us that for their honeymoon he'd wanted to take some of their friends along for sport and conversation. She was very young at the time, but even she wondered if that was the done thing. Someone pointed out to him that it wasn't, so they went along with convention.

Talking about their wedding: Naomi wrote a dazzling book about herself, *Dance and Skylark*. (This was some time after Ally died). She was urged by the publisher to write a bit more about Ally than just their meeting, which begins and ends the book, so she did, very reluctantly, but the meat of the book is her joyous embrace of life as a youngster in Scotland. If you would enjoy getting to know a glorious free spirit growing into a thinking adult, you should read it.

*

I was browned-off with my life, as a person, an actor, a friend. I was skimming along the surface of the world with only the occasional bounce to show it I was still around. With the little fame I had, I was offered a really inventive comedy role in the tour of a play, *Don't Start Without Me*, a role that had brought the actor Brian Cox to the notice of the critics early in his career. It was a very original part in a very conventional but amusing play, and just as he did, I got the best reviews around the touring theatres in Britain. In Chelmsford: 'Whoever realised seeing Kerry Gardner in *Up Pompeii!* that he had this extraordinary comic talent?' (Back-handed compliment if ever there was one). Yes, I was earning a material living, but less and less satisfied with its intellectual rewards. Because of *Up Pompeii!*

I was asked by several overseas managements to tour some West End comedies abroad, in Australia and South Africa – those were apartheid days, so I was quick to say no to the latter – which would have made me richer by far, but I had been to RADA for God's sake, done Molière and Shakespeare, and it was only because of the piffle I'd done recently on television that I'd become famous. *Boeing-Boeing* in the Outback! It dawned on me that I could end life with as much substance as a playing card – a well-remunerated Joker but intellectually as thin as cardboard.

I cast around in my mind as to what else I might enjoy doing if I gave up acting. I was in my mid-thirties and needed to make a living, that was certain. At that age, starting a career as a veterinary surgeon with its seven years of training was out of the question. Two hobbies I enjoyed were photography and painting, so I got a job working in a photographic studio somewhere off Edgware Road. To begin with, I had to learn about developing and printing film, so I was put in that department. Handing back prints and rolls of film to famous photographers' assistants who came around to collect was not in the least satisfying. At that rate, it might take ten years before I got paid a living wage to be a photographer. I stuck it for eight months.

I got a job working in an art gallery off Marylebone Road, where on the third Saturday of every month, a man would go into the basement of the showroom and, for the American market, forge the signatures of famous portraitists onto oil paintings of ancient English toffs and their molls. I still thought of myself as an actor throughout these various try-outs, so I trusted in my luck and left that shady job pretty quickly. But then, through friends, I met William Ware, an accredited war artist who had his own gallery in Sloane Street. Every month he staged exhibitions of artists he admired, ancient and modern, and every now and then hung his own paintings. He was very short-sighted, and as a consequence, his large canvasses were very Turneresque. I absolutely loved them. With regular showings of Russian icons, pottery, and sculptures, this was more like a job I could give my life to. I gave a year or more of it, loving William and Eileen, his artist wife – two of the vaguest and nicest people you could meet – socialising with them and their friends. They lived down Etchingham way in Sussex, near Moray and his wife Pam, so seeing them all down there at weekends was an added bonus. Pam and Moray gave their country home over to charity every other summer inviting the public into their large garden for a fete, where famous actors would run different stalls of their own choosing. For instance, there was a sideshow where the public had to guess the combined weights of three well-known actresses. The winner was a sheep farmer who asked if he could pick up each of them in turn and got their combined weights correct to within a pound. And I helped Robin Ellis (the original Poldark) with a stall where people could chuck enamel plates into a plastic laundry basket (underarm, frisbee-like, hurled like a cricket ball – incredibly noisy, and *very* popular because Robin is extremely handsome, so we made a lot of money).

*

I'm inclined to rush into things (it has taken me many years to realise that I'm slow-witted), so it only came to me gradually throughout this enjoyable period of working at William's art gallery that I would be about fifty years old before I could make a living selling art. I would need to know the provenance of all the different schools of painting around the world so as to be able to speak knowledgeably, off-the-cuff, about this Renaissance artist and that cubist. Acquiring that in-depth knowledge could take me forever.

So whatever I did, it had to be more immediately rewarding.

Well . . . I knew actors, and I had a good idea of how good acting was arrived at. Perhaps I could be an actors' agent – the sort I'd wished I'd had, the sort who invested their working hours in their clients. (No, no, I wasn't that high-minded at the time – it was just instinct). I needed a paying job that would last.

I made an appointment to see my then-agent, Clodagh Wallace, of Brunskill Management, went into the agency and asked her if she would take me on as an assistant. She gave me the oddest look, and

I wondered if she hadn't been on the point of firing me – I hadn't worked as an actor for more than a year. She rang me later in the week to apologise and say she had been somewhat spooked as she had, only a few seconds before I'd come into the office, put down the phone on her partner in Northumbria having told her she needed an assistant in London. 'If you would like to be that assistant let's give it a go.'

So I jumped out of my pram and pushed it for others. From baby to nanny!

But what about the dogs? Although I loved them to bits, the problem was what to do with them when I was in a 10-to-6 job. As an actor, I was sometimes able to take them into rehearsal and on tour, and at home, David would look after them, but without him, my office hours weren't conducive to their happiness or mine. Through a friend whose parents lived down in Cornwall, I was given the address of two families who would be happy to have them, so with an aching heart, I dispatched them down to the South West, each with a top or bottom half of my pyjamas to keep them comforted. Ally, the Jack Russell, was going to live next to a golf course, and Chekov, the Dandie Dinmont, at a farm. When my pyjamas were returned, washed and ironed, a few months later, there was a note saying the animals had settled down well, were much loved, and the two owners thought I may want my nightwear back. My dogs were happy without me. I was gutted.

Of course, being an agent was much harder than I'd imagined. Talking to actors on the phone or when they dropped round for a chat was the easy bit, they were only too pleased that there was yet another person looking after their careers, and when I got to know Brunskill's list of clients, I was relieved to find I already admired most of them.

The office of Brunskill Management was situated in Clodagh Wallace's beautiful modern home beside the River Thames in Hammersmith. You could drop a coin from the balcony straight into the water –so a perfect vantage point to see the Boat Race. I sat opposite her at one end of a long dining table with a pad and a telephone in front of me, but once I'd started talking to prospective employers, it seemed there wasn't much I could say that was right. With the phone to my ear, I'd look up to see Clodagh writhing in embarrassment at the far end, her head shaking vigorously, so I would pass the caller on to her PDQ and listen. What I heard was pretty much what I thought I'd been going to say, but not always in the way I would have said it. Eventually, I found it easier to stare down at my pad while I spoke and not look at her vehement disapproval. A month later, I looked up to see her getting on with her job and not taking any notice of me. I took that as a pass.

I liked my boss very much. She was balanced, matter of fact, attractive and honest, and once she'd learned to trust me, we got on well workaday and socially.

I thought I'd given up acting forever, but a few months into the agenting job Bob West (yes, the same one who'd got me into trouble before) rang the office to ask if I would understudy Jim Dale in a musical which was just about to open in London, *The Card* - choreographed by Gillian Lynne. I was amazed: 'Gilly's agreed to it?' Apparently so. I was getting a meagre salary as a fledgling agent, so I asked Clodagh if she could live with me taking time off from work for the mid-week matinee when I'd have to be at the theatre. The answer was no. 'Clodagh, I really need the cash.' 'You can't be away that long. Evenings are fine, that's your own time, but not during the working day.' I rang Bob back and gave him the reason I couldn't do it. He rang again within the hour to say the management could live with my not being in the theatre for the matinees, but I'd need to be available: so if Jim Dale was ill, I'd have to leg it across town. They must have been desperate – or not thought it through. It would take me at least half an hour to get to the theatre from Hammersmith, another quarter of an hour to get into costume – by which time the audience would have left. They would have had to cancel the matinee and refund the ticket money.

Clodagh was fine with that.

I went to see *The Card* when it opened at the Queens a few days after I'd come on board. This was 1973. Jim Dale was astounding as a singer, actor, and dancer. He seemed to be in every number, as a soloist or with the company of dancers, all Gilly's stalwarts. He was every bit as good as they (I recognised a few of them from *Once Upon a Time*). Did she really think I could do what he did?

So this is how it was: the show had tried out in Bristol before coming to London. It had been playing to a paying public in Bristol, and now, in the West End it was a critical success. Jim Dale was the undisputed star, and I was expected to play the title role should he ever be away for any reason (illness, prior engagements, whatever). I didn't see Gilly once, and as it had been agreed, I could only work in the evenings and both shows Saturday, I had almost no rehearsal. I was taken through the steps by Gilly's dance assistant, Roy, in the bar of the theatre, I learned a wheelbarrow-full of lines, worked once or twice on stage with other understudies – but never the dancers – and I was never in all those six months of the run ready to go on. I could have played the character, no problem, and sung the songs passably, but when it came to the dancing, I would have had to stand at the side of the stage while Roy performed for me. If I'd ever been forced to dance on stage in Jim's place, I would have thrown myself down a flight of stairs. 'Broken leg! Sorry.' But Jim was a trouper, and I think he would rather have died than not perform. Talk about luck. I went into the theatre for each performance, asking the stage doorkeeper with trepidation if Jim was in. He always was … but those were the scariest six months of my life.

Working for the agency, Clodagh trusted me to take on a few actors to supplement my earnings, so when I went around the drama schools, I was looking for beginners whom I thought had the potential to be 'special'. Of course, they must also, one day, make money for themselves and the agency, but as far as I was concerned, it didn't have to be straight away. Money and acquiring it for myself has never really interested me. But I was not so removed from reality that I wasn't aware that these youngsters had to eat.

I went to the performances at the many drama schools in London and chose some really interesting leaving students, and of those early ones, most have gone on to good careers and remain friends. They were mostly what you'd call 'character' actors, not necessarily pretty, but brilliant at metamorphosing into believable others. (There are lots of fine 'character' actors in this country, but off the top of my head, my first thought as an example is Kathryn Hunter. You haven't heard of this amazing woman? Make it a priority to go and see the next thing she does).

What was more than a little infuriating was that all the directors and casting directors I knew and admired, and had carefully avoided talking to socially as an actor because I never wanted to be thought brown-nosing, nearly all of them welcomed me with open arms as an agent while bewailing the switch: you were such a good actor – why the change? If the buggers had only offered me worthwhile work as a performer . . . who knows, I might have stuck with it.

No, I wouldn't have. I'd fallen out of love with the doing of it – but I was pretty certain I knew how it should be done.

Not all directors and casting directors are sweethearts, of course, but now I was a possible aide on their side of the business, most of them were encouraging and helpful. A few of them chose to be my mentors – for which I'm grateful to this day.

On the other hand, I found out, rather late in my life you may think, that bullies have to be bullied to gain their respect. Very early days after I'd started on my own, I took on a young actor from the London Academy of Music and Dramatic Art whose only ambition at the time was to be in the National Theatre or the Royal Shakespeare Company. So I wrote to Peter Hall at the National telling him of the abilities of young James and his passion to be part of the National company. I got a very courteous reply from the great man saying that that was just the sort of actor the National needed, so please ring his casting director, Gillian D, and get an interview for him. (My 'youngster' was over six-foot-tall with a beautifully modulated lower register voice). I did as directed and rang to arrange a meeting for James with Gillian, who had not registered my presence at any throng of The Biz which we'd attended together. I was a newbie on my own at that time.

When I next talked to James, asking him how the meeting had gone, he told me that Gillian had not been at the interview (she'd gone Christmas shopping) and her second-in-command had met him and hadn't more than a clue (and a photo) as to his reason for being there.

I was incensed and wrote a furious letter to Peter Hall quoting his original letter and telling him that if that was the way aspiring actors were to be treated at the National, I was certainly not going to risk suggesting anyone else – and he should sack his casting director for starters. (I realised that I may have killed my chances of ever getting any of my actors' jobs at the National after that, but I was too angry to care). Two days later I got a phone call from the National telling me that as Sir Peter was abroad, they'd taken the liberty of passing my letter on to his casting director – the one who had been absent from the meeting, shopping being more important, the one I'd suggested Peter Hall sack. I was appalled.

An ominous silence followed.

James went on to be cast at the Royal Shakespeare Company soon after, but when another actor came to see me a few months later asking for representation, he told me that Gillian had said he should see me as I was one of the best agents in London. We became friends after that.

There was another casting director, one of the heads of casting at London Weekend Television, who found it easy to ignore my presence at whatever shindig we were both at, assuming, again, that I was beneath her notice being such a newcomer in her world. If I smiled at her, she would look away. So, against the grain of everything I believed, I began to ostentatiously look away when she glanced in my direction until the day came when she came to me and said, 'Kerry, you don't seem to like me. Have I done something to offend you?' And I said effusively: 'Oh, hello, Diana. Sorry, I didn't see you there. How are you?' She took notice of me and my suggested actors thereafter. I know important people can be busy, but why do we have to play games to be thought worthy of attention? A friendly nod will do.

*

How should a young actor approach the job of acting? Apart from knowing there's nothing in life more essential to them, they should think of themselves as athletes, keeping their bodies toned and fit – whatever the provocation. Don't let disappointment add weight with food or drink. The day you leave home looking a mess is the day someone who could be useful to your career notices you and mentally puts you in the Not To Be Taken Seriously bin.

Don't be afraid. You can be nervous, yes, but you can mask that. And don't assume your interviewer is of superior intelligence. Chances are they are as inwardly shy as you, out of sorts, hungry, as short-tempered as you, and they wipe their bum just like you . . . whatever. Interview them gently. But don't let on you are more intelligent, even if you are, and don't hold onto their noses too firmly when you lead them to where you get what you want. In other words, think of them as equals, not betters. They need you as much as you need them, however pumped up their reputations.

Be your relaxed self. Be punctual. And courteous. Treat others as you would have them treat you. Because the old truism applies: be nice to people on the way up, because you may need them on the way down.

Those are the basic requirements in a nutshell.

CHAPTER 13
Luck, or What?

I'd been working as an assistant at Brunskill's for eighteen months when I happened to be in Chelsea one weekend and saw my childhood friend, Frances, coming out of a house with her husband, Richard – the man she'd told me she'd marry when we were fourteen, and he was in his late twenties. Frances was only six months older than me, but I was shocked at how different she looked now. She reminded me of a picture I'd once seen of Queen Mary – in a toque hat, elderly, wispy and regal. We hadn't met for quite a few years, and there she was, coming carefully down those front steps, Richard supporting her.

We had always liked one another, so after some jolly pleasantries, she invited me up to their home in East Anglia for the following weekend.

When we'd been eight, or thereabouts, soon after we'd first met at the aunts, she had looked to me for friendship and reassurance, particularly when it had to do with horses. She was a timid rider, whereas I was a cowboy and would jump an obstacle several times when we were out hunting to show her and her pony how easy it was. My Aunty Joyce would be with us somewhere in the field, riding side-saddle, and I was on Prince, my primrose-dumper, urging Frances and her pony on.

(I am now ashamed that I enjoyed hunting so much: riding helter-skelter over farmers' fields, the sheer exhilaration of the chase was thrilling. Not the tearing apart of the fox or hare, the 'blooding' of my face, but the freedom to ride long distances at full pelt. I am not now a hunt saboteur but calling it a sport is an immoral nonsense. And the pretences that are made that present-day hunting is different is a disgraceful sham. But then that's typical of the gentry: if the laws of the land don't suit, don't obey them. Pshaw!).

Anyway, I went up to their manor house in East Anglia after work the next Friday night. I'd not been to Norfolk for a while, and although the dinner on Saturday was pleasant enough (it was no doubt casserole of one of their pheasants, shot included), the conversation was very mundane until Frances rose from the table to go to bed. She passed behind me on her way out of the dining room and said something (inaudible) to Richard; he responded (inaudibly), and then she turned around and slapped him across the face harder than I thought possible, even in melodrama. Richard pulled her onto his lap, where she sobbed for a while before we led her up to their bedroom.

Once up there, Richard vanished. I knelt beside their bed and, with tears running down her face, Frances told me why she was so unhappy. Their story is not mine to tell, so I can only give you the outcome.

She talked, and I listened, and I got to bed at about three in the morning. Richard woke me at six. He was going to be driving around their farm, and would I come with him, please. So, what had Frances said? Bouncing about in his Land Rover over the fields, I told him. 'Ah, but . . ,' he replied.

Later that day beside the bed, I told her of his justifications. She was still inconsolable, and we talked more, she crying the while. The next weekend was the same. Three hours at night listening to her, holding her hand, six o'clock next morning driving around the farm while I told him what she'd said.

The result, after a month or so of this back and forth, was that they became the happiest couple imaginable and thought me responsible. They couldn't do enough for me: we want you close by, have a house on our estate, please, and surely you don't want to work as an agent for someone else, you must have your own agency.

I had only been a conduit between these two, and all I had done was explain one to the other, but in their renewed happiness, they wanted to lavish love and 'things' on me as a thank you. 'You must live near us; you must have your own agency.' Because of their insistence, I chose a small two-up two-down cottage with a demolition order on it, which was a quarter of a mile from their house and accepted their offer of having my own agency – my only stipulation being that they would be partners with me. And, as I couldn't possibly do it from scratch without assistance, I'd need a secretary. *Anything, darling, anything.*

We had a very happy time planning it all.

The wee cottage was made habitable, and it really was just two rooms on each floor, once no doubt housing two farm workers' families, each with their own front door with just one small room above the other. It was situated in the middle of their farmland, with a stream bordering a tiny patch of grass behind the house. I paid them a peppercorn rent for it: one penny. It was mine until I died.

So that fixed, what about the agency?

I remembered I had a friend in publishing with offices in central London, in Goodge Street, with space to let. The front door of the building was beside a Greek restaurant, and immediately above the restaurant was the room I could use as my office.

With all the goings-on, Frances had been transformed; she was now much younger than me – thirty-nine going on fifteen. She was so full of bounce and sparkle it could be embarrassing – particularly in theatres, where she would chatter happily. And she had such fun doing up that small room. She decorated it like a library in a mansion with fitted carpet, velvet curtains, a standard lamp with pleated shade, a quasi-antique leather-topped library table with, behind it, an oak refectory dining chair, the leather studded with brass. A smaller antique table with a more practicable modern office chair on casters sufficed for my secretary, Bethan. (I shared her with the literary firm across the landing). The modern phones and desktop paraphernalia were rather incongruous in that set-up. There were two other modern bits of furniture: a wickerwork-and-teak Danish sofa for visitors and a faux-teak filing cabinet. The room looked magnificent.

On 2 February 1977, I opened Kerry Gardner Associates for business.

Within a fairly short period, my office smelled of food, and within eighteen months, the curtains and carpet smelled strongly of dolmades and chips, as indeed did my secretary and I. Before I could go out in public at night, I would go home and have a bath and change my clothes. But I didn't care; I was so chuffed at being my own boss, and nobody who came to see me in that handsome room made mention of the smell. (However, within two years, I moved around the corner to above a picture framers).

Where I lived then was above the Phoenix Theatre, which was bang on the Charing Cross Road, only a ten-minute walk from work.

How had that come about?

I had been told the king of Phoenix House was Christopher Biggins, and I'd only had to mention to the kind man that it would be very convenient for me to live so close to work for him to find me a vacant flat in the block. Derek Jarman, the filmmaker, was another of the tenants. Cameron Mackintosh, in the days he was earning a living by sending out tours of *Winnie the Pooh*, yet another. But heavens was it noisy! Cup Final supporters kept the match alive until five in the morning, right outside my window. And the rugby crowd!

Now I had my own agency, I had to find working actors to fund it. I already had the few Clodagh had allowed me, but I was in the enviable position of not having to rush into choosing any but those I truly believed in. The youngsters I already had were to my way of thinking bound to be successful; maybe not immediately, but they were that good I knew sooner or later their worth would be recognised. Of course, I hoped that day would be sooner rather than in the next century, I needed to make a living, the freelancer that I now was. All of us did.

I still went to all the drama school productions (there were fewer drama schools in those days) to see students in their final year showcases, although I faced fierce competition from all the established agents there to snag the best students. For the larger agencies (the supermarket agencies as I thought of them – the ones with well-stocked shelves of actors), a student with good looks was their first requirement, along with acting ability. Being pretty can get you fancy parts early on, but if we look back, we can just about remember, with difficulty, the startlingly good-looking performers of yesteryear who have disappeared with hardly a trace. That the top agents were mainly there for the cutest was OK by me. I was only interested in performers who could convince me for the few minutes they were allowed to show off on their academy stages that they were *being* their characters so that when they went off stage, I felt cheated: *No! Come back. Tell me more about yourself.*

So I suppose it can be said that I specialised in 'character' actors.

But I found it very shy-making to approach complete strangers, the students whom I'd admired strutting their stuff, who didn't know me from Adam. Yes, they'd been coached by the school for both the performance and, perfunctorily, for this after-show party in the bar of the theatre, but however you looked at it, we were all in a bazaar. Says I, the buyer: 'I enjoyed what you did very much.' Says performer/seller: 'Thank you.' Me: 'The solo piece you did for us was by John Hopkins. I like his writing very much. Did you get to play the whole role during the term, or did you just choose that segment for today's show?' Actor looks nonplussed. Did I gabble? Me, pressing on, serious half-smile on my face: 'I also very much liked the duologue you did, that suited you too, maybe not as much, but . . . It seems whatever you set your mind to works well for you. You're very good. Do you have representation yet?' 'Er, some agent saw me last term and seems interested . . .' 'I'm not at all surprised. You are extraordinary. Well, if you don't go with this other management, I hope you'll consider coming to meet me. Well done. Oh, I'm Kerry Gardner, by the way.' I wander away, butterflies in my stomach, the other students staring at me as if I'd been a flasher propositioning a nun. After a year or so, my name sparked some recognition in the student, who would then nonchalantly re-join friends with a bit of a smirk.

This way I found a few and lost more. There were a lot of us locusts at these after-show gatherings, and I have to admit I never enjoyed them, even though the schmoozing became easier over time.

One youngster said that what he wanted most from life was to be in a *Star Wars* film. It just so happened that I was able to ring him the day after to tell him I had a meeting for him with George Lucas later in the week. They met up, and he got two parts in that particular *Star Wars* film: one, a monster, and the other a stormtrooper, both with lines. Just out of the trap and racing away, and now mine! These periodic thrills occurred almost until the day I gave up agenting. Are you surprised I enjoyed myself?

Later, because I was good on the phone and could 'sell' my actors with my smooth-and-honeyed tongue, I would find these now-working actors of mine recommending me to others in their casts.

Remembering that never once throughout those seventeen years I was an actor did an agent go out of town to see my work, I made it my job to visit all my clients however far away from London they were performing – praising, enthusing, interested, asking if the digs they had that week were bearable . . . and so on.

I thought it best to wear some sort of informal uniform: a shirt, tie, sportscoat, and pressed charcoal trousers in the winter; more relaxed in the summer – short sleeves, no tie, coat and jauntier pants. I was after all representing these actors, so I was 'on show' all day. But my outfit was never flashy; I wasn't there to outshine them.

Being responsible for other people's lives never fazed me, I don't know why. Taking calls, ringing people back, dashing from work to bathe and then travel to see clients in out-of-the-way theatres, that was exciting. Paperwork was new to me, but in the office, Bethan did the typing and my partner, Richard, did the accounting. I would take the accounts to him in the country at the end of each month, and he would do the books and pay the bills.

I suppose if I'd had to make a financial go of it straight away the pressure would have frightened me, but rather like the time I was at RADA and my father paid me a living allowance, I had my friends' financial support, and I was able to slowly build up a list of actors that employers seemed happy to use. Came the day a couple of years later that the business was self-supporting and I offered to buy out my partners (they were the Associates in the agency's title after all), Richard refused, saying that would complicate tax matters: please to think of it as mine, take it away, and enjoy it.

I changed the title of the agency to Kerry Gardner Management.

But something rather sad had happened in the meantime: Frances told me one day that although Richard knew nothing untoward was going on between the two of us, as her husband, he couldn't bear to see his wife so happy with another man. He asked she only see me in his company. 'So, come to your new house as often as you can, darling, won't you please, but you and I can't go out on our own anymore.' So my bouncy fifteen-year-old companion returned to being that much older woman for the sake of her husband, and indeed I did see a lot of them most weekends. She didn't revert to being an ancient, thank heavens, but to begin with, she and I shared an unhappy secret when we were all together, Richard seeming oblivious. The limitations faded with time, and we returned to our earlier easy friendship. However, Richard died some years ago, and apart from her asking me to read a poem she had chosen at his funeral, she has cut me out of her life. It makes me sad. I have so much to thank her for.

Throughout this period, I saw lots of my darling Naomi. For instance, we had a holiday together when I drove her around Scotland. It amused her greatly when at one hotel as I paid the bill, she overheard me being asked by the landlord if she was my mother, and I said no. So she was a relation? No. I didn't offer an explanation. Actually, I've always found people's ages uninteresting. She was my friend, for heaven's sake. My favourite human being on earth, yes, but he didn't ask that.

I took Naomi to classical concerts – Ally having a tin ear for music which he admitted to – and introduced her to Rossini and Dvořák; went with her to plays and the cinema and Events. For instance, I took her to see my favourite stand-up comedian, Eddie Izzard, and she nearly fell off her seat, she laughed so much. By now, her daughter and son-in-law, John, had moved into the main house, and Naomi lived in a small bungalow at the bottom of the garden – put up during the war as a prefabricated rehearsal studio for Ally, and later converted with bricks and mortar into a living space. I went to see her there as often as possible. After Ally died, she'd assumed their friends would fade away, but she was touched to find that we all needed her as much as we ever had.

I got a phone call from her once. She sounded tremulous. 'I haven't forgotten our lunch date, dearest. I'll be there.' She rang off. What lunch date, I wondered uneasily – had I forgotten? I rang Merlith.

Naomi had decided to do a rather arduous hill walk while on holiday on her own in Scotland, a walk she'd done with Ally years before, and she got lost. She had been away from the hotel for five hours before they noticed her missing, and a rescue party was sent out. They'd found her lying at the side of a path, unconscious, and taken her to the nearest hospital. She had hypothermia and was in a bad way. It was apparently her conviction that she and I had a date that pulled her through. So I was told. I like to think it's true.

Naomi lived for another twenty-five years after Ally died. I'm not sure there wasn't a day that she didn't miss him – certainly early on, she couldn't wait to get back to his side – but she was much cherished by us, her children. She dropped dead on her way to the drinks' cabinet one evening, glass in hand. Way to go, Naomi!

For the first three years or so after she'd gone, I was certain she was looking after me: my guardian angel. Then suddenly, she wasn't. It was very odd.

I have memories of her everywhere. Not just thoughts in my head, but objects as well. She gave me a one-person Portmeirion table setting with a strawberry motif, and I liked it so much I went ahead and ordered five more. It cost a fortune. (The Sims had their summer holidays in Portmeirion). Then there's the beautifully carved honey-wood polar bear; and the plaid mohair blanket which our present poodle, Biscuit, needs to dig through to get to Australia. And of course, poodles! I remember two of Naomi's miniature poodles, Mosca and Fly, and her telling me that if I ever wanted another dog after the departure of my terriers, Ally and Chekov, there were no more intelligent, clean and lovable dogs on the planet than poodles. I have the third of them now, Biscuit, a toy as I'm older and can't lift a grown-up dog into a car anymore, but our first two, Bosky and Jessie, were the full standards. Naomi was so right: I have been the proud owner of three through the years, and they have always been the delight of anyone that meets them.

Other 'things' Naomi and Ally gave to me (by that I mean brought to my attention, shared) were the novels of Thornton Wilder, *The Dialogues of Plato*, *The Mouse and His Child* by Russell Hoban, snooker, and comice pears, and of course, Luis d'Antin van Rooten's *Mots d'Heures: Gousses, Rames* – 'Un petit, d'un petit . . .' etc. A picture I admired so many eons ago in the Royal Scottish Academy in Edinburgh hangs on our walls thanks to them, and a set of Everyman Encyclopaedias takes up most of a shelf. They introduced me to Robin Hall and Jimmie MacGregor and 'Sailing Homeward to Mingulay', and I gave them Rossini's String Sonatas. The Sims, but especially Naomi, pervade my being – a mutual adoption which enriched my life beyond measure, the parents I eventually had.

*

My sexual forays were few and far between before and after starting the agency. Actors can be the most seductive and attractive of people, and I swore I would never take advantage of my position as a possible saviour. *And*, of course, it would be impossible to work for a performer if one became emotionally entangled – so during that time, I foreswore all temptations of thespian flesh. Once I'd settled in, I learned to separate my private and work life so I didn't impose that extra handicap on myself. Nevertheless, during the thirty years I was an agent, I never had a relationship with a client. Besides which, as I've told you already, I'd already had three failed hook-ups with actors, and it seemed downright idiotic to tempt sanity with a fourth.

(I'm revising this book not long after the Weinstein affair broke.

I really don't want to sound holier-than-thou, but it seems to me basic manners would prevent one from pushing oneself on another person. 'Respect' is a word that covers it. We do unto others what we would have done unto us, and no one wants to be assaulted, even in the mildest of ways. Insistence is just bloody rude. As Ursula Le Guin put it – she was talking to women, but it applies to us all: 'I hope you live without the need to dominate, and without the need to be dominated').

*

So, what did I think that actor/agent relationship should be?

I find it amazing that actors who crave appreciation should set themselves up to be constantly slapped: by critics and by possible employers such as directors and producers. One can understand rejection by friends or lovers – hurtful, but with those one is often the cause – but from people you are inwardly praying are going to help you? And yet there the actors are, some of the bravest and, sometimes, the sweetly silliest people I know, going back again and again for more possible rejections in the hope that someone, someday, will appreciate them enough to give them That Opportunity. So, as their agent, I was there to pledge faith and to help, whether it was on how to present themselves to prospective employers or which photographers to use to best show themselves off – really empathetic photographers are few and far between and very expensive [3] – or how to dress appropriately for auditions and, indeed, the outside world. I

---

[3]   *Spotlight* is an important part of the actor's survival kit. Two slim books of photographs, one for the men and one for the women, were what was around when I started. Nowadays everything is done online, but until recently those two books multiplied into four fat tomes, two for each sex. It was very important that you supply an attracting photograph with your agent's logo next to it, because this was the best way for prospective employers to track you down. Entries weren't cheap so it was important to me once I was an agent to find clever photographers who could make my actors look natural, rather than in those studio portraits of old. (Gauze over the lens, for instance). As an agent, Jenny Potter was my photographer of choice.

would read their offered scripts and, if asked, give my opinion as to whether their careers should go down that route; arrange their travel and accommodation if needed; be their partner. And, of course, get them the best financial deal when it came to negotiating their contracts. Yes, *and* to take a percentage of their fee, but throughout those thirty years, I never asked for more than the standard 10% – even after almost all agents were asking for more. The rent, the staff and the phone bill had to be paid.

Not true. I did demand 12.5% for commercials, but then I've always been sniffy about those. Basically, because I disapprove of advertising. It coerces people through envy or greed to want things that they can't really afford because their acquaintances want them or have them – or fashion dictates. I was ambivalent about television commercials because I was aware they were a great source of revenue for actors (one or two days' work could pay huge amounts of money), but I employed someone else in the agency to deal with that side of things. Commercials were a good source of income for all of us, even if I disapproved of them. (I'd only done one the entire time I was an actor – as a dad, for an Irish bank. I was younger then).

My clients and I were bound at the hip – and when they got slapped down, I felt the hurt as well. But, without exception, mine had to be the brave face.

I've said often enough when people ask me what I look for in an actor: I want someone daring enough to climb a hundred-foot ladder and dive from the top into a teacup of water. Too bad if you miss, but oh, the extraordinary, wonderful *bravery* of it! And when you enter the water with scarcely a ripple, the sheer wonder of it! Those are the actors I looked for, the ones with the nerve not to care too much about looking ridiculous if they didn't achieve perfection, but to go on trying again and again to get it how they believe it should be.

If someone gives them the chance.

Which brings us to LUCK.

Pam Ferris, when she was a client of mine, was wonderful as a hard bitch in *Connie*, an ATV series she did with Stephanie Beacham, which didn't find favour with the public. A few years later, she played Ma Larkin in *The Darling Buds of May* – which was a mega hit. So for a long period afterwards, she was offered earth-mother roles – but if the earlier series had been a success, she'd have been sent scripts of nothing but hard-bitten manipulating schemers, and it's unlikely anyone would have thought of her when it came to casting *The Darling Buds*. She's a versatile character actress, so that's how come she had two bites of the cherry, and, as I've said (probably too often), to hopefuls: 'Cream does get to the top eventually'. It does – she has. But those lucky breaks come far too seldom for most.

With his permission, I'd like to use Bill Paterson as a template of what I love most in actors. He was one of the first I took on in those early days on my own. And it came about like this: I went to see a female client, Jenny Lee, in a play up in Edinburgh and said to her (this was after the show in the theatre bar) that as well as her performance I'd very much liked Bill Paterson's. I didn't know him from a bar of soap then, but this Scottish actor was extraordinary in this particular play. It so happened that he was interested in meeting me as he wanted to take his career to London and see how well he could do down there. Jenny brought him over, and we got on a treat. He's a lovely fun guy as well as supremely talented. But nothing apart from laughter came of that meeting.

The next time I went to see Jenny, maybe six months later, she was in London in another modern play at the Shaw Theatre, in which there were two actors apart from Jen that I admired – Bill being one of them. Because of my work schedule (and bathing), I often didn't get into the theatre till just before the lights went down, so I seldom saw a programme. We all met after the show, and it turned out he'd played *both* the parts that I'd found outstanding. He was that versatile I hadn't recognised him in the second role. He obviously found my enthusiasm for him enough because he said he'd like to join the agency.

I just want to share one more snapshot before I come to the point: some years after this, Billy played the eponymous hero in *Schweik in the Second World War* by Bertolt Brecht at the National Theatre. In the theatre bar after the first night performance, there was Billy, his exhausting work done, surrounded by the smartly attired casting directors out for a gala night. He stood there, in his down-at-heel, slightly off-white cricket trews – the hem on one of his trouser legs had become unsewn so it was, literally, dragging on the ground – his less-than-white gym shoes, and a shapeless greenish linen jacket. There he was, making the bees around his honeypot laugh. *That's my boy*, I thought with such pride. *That's why I love this job!*

Billy is rooted in reality. For people of imagination, that's essential. You have to believe in yourself, of course you do, but as a questing human, if you believe all the praise that's heaped on you, that way lies disintegration. Reality keeps your vision sharp in the here and now. But with his tap-root in the earth, Bill's imaginings can soar and create fantasies, yet the core of him is never far from the absurdity of it all; he doesn't take himself too seriously during and after giving a wonderful performance. (If you haven't read his book about his childhood in Glasgow, *Tales from the Back Green*, you have joy in store. That's two books about children growing up in Scotland I've recommended now, Naomi's and Billy's. What is it about these northerners in their chilly climes?).

I got many rewards from my job. My favourite might well be that years later Billy Paterson sent me a message: 'BAFTA Scotland gave me a "Lifetime" Award this year!! No small part due to you, Kerry!'

But can you beat this: Bill Armstrong made me the guardian of his firstborn?

Billy P. came to the agency, and his reputation down south grew quickly, which helped my agency's, which meant that I started getting prominent performers coming to *me* asking for representation – and it didn't take very long for my now-impressive list of clients to attract the notice of famous employers.

While we're talking of Billy, here's an anecdote to do with him, giving you a glimpse of an evening's work for me. Bill took over from Tom Conti in *Whose Life is it Anyway?* in the West End. Knowing that George Gallaccio, a television producer I'd recently met, was looking to cast the lead role in a new series for the BBC, I invited him along to the Savoy Theatre in London where *Whose Life* was playing. You may remember from a theatre production or the film that the story is set in a hospital ward. So, it started with Billy centre-stage in a hospital bed, and twenty minutes into the dialogue, George murmurs in my ear that he has to go to the loo. Couldn't he have gone before, I wondered? We're sitting in the centre block of the stalls, row eight, so not a little distracting to the actors on stage when he gets up to leave. Just when it occurs to me that George is taking a long time in the lavatory, a St John Ambulance man taps me on the shoulder: my friend has been taken ill in the stalls bar, and would I come with him, please?

I find a white-faced George lying on the carpet in the plush bar-room with two other ambulance people beside him. They explain that he fainted. He's lying there looking up at me, his eyes blinking through his skewed spectacles: 'You feeling better, George?' He murmurs, and it felt wrong to be towering over a guest when he was so vulnerable, so I lay down on the carpet beside him. We lie there talking calmly – and then he struggles to his feet while the ambulance crew recount with some relish that a lot of theatre-goers have felt ill watching this hospital play: one American gentleman was sick all down his front but didn't want to cause any inconvenience to anyone by getting up and leaving, so sat there in his seat for a good half hour before the lights came up for the interval. Then there was the time .. . 'Don't you worry sir, lots of people have been affected the way you have.'

George came back to watch the rest of the play, brave man, and the next day offered Bill the lead role in his new TV series. It was a pretty unexceptional script, we refused with a polite thank you, and when we saw it the following year on the box agreed Bill was well out of it. But George wasn't offended and continued to offer work to my other actors through the years.

Another instance of one of my clients bringing an unknown

into the fold: James S was working up in Manchester at the Library Theatre in a production of *Tom Jones*, and as was my wont, I drove up to see him. He was excellent playing Blifil, the baddy in the piece, and there was a blonde actress alongside him playing Sophy Western, our heroine. Her name was Miranda Richardson. She played it very still, so it was mesmerising. You seldom go backstage after the show in repertory theatres as it's a nightmare to navigate and the dressing rooms are communal, so the usual place to meet after the performance is the theatre bar, and it was there James asked if I'd liked Miranda's performance as she was looking for an agent. He brought her over, and she joined the team. (A golden moment to treasure: I once raced up the Royal Court stairs to the actors' dressing room to tell Miranda that Sam Goldwyn Jr. was right behind me, wanting to congratulate her on her performance – to mocking laughter from everyone in the room. Until he walked in).

Much the same happened with Imelda Staunton. Billy told me she wasn't very happy with her representation, he recommended me to her, and she joined up. Sometime later, when he and Imelda were doing *Guys and Dolls* at the National, Billy recommended I meet Jim Carter, who was playing Big Jule in the musical, with the idea of perhaps representing him. I already had a tall heavy-set actor, so I declined. This was sometimes the problem: however much you admired someone's work, the chances were you already had someone of the same 'type' in your team of actors, and it wouldn't be fair on the first on board to take on another who would be competing with them when it came to casting meetings. Competition for parts was fierce enough without it coming from within your own agency.

Not that long ago, when I was no longer an agent, Julian Fellowes tapped me on the shoulder and reminded me he'd once written to me for representation, and I'd turned him down. I tried to laugh it off: 'I hope I replied to your letter.' 'Oh, yes.' (Thank heaven! He'd obviously sent a stamped addressed envelope). 'You were very polite.' 'And did I say I couldn't look after you because I already had someone on my books who was too like you for me to be able to take you on?' 'That's right', he chortled. He's a very nice understanding man – and didn't do too badly without my help. Neither did Jim.

Reading letters from actors asking for a meeting, I would only reply to those that had a direct or amusing tone without a hint of pleading. The formulaic dull ones were from the unimaginative. For heaven's sake, these strangers were on an equal footing. Letters to Ms Kerry Gardner got the bin!

I have to blow my own trumpet here for a second, although I have always been hesitant about promoting myself. Manners inhibited me from pushing myself forward as an actor, and I edged away from people who could help me in my career – *and* I'm not good at cap-in-hand. But despite hating being at public school, that sense of entitlement must have rubbed itself off on me because for my actors, I had no qualms in promoting *them*, shouting from the rooftops: I HAVE THE BEST. COME AND BUY! And because the quality of my produce was so superior, they did.

I'm very cavalier with money with regards to my own, but I was always determined to coerce proper salaries for my clients. The thunderous silence I used occasionally on the phone after an offer, which meant, 'They are worth more than *that*! You should be ashamed of yourself!', worked a treat, as did the little snorts of derision, but doing one's homework as to how much there was in the budget and how much had been allocated for the role was more important. It was a challenge to see if I couldn't wangle more out of the employers than they had intended to pay. There's not much leeway in theatre salaries – except for the stars – but with the commercial television companies – *en garde!*

Mind you, I did take one fearful risk fairly early on. I had this client who had been offered a risible rise in salary after she'd done two series of a very successful television series. Before series one started, she had been bound by a two-series contract to have a percentage rise on her fee should the first series be successful. Well, it certainly was, as was series two, so come the time for series three, I was free to negotiate. Before I could open my mouth, I was offered the same percentage rise as before. This actor had become a household name by the end of the second series, was playing a role not that much smaller than the lead, so was in comparison being offered a pittance. I told the casting director, Malcolm Drury, that she should be paid the same as her co-star. He laughed and said the company wouldn't stand for that – the co-star had played the lead in so many series before this one – but he did offer her a little more. I doubled the sum he suggested, said that's the least we could accept. 'We', you notice, the actor and me. He said that couldn't be met, so the company would have to recast. I gambled on the public success of the series and of her importance in it and said, OK, recast, but before you do, ask the company whether the story can afford to do without her.

I had in the meantime told my actor of the second offer, which was better than she'd been expecting, and told her of my rejection of it. She was undecided but agreed that just because she was a woman, the disparity with the male lead wasn't fair, so, 'Go for it, Kerry.'

There was ominous silence thereafter from both the casting director and the television company being held to ransom. The artist had booked a holiday abroad in anticipation of coming back to work, so a few weeks later changed her mind. 'I was looking forward to working when I got back. I couldn't be happy out there in Australia knowing I might have nothing to come back to, so I want you to agree to what they offered, please.' 'You're sure?' 'Er, yes.' 'All right, I said – and did nothing about it.

She'd been away two weeks of her three-week holiday when Malcolm rang and told me of the dates she'd be needed for costume fittings. 'The company agreed to the fee I asked for her?' 'They're pretty bloody angry, but yes.' My resolve had been so shaken since I'd disobeyed my client's instructions and held my nerve, if not hers, that he could hear my exhalation of breath over the phone. 'Canny bastard,' he said and laughed. 'Well done.'

I had a series of clever assistants. Whenever the agency was doing exceptionally well, I would take on another helper, so the actors had more people looking after their needs; and after ten or so years, I determined that what the agency needed was someone looking after writers and directors, both for their talents, and the usefulness they could be to each other and the actors. Pauline Asper had already been my assistant for many years, and now I put her in charge of what I thought of as the agency's Literary Arm. I'd already taken on a few writers and directors, and she began to look for others. After all, everything I saw my actors do around the country had been directed by someone – those someones often being very talented. And, of course, there had been writers involved – and if the scripts were good, I attempted to meet the authors too.

Another plan I had, more of a wish really, was to own a building which could be converted into two studio theatres, seating maybe 250 in each, and a third auditorium of similar dimensions in which to show films. Because I so often visited my actors in far-away cities, and some of the plays and the casts with them were first class, it seemed a shame sometimes that one couldn't transport the shows exactly as they were into London for a short run – for, say, three weeks. The actors would be paid the same provincial wage, but in London, they'd get the exposure and the reviews in the national papers. If the production attracted enough attention and was successful, I could transfer the play with the original cast into the second auditorium of identical size and shape for a longer run, three months, perhaps – with enhanced salaries, of course. Then, should any London management want to take it further it was theirs, ready and successful, for the asking – and the money from the deal would be ploughed back into the building. That second auditorium when not in use, would be used for conferences, meetings, whatever, thus paying its own way. The cinema, the same shaped room as the other two with the same number of seats, would start early and at weekends would go on until the late-night film ended, about three in the morning. The building would open early, and there would be two restaurants within the complex – the first an affordable café-bistro, the second serving expensive up-scale food, their rack of lamb and beef Wellington for dinner turned into tomorrow's lunch of shepherd's and cottage pie in the café. This would also be a meeting place, serving coffee and tea and snacks with chess and draughts boards and sofas. The walls of every room and corridor would be used for saleable art. And everyone employed to work there would be a shareholder, so it would be in everyone's interest to keep the place spic and span – somewhere to be proud of.

Arranged by a friend, I went to a meeting around a long mahogany table somewhere in the City of London, and without too much effort, we got together a consortium of businessmen who volunteered to make it happen.

They made bids on various London properties: one of them, in Wigmore Street opposite the concert hall, had not long before been a department store, Debenham & Freebody. In my mind, I imagined the public, the scruffy and the couturier-clad, passing each other on those faux-marble stairs or sharing the gilded lifts up to our complex above (the rest of the building could be offices which would support the theatres – but as to which businesses I didn't want to be involved, that was up to the consortium). When that particular building came to be sold, there was a Dutch Auction, and we didn't bid enough. Then there was the building on the Waterloo roundabout, the Hospital for Women and Children. I asked Alan Ayckbourn if he'd be interested in being the Artistic Director of it, along with his being the director of Scarborough's Theatre in the Round, and he thought mischievously it would be fun to run a theatre in competition to the National, which was only a stone's throw away. Our consortium didn't bid enough for that building either. It is now a School for Languages.

One of the people I approached as to his possible interest in my scheme was Prince Edward. He was working in Andrew Lloyd Webber's Really Useful Company at the time, and there was talk, maybe just gossip, of his branching out on his own. I took him to lunch in a curiously empty restaurant behind the Wyndham's Theatre (him and his bodyguard who sat four tables away) – and we were the only people there. He was uncommunicative, and the lunch wasn't a success. The food was good, and the place had been thriving when I'd been there before – that's why I'd chosen it. Had someone bought it out so as to be cleared of customers that lunchtime in the heart of town? Talking to someone across a small Soho table with only one other (armed?) person in the room didn't make for easy chat.

I had plans to call one of the auditoriums (auditoria?) The Alastair Sim, but after those two tries, the businessmen who had offered to help realise my dream got discouraged, and that was the end of Ally's Theatre. Others have been successful with less grandiose but similar ideas since.

Pity, really. The actors in the agency would have had their own theatre where they could have tried out any of their conceits (one-person shows, plays they'd written), their own audition rooms where they'd have felt at ease, a forum in which to meet and plan, a sort of club of their own with us, their representatives, down a nearby corridor. Never mind. I had great fun planning it, and I've heard said it's better to travel hopefully than to arrive. Bollocks. Arriving would have been thrilling.

But for the longest time, life was filled with success. I went to one showbiz jamboree after another. Huge ballrooms inside huge hotels (in London: the Savoy, the Grosvenor House, the Dorchester . . .) filled with overheated people sitting at fifteen enormous round tables or more, congratulations and commiserations and gossip, speeches, award-giving, ordinary food, and massively noisy – all that voice training! Those award ceremonies could also be in huge cavernous theatres like the Drury Lane, the Coliseum or Covent Garden. I was only ever there because one of my actors was up for some prize, and I met mates and performers I was in awe of, and lots I thought overrated. These bashes were fun, and I was always proud to be part of this rarefied world. Picking up Helen Mirren's bag which she'd just dropped when I opened the hefty front doors of the Drury Lane for her; being tapped on the shoulder by Jeff Bridges and asked if I'd be so kind as to introduce my client Miranda Richardson to him; being asked by Johnny Depp if I wasn't proud to be Miranda's agent – to which I replied that of course I was, and 'I'm sure she's as proud of me!' Meeting the gorgeous Catherine Zeta-Jones at a Variety Club Lunch; and sitting opposite the fabled Celeste Holm at the Russian Tea Rooms in Manhattan, who didn't think I would know her (I was astonished: 'you've been one of my idols all my life,' I gushed emotionally – and truly meant it). Or Tony Randall inviting me to his New York apartment in the Dakota building to see if I could help with some casting he was doing for his theatre company. Or going to a birthday party thrown by Tom Hanks in Los Angeles for his friend, Gary Sinise.

Lots and lots of chance encounters which seasoned my working life, making it extraordinary and ridiculous fun.

CHAPTER 14
My Dearest Dear

I've been having some trouble getting further into the book because the first seventeen years of my adult life were as a performer, so, even without a diary, dates and incidents aren't too difficult to recall – but once I'd morphed into an agent?

I was an actors' agent for just under thirty years, and most of my life as a carer of others is a blur because there was so much of the same old, same old in the way of answering the telephone, haggling over offers, reading scripts, going to screenings, advising, and always being ever-so-amenable to people you have to have time for, for the sake of your clients, *and* – never-ending – telling your darlings of their acceptances and rejections. For the first twenty years or more of my agenting life, I loved the work and found it very satisfying.

In those early days casting directors were comparatively thin on the ground. Casting directors or 'casting' are people who are there to suggest actors to their directors for various projects – be they for screen or stage. Most theatre and television directors worth their salt have a very good idea of the actors they want for their lead roles when they take on a project. But sometimes their favourites aren't available for the dates they're needed. To give you an example: my pal Corinne Rodriguez, who worked for London Weekend Television, would suggest actors to her directors for the leads *and* the smaller supporting parts needed to complete their casts because screen directors in particular couldn't be expected to know all the up-and-coming actors from around the country. That's precisely why I would take casting directors to see my clients working here, there and everywhere so these folks would remember them when the next casting session came up.

And driving around the country seeing my actors perform, taking carloads of these useful casting directors, was a full-time job if ever there was one; a bit like trying to amuse a table full of dinner guests you only know on a superficial basis – looking straight ahead while steering your plate. The meeting and greeting after the performance of your actor is satisfying because that's the time for the performer to show their agreeable other side (*Such a good actor and, my, wouldn't he or she be fun to work with!*), but then you've got to take the same troupe back to town. For instance: I made three journeys to the Bristol Old Vic theatre in two weeks in my car, packed each time – so nine casting directors all told – to show off Miranda Richardson to those I thought might be useful to her later career.

Another example: there was a journey I made with one of my favourite casting directors, Derek Barnes, who when we first met, worked for Associated TV (he's now with the BBC). One Friday morning, I drove us up to Newcastle to show him one of my clients in Shakespeare's *Twelfth Night*, stayed there overnight, and next morning we dashed down south to Harrogate to see another client in a matinee of *Ashes* . . . before belting eastwards to Scarborough for the evening performance to see yet another client in yet another production of *Twelfth Night*. We got back to London around four on Sunday morning.

(What with prep school, RADA, and rep, I've played every role in *Twelfth Night* except for Maria. I wonder how believable I was as Viola in the St Wilfrid's production, aged eleven? It obviously didn't light my fire. When I played the clown, Feste, at Farnham Rep, Edward Fox played Sebastian – his first professional appearance he later told me. When I played Sebastian at the Old Vic a *Dame* played opposite me. And Tom Courtenay played Feste – bloody difficult as it is. OK, so I'll admit he was more interesting than me in that role).

With all that dashing about the country, you can tell why I kept as many dependable personnel in the office as the company could afford to look after the actors. And why I kept in touch by telephone throughout my trips away. No mobiles then – it had to be coins in the box.

One great satisfaction was when I could compose a winning letter to get clients seen – once they are through the casting door there's nothing more one can do for them. Badgering is unsubtle, not good form. Not every casting director had an imagination to go with their very necessary memory files, so persuading them to meet a client could be very frustrating. If I couldn't inveigle a common-or-garden meeting by telephone, I had to use other wiles.

Steven Waddington (I surely don't need to put 'a glorious actor' after every client of mine, because they all were to me) was an obvious choice for a part in the film of *Edward II* which Derek Jarman was about to make: tall, strapping, good to look at, he would be perfect, surely, in that historical story full of scheming barons, courtiers, army men etc., so I urged Susie Figgis, the casting director, to meet him. 'No point. There's nothing for him in *Edward*, darling.' Oh, come on, I thought, I know my history – and the play by Marlowe! A few days later, Steven rings me to say he'd met Nigel Terry, one of Derek Jarman's favourite actors, who'd said to him: 'Get your agent to put you up for this film, mate; there's lots in it for you.' (Of course there bloody was!) These were earlyish days on my own, so etiquette had prevented me from going behind Susie's back, but this spur was all I needed. I rang Derek (if you remember we used to live in adjoining Phoenix House flats) and told him of my problem of not being able to get past his casting director, when I knew, and Nigel Terry knew, there was bound to be some role for Steven in his film. Would Derek meet him, please? 'I'll be in the office tomorrow morning, get him to call in,' says Derek. Steven called in, without an appointment – and was given the leading role of Edward II. At the first screening of the film Susie came up to me to congratulate herself: 'Didn't we do well!' I smiled, my teeth clamped, and wanted to knock her down. 'There's nothing for him in *Edward*, darling.' Really?

All this taught me early on to go straight to the horse's mouth – when I knew the horse, or in this next case, even if I didn't. I'd read in some trade paper that the creative team for the film *Dance With a Stranger* were having problems finding their lead, Ruth Ellis, having seen every leading actress in the country. I sent off one of my most artful letters, bending the truth somewhat, telling the director Mike Newell and his casting lady, Celestia Fox, that there was no one in England who could possibly be better in the role than Miranda Richardson. I even hinted that Ruth Ellis's early background and Miranda's weren't too dissimilar. That was tosh. The letter got her an interview, she got the part, and I got the most enormous bouquet of flowers by way of thanks from Celestia, with a note saying Mike Newell had said that from now on he was to be alerted to any suggestions I might have.

Two down, one more anecdote along these lines to go: the Head of Casting for Anglia Television rang me in a fury. 'I'm not your secretary, Kerry Gardner!' Why? I had contacted a new-minted friend of mine, that very fine screen director John Gorrie, to ask him to meet someone for a role in his next television production – I'd seen the cast breakdown, of course, so knew what I was talking about. They'd met, and John had offered him the part. The casting director was ringing ostensibly to tell me of the offer and to talk fees. But she was furious I'd sidestepped her to go straight to her director. 'I'm not your secretary!' She never took my calls again, but luckily for my actors, she retired not long after.

*

Some of my actors were more private than others. At least with me. They thought our relationship was a business one: fine, it was. We still had an agreeable and satisfactory working relationship – usually with lots of laughter included. (I did need a sense of fun from my actors – and indeed in real life, in everybody who could be a friend). But there was an extra satisfaction for me from the others who completely trusted me with their lives and their thoughts. Thinking about it now, I suppose the balance was 50/50; those that didn't trade their inner selves with those who did. I still have beloved client-friends I see to this day, but, workwise, of those who did, I suppose Billy and Miranda were the most fulfilling through the years. Billy I still see. He married a wonderfully gifted woman he met doing a play at the ICA theatre in which he spent most of the time in a hencoop dressed as a woman. Hildegard, his now-wife and mother of their children, designed the set. How sexy is that!

As the agency's reputation grew, the money offers that came in were more respectful, and a lot of my clients had offers of work made to them outright – meeting unnecessary – because of their growing status. That didn't mean we didn't still have to scour all the trade papers at the agency – join the dots of disparate conversations, follow up rumours, on behalf of my less prominent actors, certainly the young ones. In fact, looking after youngsters was almost the most fun: talking people into meeting them for work, taking people to see the work they did, promoting that work to others until the day came when the scripts came for them with an if-you-want-it-this-is-yours offer. My work wasn't finished, by any means, but my belief in that actor had been vindicated, and a decent career – bar accidents – was on its way. By now, there were assistants in the agency who would arrange all the subsequent costume fittings, call times, check the required paperwork, and so on. It was very important that each and every acting job was known about by everyone in the agency – and the first thing we did every morning before the day's work started was to go through our notebooks and tell each other what had happened the day before – so the cross-checking that went on was endless, but still, very occasionally, a client would ring and ask crossly why the wrong headshot had been sent to the casting director, or the CV we'd sent hadn't got their last job on it, or the place of the meeting hadn't tallied with the office they'd been sent to, and didn't we know the part we'd put them up for was for a sixty-year-old and every actor there at the casting call was wrinkly and old. (The fact that our client was sixty but hadn't ever publicly admitted to it seemed by the by). All my fault.

Talking about 'accidents': one young man who was On His Way stopped to have sex with his girlfriend on the Common near his apartment. (Why they didn't take the extra steps to get inside one can guess at, but at least it was dark). They were in *flagrante delicto* when a passerby patted him on the back. It wasn't until he was having a bath a little later, he noticed the line of bubbles coming up from his body. He hadn't been patted, he'd been stabbed. I went to see him in hospital. 'You shouldn't be here, you should be looking after your clients,' he said. He was the same guy who'd asked me in Leicester when I'd driven up to see his first night: 'What the fuck are you doing here?' My idea of the agent-actor relationship obviously didn't tally with his. We parted company soon after. But he got better, put on weight and is doing very well.

There was one actor who didn't fare so well. This youngster to whom I'd been recommended came to me after he'd played Hamlet for the Glasgow Citizens Theatre – the Citz, as it's called in the biz, a highly respected repertory venue. To be asked to play Hamlet at such a young age was extraordinary. Andy, my new young client, was great to be around: sharp and funny and very sure of himself. Let's face it: he was an arrogant sod! I remember well the day when the phone rang, and it was Michael Attenborough at the other end (Michael was the artistic director of the Hampstead Theatre at the time. It was where Andy was being auditioned for a new play). 'Your actor, Andrew X, may be the most exciting prospect the world has ever known, Kerry, but he will never work in any theatre I run, now or in the future.' Bloody hell, whatever had he done? It turned out Michael had wandered into the back of the stalls of his theatre while Andy was auditioning, and Andy had objected to his presence: 'Who the fuck is that?' Robin, the director he was working with, tried to placate him by suggesting they get on with the audition, but, 'No, tell fucker to leave. I'm not going on with him here.' Michael, 'the fucker', left – and rang me. Andy didn't get that job. Nor did Michael ever employ him.

It wasn't that he didn't do some amazing work, both on the stage and screen, all the time he was with me. But he just lost his sense of proportion too often.

In the middle of a job he did get with Granada Television, he and a fellow actor had Super Glued their hotel bedroom doors shut after pulling all the furniture out into the corridor. Funny jape, but Granada TV was told that that particular hotel chain would not be accommodating any of their actors in the future.

Another time he was working overseas on the film *Mutiny on the Bounty* when Anthony Hopkins suggested to him he lay off the booze because it could ruin his career. 'What the fuck do you know about anything?' Hopkins was told. This was reported back to me by the film company.

He left London eventually to go and find himself in Yorkshire, and I've never heard from him, or of him, since. Shame: he was a bonus of a guy and a thrilling actor. He'd have done the world proud.

*

For various reasons I moved my office from place to place, trying always to be in central London. I went from Soho to Chelsea, from Kensington to Pimlico. Another ploy: I thought that maybe, as an agent, there might be safety in numbers and made one fairly disastrous decision to join forces with two other agents, Norma Skemp and Nina Quick. When I say join forces, I meant only to share premises with them – I'd found a really nice building in King's Road, Chelsea, my stomping ground from those many years earlier. But from the joint party we gave at the beginning of the amalgamation onwards, I realised that those two other agents' clients thought I was going to be working for them – which was never my intention. Sharing information, the loos and the kitchen, yes. Nothing else. It didn't last long. We broke up the partnership after a couple of years.

The office I then took in Kensington was opposite the Kensington Gardens Hotel which abuts Hyde Park. A cramped space halfway up the building, but great at lunchtime because one could take one's sandwiches into Kensington Gardens just across the road. And the shops nearby in Kensington High Street were very varied, good for mooching through in one's lunch hour. One early morning, walking to work – I now lived up the road in Olympia – I bumped into a tall gangly girl who was walking briskly towards me. It was only when I apologised, and she smiled brilliantly at me I realised she was no other than Diana, Princess of Wales. She seemed happy, so it must have been early days in her marriage.

That same glorious, scatty, but wonderful woman, bench-tested to destruction, died while I was still at that office, and it was because of her that from my window I witnessed the most astounding outpouring of communal emotion. People from all walks of life, of all ages, all carrying flowers, trooped past on the pavement opposite: dressed in tweeds, in hippy clothes, in uniform, some with sticks, some inching along on Zimmer frames, with prams, babies in slings, black, white, citizens of every hue. Silent. From early morning through to when I finished work at six, this endless line of mourners went past, most with their heads bowed – and it went on for two days. The office was a sombre place: what was happening outside was unbearably moving.

My curiosity took me the hundred yards from the office to the great sweep of the park in front of Kensington Palace after that first day of pilgrimage, and I went again three days later when you couldn't see the grass for flowers, most of them still in their cellophane, which stretched for, what, 200 yards between the railings beside the road where I stood up to the Palace where she'd lived. And the railings had messages of love, and teddy bears, and toys, and flowers pinned to them, and groups of people standing with their heads bowed around lit candles. I didn't sob out loud, but it was difficult not to. I hope never to witness anything like that depth of grief again.

*

I had various assistants during those years, from the tough and funny Ruth and Mo, Griselda and Pauline, and Sean from the States, to the strange and ladylike Elaine from Australia. I say strange because it was twice reported to me by others in the building that she would search my waste bin at lunchtime looking for evidence that I was having affairs. With whom I never did find out, but as I had a lovely partner by then, it's really beyond me to know what on earth she was trying to prove. Her disloyalty lost me a treasured client, but I only twigged later after she and I parted company. She went back to

Australia, where I was told she died of a brain tumour. And then there was my long-term accountant and friend, who heeded the bank's encouragement to borrow, borrow, borrow because the rates were so good, but eventually had to ask me if I could pay her year's salary in advance to pay off her debts – which, of course, I couldn't, the money wasn't mine. From that day on my 'friend' bad-mouthed the agency and because some of my actors had made her their accountant too, she lost us more clients. One of my actors worked for her on a part-time basis, so I know what I say to be true.

So it wasn't all a bed of roses.

*

As that 'lovely partner' entered fairly early on in my time of agenting, I should put him centre stage now. Because I met Martin Lovell only four years after I started Kerry Gardner Associates – soon after it became Kerry Gardner Management – he seems always to have featured during that entire period. He didn't. The agency was on its way when we met, but as so much of what I'm going to tell you from now on involves him in its woof and weft, I had better introduce you.

On 1 November 1981, I'd been invited to dinner by a part-time client from Argentina, expecting to meet some friends of his who had recently come over from South America. His guests were late and, as they hadn't had time to install a telephone – we were still without mobiles – he couldn't call them to find out the reason, so after half an hour's wait, he went to get them, leaving me on my own in his flat.

Twenty minutes later, in through the door came the most beautiful man I'd ever met. He was English, hence very apologetic. His friend hadn't been able to come, but here he was, thanks to his host. Hello. His name was Martin. He was my height with dark hair and hazel eyes. His smile could have melted the ice caps. Looking back, I remember the evening as so amazing it now seems almost artificial. How could a celestial being have just dropped by? The three of us chatted away, although I remember little of what was said. It turned out Martin had just recently arrived from South America with a friend – I hoped it wasn't *that* sort of friend, but I didn't ask. His parents were English, his father teaching English at Argentine schools. He'd been at prep school in Sussex with his brother, Dorian, before returning to Buenos Aires to enter the Naval Academy there.

He was an avid enough listener for it to be flattering. As you've read this far, you'll know the sort of things I told him about me, so we won't waste time repeating it.

I so enjoyed him that evening when we met – he had a wonderful sense of mischief and, I suppose, I was flattered that the godlike being opposite me enjoyed my company so much. Intelligent, wry, witty *and* discerning!

His parents had divorced, he didn't like his mother's choice of second husband, an Argentinian diplomat with whom she'd had two further children, both girls, and . . . slowly, through the evening as we talked, our faces seemed to grow closer until they were only inches apart – although they were in fact separated by a table. Because we had been brought up properly, we must have included our host (also called Martin, coincidentally) in this exclusive bubble his guests were in. By the end of the evening, I was hopelessly smitten and wanted to be as one with this stranger forever and ever, amen.

I must have stuck around after he'd gone home because our host told me that there *was* something between the divine man who'd just left and his friend, Jorge, but the reason Jorge hadn't come to dinner was because he'd preferred to go clubbing.

The next day I couldn't believe that I wouldn't be rung back, just too much that had been unspoken was surely still to be resolved, and indeed, the English Martin rang me two days later. Could we talk, please?

We met at my home above the Phoenix Theatre.

He and Jorge were only together because they had both wanted to leave homophobic Argentina, and while Martin wanted our culture, Jorge wanted our country's permissiveness. The evening when Martin and I met, Jorge preferred to go out and dance with strangers. As far as Martin was concerned, I was The One. If I felt the same, he'd part company with Jorge. I was already excited beyond telling by this man, so of course I said yes, please.

I suppose the meeting I've described was about the time of the Aids scare, but throughout my life, I've never had reason to suspect – or had it brought home to me – that anyone I slept with was diseased.

Once we lived together, I got to know this beautiful newcomer to my life – and the depths of this fun guy's unhappiness was a real shock. Mother-dependence was not something I knew about, but after three months of togetherness I did. He would sit at my feet and pour out his woes: his darling mother had died of cancer a year before, and he was distraught. The more he told me, the deeper his distress. Of course, I commiserated, but this endless misery got me down. I had actors to look after and their problems were mine too, so I told him that first Christmas I couldn't cope with it – we had to part after the holidays.

He worked at the time at the Chase Manhattan Bank, an American company that kept American customs, and Boxing Day wasn't a holiday for them. So he went to London for the gap between Christmas and New Year's Eve, leaving me in Norfolk feeling as miserable as I'd ever been – and when he came back, he was the man I'd first met: controlled and fun, seemingly without a care in the world. What was not to admire? A miracle of self-will.

But, of course, it had a cost.

What to say about this most beautiful of men without being crass and obvious. He was startlingly handsome but didn't know it. He was gentle and mischievous: he would make his witty asides with a completely serious face, and he was a wonderful cartoonist. He was a man of his word. He had a prodigious memory. He was never cruel in his observations of others. And from that first meeting onwards, his warmth and obvious approval of me meant there was no question that he loved me as much as I loved him.

Martin's parents couldn't afford to send both their boys to public schools, so for a time when his stepfather Alfredo was working at the consulate in Moscow, he was enrolled at a school there – where not a word of English was spoken or understood. He was also assigned a fellow pupil, a girl, who followed him everywhere and reported on his doings to the authorities. So he muddled through as best he could, and being the boy he was, ended up speaking Russian. Then later still, Alfredo having been posted back to Argentina, he got into the Naval Academy in Buenos Aires on a scholarship (Dorian, the firstborn, all this while at Downside School in England). It was important financially to his parents that Martin maintain his grant and, brainy lad that he was, he came either first or second in every subject he sat throughout his time there. Because of this, he was known as The Rock by the other cadets – I was told this by one of his classmates who came to visit us here with his family not long after we'd met. Martin told me rather scornfully that the Argentine teaching was far superior to the English: 'We took twelve subjects, and when we were tested, if we didn't pass, we had to re-do the whole year again. Here you do eight or nine at most, and even if you don't pass in any of them, if you went to the right school you get a good job in the City.

'And what's this about British politicians being Ministers of This or That in the government when they know next-to-nothing about their briefs? In Argentina, the people put in charge of the country's interests have been specialists in their various capacities: bankers in charge of the economy, agriculturalists in charge of farming, doctors taking care of health, and so on. Here in the UK, they have five minutes to learn everything about something very important on which the country relies before being whisked off ten minutes later to some other Ministry because they've made such a botch of their last brief.'

But he was also proud to tell his Argentine friends that in London, people would put their payment for any newspapers they took from the street stands onto the pavement. His pals were astounded: in Argentina the money wouldn't be lying there long.

Martin really disliked his stepfather. He did his best at school so as to not let his mother down. I think it probable that if she hadn't died when he was thirty-two, he would have stayed wherever she resided – and consequently, I wouldn't have met him. But at a marquee party we gave for a hundred guests for our Noughties Birthday (he was sixty and I was seventy) when it was time for us to say a few words to the assembled company, he stunned me when he said: 'My mother told me I'd be a failure when I grew up, and' – indicating our guests with open arms – 'look at you.' I choked up and couldn't say anything to follow that, except thank everyone for being there. It's possible of course that his mother meant, without expressing it in so many words, that as a homosexual he'd fail in life. But whatever way she meant it, what a terrible thing to say to one's son. And there in front of him were a hundred people to prove her wrong.

And I heard only the other day from a lifelong friend of his who now lives in New York that he'd said rather sharply to her of his mother's love (and I quote): 'She always showed more affection to the dogs than her children.'

Never mind, her hold over him was insidious.

When the naval cadets were going to the cowboy or war films, Martin would secretly sneak off to see the latest Doris Day. It helped that he was bilingual in both Spanish and English. (Although it was one of his buddies who first introduced him to opera, so it wasn't all hazing and macho at the Naval Academy).

He brought his passion for opera and singers – Doris Day included – into my life, and over the years inspired me. Eventually, I could tell most times who the unknown singer on the radio was: of the tenors Tito Schipa and Fritz Wunderlich were obvious – very distinctive – but Domingo, Pavarotti, Corelli, di Stefano, Gedda and his favourite Jussi Björling were difficult to separate by the sound, so I sometimes had to guess by their different ways of delivery from those earlier days of singing and now– but he taught me that too. He loved Callas, Elizabeth Schwarzkopf, Victoria de los Ángeles, and Montserrat Caballé. He played me Isobel Baillie's *Never Sing Louder than Lovely* – what a title, what a sweet voice. We discovered together and fell in love with Jessye Norman, Natalie Dessay, Jonas Kaufmann, and the peerless Lorraine Hunt Lieberson.

And I 'gave' him: Richard Strauss, Peter Skellern, Ivor Novello, Edward Elgar, Carly Simon, Michael Feinstein and Sibelius, as well as theatre and contemporary dance. We took it from there over the years, but I could never convince him that chamber music was worth persevering with – something I'd not that long before come to appreciate myself. We shared his passion for Beethoven, but I was never fully won over by his adoration of Mozart; because Wolfgang is played on Radio 3 so relentlessly, I always seem to know which note is coming next. (Talking about that: what about Bruckner – so well regarded, so endlessly repetitive? Some of what he wrote is without doubt beautiful, but the word 'bombastic' must have been coined for him).

Martin had a special love for the countertenor voice. He told me of going to a concert in a cathedral in Buenos Aires; the weather was very cold so that when Alfred Deller and his sons appeared in their fur coats and started singing, the audience looked about them. Where was this extraordinary sound coming from? Surely not from those three burly bearded men standing on the steps in front of them. Personally, I'm still struggling to fully appreciate the countertenors' strange neither male-nor-female voices but have just heard someone select Philippe Jaroussky singing Vivaldi for his final choice of music on Michael Berkeley's *Private Passions*, so I've done the extravagantly easy thing, and I've ordered the CD from Amazon. I'm still working on it, Martin.

And, I suppose, the easiest way to reduce me to tears is to play the *Four Last Songs* by Richard Strauss, sung by Jessye Norman. I once played them to a dear friend in the kitchen and embarrassingly found myself sobbing uncontrollably between the fridge and the sink. 'You'll love this,' I had told her cheerfully beforehand, and she was dumbfounded at what that word meant to me.

If I was only allowed one composer's work on a desert island, I would find it impossible to choose between Schubert and Haydn. I suppose I'd have to plump for Schubert even though there would be so much less to listen to than the Haydn. But Schubert for the romanticism, I guess – and of course the chunes. Ah, but Haydn for the fun!

I infected Martin with my adoration of Ivor Novello's music. We'd sit and listen to a double CD of his songs sometimes, and one of our favourite parts of it wasn't the music of 'My Dearest Dear' from *The Dancing Years*, although that is lovely, but the introduction Novello had written for it. It would always make us chortle, and through the years, we found so many different uses for different parts of it in everyday conversations.

Ivor Novello is the composer, Mary Ellis the singer. It goes:

Her: And now let's do some work. I can't get the last page of that gavotte. Have you got it there?

Him: No, but I've got something else I'd like you to try. Something I wrote last night.

Her: Oh, I know, another waltz.

Him: No, no, not another waltz, no. It's just a simple little tune – not a money-maker. I wrote the words too. See if you like it.

Her: It's dedicated to me!

Him: They are all dedicated to you.

Her: Oh, Rudi, your writing. Really! Say them for me. I don't want to spoil it.

Him: 'My dearest dear . . .'

Of course, the pronunciation is very laid-back English 1930s/50s, and we would quote bits of it to each other in public when appropriate – and it had to be unexpected to make us laugh out loud. Did I tell you my partner was also a wonderful mimic?

Anything else I've not told you about him? He could speak English, Spanish and French fluently and had a smattering of Russian and Italian. But, marring his utter perfection, he was also a hypochondriac. And he was a teetotaller. But he thought his countrymen were more fun when they'd had a drink, so I was OK.

There's a lovely anecdote of him as a boy which I asked him to repeat in front of folk every now and then, it gave me such pleasure.

Martin was eleven, his brother Dorian twelve when they were sent back from Sweden, where Alfredo, their stepfather, was stationed, to their school in England. They were put on the train to the port of Gothenburg, from where they would take a ship to Tilbury. Onboard the train, they palled up with another youngster, and because they had nothing better to do, the three of them went to the end of the train to look out of the last carriage. They arrived at the station of Laxa when Martin decided to go back to their compartment. He'd been sitting there for some time when it occurred to him that his brother and their Swedish friend had been absent for rather longer than expected, so he went in search of them and, getting to the end of the train without finding them, wondered why the walk he'd just made seemed that much shorter than before. In the meantime, and this was told to me by Dorian, the two lads, on deciding to return to their seats, found the train had divided, and from their now-first carriage could see Martin's end of the train disappearing into the distance. They got off at once, pretty damned scared and the station master – who spoke perfect English, wouldn't you know – flagged down the next train, an express to Gothenburg, where the three of them were reunited. Asked if he wasn't frightened, Martin, aged eleven, replied, 'Why would I be? I had the money and the passports.' So young, so cool.

A new relation of Martin's would pop up every ten years or so. The family he introduced me to initially was his brother, Dorian, the QC, his Argentinian half-sisters, Laila and Dianna . . . and then, on a fairly regular basis, more turned up. His father must have sired willy-nilly outside his marriage, and there was little surprise when the phone rang to hear someone new lay claim to kinship. Martin didn't know of his half-brother John until he was thirty (it was to John's and his wife Pauline's flat we went to in Cape Town) and then another half-sister turned up – this was the adorable Carmen – and then later still an ex-policeman from Liverpool contacted Dorian, having seen his name in the papers . . .

Once we were 'an item', I took him to meet my depleted Sim

family. Naomi took him to her heart, but Merlith didn't. She thought he was a bit camp, which pissed me off – he was an impossibly perfect man to me.

I've always rather enjoyed tales from the supernatural and been intrigued by people who 'see' things. And, I *think*, I envy them. But it came as a shock when, that first weekend evening at Forrigan, Martin told me he'd met Ally earlier in the day, Ally being long dead.

Apparently, I had been painting at my easel in the conservatory, and Martin was on the sofa next door, reading. This was just after lunch, and the rest of the family were having a siesta. Ally came into the room wearing a dressing-gown and sat down in his usual chair at the fireplace. Martin had risen when he came into the room, and Ally indicated he should sit, saying, 'Let's not interrupt Kerry, let's you and me get to know each other.' And it had gone from there. The most natural conversation as to how we'd met, were we happy where we were living, how it must be very different for him after his time in Argentina – a little as I imagine a father might interrogate a new son-in-law. After a while he left the room.

Martin asked Naomi later that afternoon if Ally had ever had this long blue tartan dressing gown, and she had told him it was his usual attire in the mornings. She accepted what he'd experienced without surprise – although Martin could never have seen that particular piece of Ally's wardrobe. I should have been spooked I suppose, but I wasn't. That my adopted father approved my choice of partner – no surprise there. And even then, the whole incident seemed everyday believable – probably because both he and Naomi were so matter of fact about it.

Martin was more in tune with that other world than me, although he never reported anything else that had happened to him along the same lines. (My mother heard the sound of massive wings beating just after my father Geoff Gardner died in their house in Ireland). The only thing I remember happening to me was when Martin and I were in a rented gîte for one night in France (we were thinking of buying a house over there), and I woke up at three in the morning because it seemed Martin was walking noisily across the room in the pitch black. 'Are you OK?' I asked him. 'What you say?' came his sleepy reply. 'Where are you going?' I asked. 'What do you mean, I'm in bed,' he said. Oh, that's odd, I thought and went back to sleep.

Apropos my mother and 'things that go bump in the night': when she lived in Ireland at Piper's Hill with Darell, they'd been invited to dinner by their neighbours in the farm across the road. This farm was on land owned by the firm of Lily & Skinner (one or the other kept their racehorses there), so it was of considerable acreage, and it was looked after by this middle-aged couple. Soon after my mother and Darell's arrival at their house, so early during the conversation before dinner, the wife had told them that some very odd things had happened when she and her husband had first settled at the farm: for instance, she had been at the sink one morning when a rather cross looking man appeared at the window in front of her. The sudden appearance of his face was quite a shock, but as the man beckoned to her to come out, she went to the kitchen door and opened it expecting him to be there. No one. She stepped out into the snow and looked for him. No sign. So she went to the spot where he must have been standing to look in through her window . . . and found footsteps in the snow right up to that point, but no footprints going away.

Another time the small table on the upstairs landing had fallen down to the hallway without apparent reason, and her husband had gathered up the pieces to see if he couldn't mend it the next day. In the morning, they found the table back in its place at the top of the stairs, completely unharmed. While the couple were recounting these tales, the lampshade from the standard lamp flew across the room and banged against the wall opposite. 'Please don't worry, these things are always happening,' the wife had said. She picked up the shade and replaced it. 'Quite harmless. It's never directed against the living.'

That same woman had also sometimes seen, during the misty days they often had in those parts, troops of strangely dressed men tramping across the field opposite. Intrigued, she'd done some research on the house and found out that the Romans had once been in the area.

I know it's stretching credulity further, but I'm just reporting what my mother told me: so that same evening, they had just finished their pudding when there was a huge thump at the windows but, drawing back the curtains, they couldn't discern anything outside in the pitch black. However, there were quite deep scratches in the glass. (I don't know how Darell coped with all this – I'd have been long gone).

At the coffee stage, my mother needed to go to the loo, which was upstairs. She had just sat down on the toilet seat when the lights in the room dimmed and looking up, she saw one of the bulbs on the small wooden chandelier was blinking out. Ten seconds later, another faded before going out. By the time the third dimmed, she was racing for the door.

Before they left, they went to look at the window glass, and the scratches had disappeared. I don't think my mother and Darell socialised with the couple again.

*

While we're about it, I'll finish my mother's story: She returned to London from Ireland once she'd divorced Darell and lived way beyond her means in possibly the two most expensive neighbourhoods in Central London, first in Knightsbridge near Harrods, then a hundred yards from the Thames in Tite Street, Chelsea. She married a fifth time, and it can only have been because of the double-barrelled surname he had, which she'd always wanted, because five years after they got hitched, she got rid of Mr Try-Out by changing the locks on her flat. She kept every single one of his belongings, including all his first edition Henry Williamsons (of *Tarka the Otter* fame). The last time her fifth and last husband was sighted in the City, he was looking the worse for drink.

I say that about the double-barrelled surname because after that last husband's expulsion, she reverted to calling herself by Darell's surname, Farmer, adding, without asking his permission, his second Christian name, thus becoming Mrs Eline Langford Farmer.

Affected? Ma mère?

By the time she moved down to Dorset, my brother and I were having to support her financially. Came the day when she informed me that God had told her while she was watching television that she should go on a Caribbean cruise for her health. She handed me a travel brochure: 'Which of these do you think would be nicest, darling?' Bloody hell! All five cruises were exorbitantly expensive. I chose the second cheapest ('lovely, good choice, darling,') and she booked the second most expensive. She had been living a lonely life in Chelsea, and I was earning then, so I didn't really begrudge her the trip. But I was startled she suddenly had a hot-line to God. My bank balance was grateful God didn't have any later pronouncements.

At about that time, because my friends and benefactors had moved from their manor house in Norfolk to a smaller villa by the sea, I thought it only fair to give them back the cottage they'd rented-me-for-life so that the estate they were selling didn't have this little plot of land with me in the middle.

My mother decided to move from Chelsea to Blandford Forum in Dorset because it wasn't far from where my brother and his family were living outside Salisbury. I had loved Dorset from the time I'd been working on Bournemouth Pier, spending that perfect working summer in Slepe, so now without the place in Norfolk to go to, and as we felt our weekend visits to the country were essential to our well-being, I suggested to Martin we buy somewhere not too far away from her and Mark. (Mind you, not too close). So that's what we did. Martin didn't really like my mother – I'm sure my attitude to her biased him somewhat, but it didn't help she thought to her dying day that he was a 'dago'. That I wasn't an Indian despite being born in India of English parents and that the same criteria should apply to him never impinged.

My love put up with a hell of a lot for me.

Martin and I once went to my brother and sister-in-law's house for a Christmas dinner, and our mother who was staying with them over the holiday was there. We were all dressed as for a banquet, a tradition she's insisted on even when she'd been with us in our tiny kitchen in Norfolk. So there was our mother, who'd been to the hairdressers the day before, looking glamorous in her turquoise full-length housecoat, jewels sparkling – this time in their kitchen. We were halfway through the meal, their baby Eleanor in her carrycot in a corner, when my mother remarked, having been told that her daughter-in-law, Angela, was still breastfeeding: 'You know breastfeeding is an affectation?' Angela was very upset and swept up the carrycot before leaving the room. My mother, instead of apologising, was trying to justify her views to those of us left at the festive feast when I was astonished to feel the table tilting away from me and the plates and cutlery sliding off onto my mother's gown. What the hell . . .? My mother, still sitting, was now covered in detritus from the meal. Indomitable spirit that she was she went on trying to justify herself, seemingly unaware of the food, plates and cutlery on her lap. And my brother, sitting on the same side as Martin and me, bent over the table, found some butter, scooped up a handful, and leaning over, slowly and deliberately smeared the butter over our mother's face and into her hair. It's a shocking image that will stay with me till I die.

The above reminds me of another Christmas holiday when she was with Martin and me in our tiny two-up-two-down cottage in Norfolk. It was New Year's Eve, and a row I was having with her escalated to the point where I had to leave the room and go upstairs, I was in such a fury. But I could still hear. So when she turned her guns on Martin, I rushed down the steps into the living room, shoved her out through the front door into the snow, and banged it shut, making sure she heard the key turn. I was heaving with hatred, but the sight of her in the snow, in all her finery, sobered me up enough to realise the enormity of what I'd done – but just like her, I was damned if I was going to relent. Martin sat me down and tried to pacify me, but I was having none of it. 'I won't have you spoken to like that!' It wasn't until we heard my mother's car returning twenty minutes later that I realised what I'd done had been pointless because, one, she wouldn't get far in the deep snow, and two, she wouldn't have been able to find an open petrol station at midnight. So in she came, talking about not having enough petrol to go far, I mumbled, 'sorry', and we had another couple of 'tiptoe' days before coming back to London.

*

My mother had a lumpectomy on her left breast and was assiduous in doing the arm exercises given her by her physio. Ten years later, so not long after she moved to Dorset, the sore spot in her mouth which wouldn't heal was diagnosed as cancer. The surgeon offered her two options: cutting away a part of her cheek and tongue, so she would have to learn to speak again or drugs. The thought of the disfigurement was too appalling to this still attractive woman, so she decided to go with the drugs. From hale and hearty with a sore in her mouth to a bag of bones that could only ingest slivers of ice took just six months. Don't believe doctors when they tell you that drugs can control the pain. For the last weeks of her life in Blandford Hospital, my mother was in agony and desperate to die. She begged us, her two sons, to have her killed.

She died many years ago. For the first seventeen years of my life when I only saw her once a year for an eight-week holiday, I thought she was the most wonderful person in the world. Once I got to know her, I found it more and more difficult to cope with her snobbishness, her racism, her deep-in-the-bone self-centredness with its utter disregard for other people's feelings. So although, I knew the excuses for her behaviour were in her upbringing, her beauty, her treatment by husbands who loved her well but not wisely, her superior manner towards the rest of humanity drove me wild.

She was clever, no doubt; the year she applied for a Blue Badge Guide, out of the hundred applicants who sat the exams, she was one of only eight people who were awarded it – which meant she was officially allowed to show coachloads of tourists not only around all London's historical landmarks but around the British Isles as well. Intelligent and opinionated, but without an ounce of wisdom. – in my opinion.

Now I don't get to meet her and see her only in my mind, I am just about getting to tolerate her again, warts and all. But along with all the fun and charm she could dispense, she caused a lot of hurt, so I might not make it to loving her again – and I don't feel guilty.

CHAPTER 15
Diva

I started the One Two Three game with Miranda. These are the rules: you agree the amount of time you need to read a script, whether it's an offer or a 'would you be interested?' one, and at the designated hour, you ring each other, and on the count of three say, simultaneously, Yes or No – accept or not. I can only remember one time when we disagreed, and I persuaded her to change her mind. She was nominated for Best Actress by BAFTA for that.

I tried not to persuade actors against their choices unless I was sure they were wrong, but as with my example above, Marcia Warren was another I urged to accept the larger of two roles she'd been offered in Richard Harris's *Stepping Out* – and she won a SWET Award. (Nowadays, they're called the Oliviers).

While she was with me, Miranda was twice nominated for an Oscar: once for Best Supporting Performance, and a few years later, for Best Performance – along with nominations for Golden Globes, BAFTAs, *Evening Standard Awards*, New York Critic's Circle Awards, most of which she won, (I may have missed a few out). The Oscar and Globe nominations were for *Damage* (Best Supporting) and *Tom and Viv* (Best Actress). She and I were flown over at great expense by the film producers for these films – and it wasn't just one trip per film, but several, all of them to promote the product before the awards were voted on. It was for the Best Supporting Oscar – the first of two Oscar visits – that there was a third ticket offered, which Miranda generously offered Martin.

What to say about these promotional freebies – which the actor well and truly earns, because they are *hard work*?

Imagine a small hotel room with a couple of gilded chairs, spotlights and a camera. The performer would sit in a chair opposite a representative from any one of a multitude of national US television companies, who asked questions while the camera recorded the interview over his or her shoulder. After five minutes of this, the representative was given a tape of the chat, which they took back to Chicago/Dallas/Des Moines/New Orleans/wherever they came from, and a small snippet would be shown there by that local public broadcaster, basically to snare the interest of the viewers in the upcoming film. Back in the hotel suite, the next interviewer would come in and ask much the same questions, be given a tape . . . *ad infinitum*. This could take up a whole morning, interviewers coming from all over the States, five minutes for each. Or, maybe another time, three large round tables would be set up in a hotel ballroom around which sat representatives of various national newspapers, and at each table one of the leading actors of the film joined them, and those same questions were asked – maybe twenty minutes of questions per table before the artists vacated their seats and moved to the next table. (The three interviewees at the one I attended were Juliette Binoche, Jeremy Irons and Miranda. That was promotion for the Louis Malle film, *Damage*).

The questions were roughly the same, of course they were, but the performer couldn't look bored – each had to be given thought as though new-minted.

Then there were the very early morning radio interviews in various parts of town, photo sessions and, for Miranda, a very successful television appearance on *Saturday Night Live*.

I was basically a dogsbody, trying to make sure she had everything that could make life more bearable in these bizarre situations – but I was a very pampered pooch because alongside her, I travelled first class, was put up in the best hotels in town, with a car and driver whenever needed, tea at the Russian Tea Rooms in New York, parties in Tinsel Town, etc. etc. Hard graft but, for me as a once-actor living vicariously, huge fun. Well, I guess 'huge fun' at the Oscars was only true the first time around.

Being treated like celestial beings with no expense spared made me cynical. Many years before I had lived for ten months in New York with no money, and I was almost invisible. Now, when Robert De Niro came into his office in SoHo while Miranda was being met by his representative, and asked me, *sotto voce*, if he should agree to an interview with the English *Guardian* newspaper, and I told him he should because it was a journal which I personally read and trusted, he appeared to value my advice.

The couturiers vied to dress each and every nominee for the publicity it brought their clothes. For Miranda, Valentino, Donna Karan and others. For one of her promotional visits, she and I went to Calvin Klein's vast workshop in lower Manhattan where Miranda was gifted several outfits: for daytime wear, cocktails, dinners, for the ceremony itself. When I asked, I think innocently, what the men wore on these occasions, Calvin, who had been looking after Miranda personally, ordered up a dinner suit which he had recently designed, fitted me with it, and got the assistant to bring the accoutrements – tasselled scarf, tie, and all. At the risk of sounding ungrateful, the legs of the trousers could have accommodated another set of limbs as well as my own (imagine a sail flapping idly when a yacht is becalmed), but I wore them all with pride on three visits before lending the DJ to a covetous friend of my dimensions back in England. (Martin didn't want them, although in shoe size, trouser length, and height, we were identical. The trousers were a bit OTT – but the whole looked expensively smart, which was exactly right for the showbiz cameras). Back in England, the friend to whom I lent the suit was sick all down the front of it. I gave it to him to keep.

There was a young guy in Los Angeles, Joe Simon, who was assigned to us by the film company to take care of our wants. Not only was he good to look at, his other attractions as far as I was concerned was that he had an adorable, waist-high slobbery dog and carried a ferret around inside his shirt. Once, when I'd told him Miranda's birthday was the following day, he came up with the suggestion that as it was also David Hockney's birthday, perhaps we would like to go and have dinner with the artist up at his home in the Hollywood hills? Effing hell, of course we would! So the next evening found us sitting in the setting of one of the artist's paintings – I've seen that painting since on Tate Britain's walls – listening to the great man talking about a trip he'd made in a Winnebago through Death Valley. He is an enjoyable genius to hang with, and the dinner was fun with the eight of us and his dachshunds. After dinner, he asked us if we'd like to visit his studio. Really? We all trooped outside into the dark to what looked like an ordinary garage, but it was the TARDIS inside: a vast space with, at the far end, steps leading up to a gallery, and on the walls all around hung huge portraits of his dachshunds in various poses. I once went into a room at the Royal Academy in London and saw a roomful of Monet's haystacks and was so overwhelmed I began to blub. I wasn't quite as emotional looking at Hockney's dogs but had that same feeling of awe. What commitment and love there was displayed on those blank walls. When I went around one of David Hockney's most recent exhibitions in London, I got that same sense of *joie de vivre* from his drawings and paintings, and I noticed that everyone looking at his work was smiling. An artist who communicates directly to his viewers without complication. That's not to say he's unsubtle. So, yes, a copper-bottomed national treasure – and I got to see his dachshunds before the general public!

American film companies put you up at some of the most splendiferous hotels when they need you to help promote their wares, whether you're over there for the prize ceremonies or the press junkets. I remember gratefully the Four Seasons, the St. Regis in New York, the Nikko, The Peninsula, the Hôtel du Cap outside Cannes, and I met, breakfasted, lunched and dined in the lobbies, coffee shops and dining rooms of many more. Breakfast meetings were very popular at the time, probably still are, and it was often a battle to keep one's face alert so early in the day. But baskets of fresh pastries were everywhere you looked – that was my reward.

The companies don't merely pay for your accommodation but are happy to book you a suite. Two sumptuous rooms with a big softly lit marbled bathroom (with even softer towelling) with use of gym, sauna, pool and masseurs just down the hall. You get a daily allowance too – but they work you so hard there's not much chance of spending it. They also pay travel expenses. Transport is at your beck and call morning and night. You have a wonderfully cushy time in the evenings, but you are *very* busy during the day. Make-up is applied to your client on what seems like an hourly basis before she talks to producers, photographers and admen; more make-up before a photo opportunity in Central Park or a roof pool in LA; phone interviews with journalists from all over the world; journeys across town for fittings. Yet more make-up for magazine photoshoots; meetings set up by your American agent-partner in Downtown New York or LA with actor-producers; 45th-floor television chat shows in front of audiences in studios looking down at the ice-skaters in Rockefeller Center; rehearsing a couple of spots to slot into the *Saturday Night Live* television show; workouts in the gyms because you really get no exercise – and that's where you find yourself pedalling away on the exercise bike next to Andy MacDowell who's pounding the hell out of a running machine beside you. Who's complaining? It's glamorous, tiring and out-of-this-world unreal.

I was looking after Miranda during one of those marathon small-room hotel interviews, made sure she had everything she wanted, and suggested I might go out to get some air for five minutes. She couldn't come with me, poor love. Outside the hotel, I found myself at the top of Rodeo Drive, so I wandered down it looking at the fantastically expensive gowns in the couturier windows, until I saw a Barneys, an emporium I knew from New York, so in I went. The most beautifully coiffured female slid towards me, deliciously scented, and asked me if she could help. Not wanting to look like a gormless tourist, I asked her if they had a plain white sweater. (Martin had always wanted one, and the only ones I'd found in England were either patterned or the knobbly cricket-type). So this subtly perfumed vision led the way to a glass display case, and there was the perfect gift: a plain ivory-white sweater. 'That's great,' I said. 'Could you please have it gift-wrapped, and I'll come back to pick it up in an hour or so.' An hour later, I went to another counter at the back of Barneys to collect the sweater, was handed the parcel and told the price. I nearly fainted, but not wanting to look a complete nitwit, paid for it with a dead-pan face. (My eyelid might have flickered). He loved it, did Mart. It was his to do with as he liked, but the next time I saw it, it was nestling with his muddy boots in the back of his car. Of course, I didn't say anything, and so he never knew that this vicuna and wild-silk sweater, so perfectly plain in its display case, nearly gave me a heart attack.

'Please don't interact with the animals. It could be dangerous.' This was said to me on entering a huge studio loft in Manhattan prior to a magazine shoot. There was an open cage with a parakeet inside, and the animals around were a *beautiful* Saluki dog and a gorgeous, rare, furrrrry cat, brushed and manicured to the tips of its toes. After what seemed an hour of waiting while Miranda's make-up was being seen to, I got very bored, so started sucking my teeth for the bird – which attracted the dog, and not to be outdone, the cat. The parakeet was very intrigued and flew out of the cage onto my shoulder, from where it roamed over my head, the dog by this time leaning against me while I rubbed its ears, and the cat climbed up my body to the crook of my left arm. When the photographer, the owner of these gorgeous creatures, next looked my way, that was what met his eye – a leaning-post with a bird on its head. He gave me a disgusted look, but his animals were so obviously content he didn't say anything, just raised his eyes to heaven. (Perhaps it's not too late to be a vet).

Photographers. Everywhere we went outside the enclaves of our hotels betting was that at least one person would take photographs. The big melees seemed to consist of shouts (This way! Over here! To me, to me!) and blinding flashes. But away from the venues, the stars were constantly asked by strangers if they'd mind being photographed with this child, or him, or her. Then there were the others, the guys who already had several studio portraits of Miranda and wanted her signature on them – sometimes as many as four each of four different poses. (I'd never seen some of those pictures of her before. They certainly weren't supplied by my office). We were told that these photos were sold on, and I suppose it depended on how famous you were as to how much the vendor could ask for them. So the performer, by signing these portraits, was helping these parasites make a living. One of the most distressing sights burnt forever into my memory was when Miranda was followed to the Departure gate at LAX Airport by a man who screamed at her disappearing back, 'I hope you die soon, you English cunt!' as he threw a sheaf of photos after her. What had she done to deserve this bile? She'd refused to sign the photos.

Parties. The studios spend a fortune on these. Part of the sell to be sure. The food and drinks are expensive but not very interesting, it's who's there that matters. Schmoozing and business, that's what these jamborees are about. Which means that if you're a newcomer to these scenes of excess and don't know who's who, they become interchangeable in your mind. The venues themselves: sometimes huge rooms, sometimes small restaurants, or marquees on the beach at Cannes or Los Angeles. Glare and noise, everyone eyeing up everyone to see who's important, smiles from gleaming facades, or beautifully gowned down-the-nose aloofness, sincerity/insincerity – who knows? – rapid-fire quips, glad-to-be-here smiles till your face aches.

The Governors Ball after the Oscars: on every table a winner – and a chocolate Oscar centrepiece. Conniving people, beautiful people, mannequin people after your endorsement. The actors were products, like the goody bags which we'd find at our table settings, or on theatre seats, with the most extravagant prezzies inside. Actors were there to catch the eye and sell the films, along with clothes and accessories. Miranda wore gems worth multiple thousands of dollars lent to her by the big jewellers. Some sheikh from Saudi Arabia bought the fabulous necklace and earrings she wore at the Oscars. Sitting in Jeddah, he'd seen them on television and got on the phone.

(It was at the dinner after one of those ceremonies that Martin decided the chocolate Oscar in the middle of our table was going to go to waste, so he stole it for his friend Lucia back in England. He got it from Los Angeles to London intact, and then travelling to meet her, dropped it on the platform at Waterloo Station).

Travel. Long, low stretch limos, ugly in their absurd ostentatiousness – scrambling to get in and out of what seems an enlarged cigar-tube-cum-conference-room with cut-glass decanters, television, music and black glass which makes the world outside charcoal grey, is effortful.

Stars arriving late for screenings. Impressive, or just fuck-the-rest-of-you vanity?

Then there are the on-the-spot interviews you hadn't been told about. The studio publicist having made sure their clients look the dog's bollocks, they scramble out of the stretch looking as though their clothes have been in a brawl. They smile at strangers who stand around the outside doorway chattering excitedly at the Star Coming Among Them, and with their minders make their speedy way through empty halls towards the clatter and hum of caged humanity, and once nearly there, having been filtered through Security with passes checked, the actor is buttonholed by someone who pulls him or her away from the group who have tethered them to some sort of normality. 'We need you to talk to the press before you go into dinner. This way.' And, smiling all the while, the Star, in dressed-to-kill crumple, is taken to a large room in which maybe twenty to thirty men and women are standing, cameras flashing, and they're led to a lectern where they are asked, in an abrasive, jocular way (because this is the thirteenth someone they've talked to that evening, and there are probably ten to come) about their clothing, their belief in themselves, who they came with, 'are you going to win, and if not, who do you feel should win?' and your credentials for being a Brit in Tinseltown. Smiling answers, ducking and weaving, the performer finishes by thanking the tormentors for the grilling. The gang chorus 'good luck'. After the ceremony, if you've won, the same group are thrilled for your success, ask congratulatory questions, and you kiss and fondle the trophy till it is dull with sweat and lip-prints, as all the while those ubiquitous cameras flash.

The Oscars. Remember the Oscar ceremony takes place at midday, so you come out afterwards into the dusk – twilight comes early.

You get up early on the day, your mind detached, dreading every moment to come, excited as hell. You shower in your immense bathroom, making sure you clean carefully between the toes.

And then suddenly your bedroom with its nice view seems full of people, all nervously excited, the banter so over-the-top, which fades to dead silence as it gets nearer to the off. Absolutely everyone is winsome, and your shoelace just broke. You're ready for a mental breakdown as your hair is teased to look natural and sprayed hard to make sure it stays natural throughout the long day ahead. Someone knocks on your door. 'The car will be here in half an hour. Will you be ready, or do you need more time?'

Dressed in our bespoke evening clothes, the sun scorching outside, Miranda and I go down in the packed lift to meet our group. I meant to ring Room Service for a sandwich but imagined the gaps in my teeth filled with gunge as I smiled, so didn't. I'm feeling sick now, so who needs food? That man in the lift with us is staggeringly good-looking, but then what do you expect, this is Hollywood? Oh, hold on, it's my partner, Martin! Bugger, I stood on whoever's behind me's toes. No one's complained. I look round. No one to be seen. Odd. I've trodden on something. I leave the lift and after me, dressed like a western gambler, Sylvester Stallone comes out. Those must have been his toes. Did his cowboy boots have steel caps? Heaven's he's small! But so brawny! From his massive shoulders to his mashed toes, he's a lower-case v.

After the ministrations of a dozen people, Miranda looks like the national treasury. We smile at each other wanly.

We've asked for a town car – as against a limo – and it's escorted by overhead helicopters through deserted streets to the venue. We become part of a long line of cars inching along the road to the red carpet.

And here we are. We step out of the car into a blast of heat, and lights and NOISE and the continuing thwack-thwacks of the helicopters above. A red-carpeted valley bottom has been created between raised bleachers where the public stand *and* SCREAM. We walk the scarlet floor, looking to left and right, waving, pointing to imaginary friends in the joe-public crowd through the pops and dazzle of cameras and arc-lights. We have to walk slowly because the stars who've been set down just before us, and the ones before them, are moving towards the man with the microphone at the far end – and his voice is amplified so it can be heard above the pandemonium. And then it's Miranda's turn, and she's asked . . . I've no recollection.

Then into a huge glass foyer which seems cavernous in the silence, and there we see a snaking line of couples, maybe thirty yards long – evening-clothed men and women dressed like us, standing two by two in Indian file. 'Who are they?' I ask. No one answers me. I'm invisible. And then we are ushered into the vast auditorium, where we're shown our seats. And because she is one of The Nominated, we sit at the end of a row near the stage to make it easier to get out, walk down the aisle and accept an award – should it come to that.

The auditorium fills. The Games at the Colosseum must have been like this. Countdown for the television cameras, and then we're off. The compere comes on to face the four thousand people present, but he's brash and funny, and the laughs he gets are genuine.

There are a couple of breathtakingly zippy musical routines from film scores, one of them to a song from Alan Menken and Tim Rice which, two hours later, wins Best Song. Though I'm wound tighter than a watch spring, I'm sort of enjoying myself in a hideous way observing all this costly glitz, my body radiating heat, and feeling sick to the pit of my stomach – where a bass drum seems to have set up house. This is life in a parallel universe.

The number of nominees, the number of categories, the whole thing seems to go on for a weekend. There are commercial breaks in the televised show, and that's when members of the elite in the front half of the auditorium can leave to get a drink or have a pee. (Why would the technicians who are competing want to know the actors' results, and vice versa?) We can get a drink and watch what's on stage on the monitors in the bars. So people are in and out of their seats whenever there's a break in filming – and that's when I understand the reason for that long line of waiting couples in the foyer before the show started. They're there to fill the vacated places during the commercial breaks, so when the cameras start again for the next segment of the ceremony, it looks to the public watching at home as if the place is still jam-packed with the well-known. I felt sorry for the two pairs of people who were turfed out of our seats when we came back from our sorties to the bar. Seated with the celebrated one minute, then back to the foyer and the end of the line the next.

The Best Actress award eventually arrives. 'And the Best Actress Award goes to . . . (endless opening of envelope) 'Beatrix Potter'. (Or whoever. Miranda didn't win, so what did I care? On the other hand, when, for the Best Supporting Actress Oscar, which a few years earlier Miranda was also up for, they announced that MARisa Tomei had won it, there was one dizzying moment as the name was announced when I thought Miranda'd got it).

But the feeling of mounting dread beforehand, the silence as the nominee's names were read out and snippets of their performance were shown on the huge screens behind the announcer, the cheers by the public for their favoured stars, well, the reason I'd been born became surreal. How could a balanced life lead to this?

Our party went to the Governors Ball afterwards, where everyday Hollywood studio life became recognisable again. 'So sorry . . . you deserved to win . . . have you got anything else coming up? . . . I'm sure there'll be something else for you soon . . . get your agent to get in touch with . . . better luck next time.'

Faces came into sharper focus at the later parties we'd been invited to, the fabulously famous, the soon-to-be-famous, the wannabes – make-up shining, glamour, make-up smudging, glamour, sweat, more make-up and more glamour. All I wanted was to go to bed. Terror, however suavely masked, takes its toll.

Aaaah . . . when I am in bed and about to fall asleep, I remember with a shock that I've signed a chitty for Miranda's priceless jewels which she is no doubt jiggling about on a dance floor somewhere – and where I am now, I can't lay down my life for them.

A long flight back to England and, as though nothing untoward had happened, I'm back at work doing my stuff, the hours jumbled with jetlag.

*

It was at the Cannes Film Festival that I waited with an impatient French audience for one of the *Charlie's Angels* to arrive for a screening of a film in which she'd co-starred. We'd been tipped off that she'd had her stash of drugs stolen from her hotel bedroom, so wasn't sure to turn up. She arrived eventually, twenty minutes late, stoned out of her mind, tottering on the highest of heels, giggling girlishly, and excusing herself in half-formed Franglais sentences, but with a pussy-pelmet that showed off her still-gorgeous legs. The grumbles died reluctantly as the *ooh-la-la* took over.

*

I wasn't just passive in my efforts to enjoy the work I was doing. I often tried personally to create it – as with the theatre complex I told you about. That wonderful playwright and poet Christopher Fry wrote a four-part series for Yorkshire Television called *The Brontës of Haworth*, which I absolutely loved. It was cleverly realised with first-rate performances, and after its transmission on screen, whenever I saw Christopher at Forrigan, I urged him to adapt it for the theatre. He always demurred, saying he couldn't see how. Many years later, when Alan Ayckbourn told me he wanted to do a *Nicholas Nickleby*-type production on his stage at Scarborough (*The Life and Adventures of Nicholas Nickleby* - or *NickNick* as it was known in the business - was a stunning RSC staging of the Dickens novel directed by Trevor Nunn, the whole story being told over two full-length plays), I suggested he contact Christopher and ask him to adapt *The Brontës of Haworth*. Alan got very excited – Anne Brontë was buried in Scarborough. Christopher said he couldn't do it, so I asked him if I might try. 'Well, if you think you can, why not?' was the reply.

So that's exactly what I did, cutting and pasting (in the days before computers) Christopher's television scripts, even incorporating his introduction to the four episodes by dividing up the sentences between a cast of twelve so as to set the scene before the play-proper started. I re-jigged some of the incidents in the story, using only Christopher's lines – except for a single sentence which I composed because I needed to make sense of a change. And Alan made a superb job of staging it. It looked wonderful and was beautifully acted on the Scarborough theatre-in-the-round stage.

I had worked late into the nights and at weekends to do it, but it was exciting and a labour of love. When Christopher's agent rang and said we should talk about money, I had forgotten that side of things. 'What do you suggest?' she asked. 'Um ... 50/50, do you think?' says I. 'I mean, only for this showing, but if it hadn't been for me, there wouldn't be a stage play. So ... I don't know. What do you think?' She said that sounded about right and rang off. Next day she called again. 'Christopher can't believe you have demanded that much for what is after all his work. He could easily have done it himself. We think 1% of Box Office is more than enough.' I was outraged. 'No, he can pay for the secretary who typed it out for me – not a penny more!' She sounded embarrassed, 'I was afraid you might say something like that.'

It reminded me somewhat of the story told of the composer Brahms. After he'd heard his friend Dvořàk's cello concerto, he was reputed to have said, 'If I'd known it could be done, I'd have done it myself.' Well, Christopher, you didn't, and I did. Using all your words and with Alan's help, I turned four of your television plays into two evenings of superb theatre.

When Christopher next saw Naomi, he asked why I'd been avoiding him on that first night. Naomi, who knew the story, said something diplomatic, to which he replied, 'I don't understand. He was paid.' Remarkably stingy – but I remember every moment I worked on that adaptation as deeply rewarding.

Scarborough rep was one of the many places where I had actors appear (I think fifteen throughout the years, and I went up there to see all of them). Alan seemed impressed with my clients, and as I thought he was a remarkable director as well as a once-in-a-lifetime writer, I was proud to have them work with him. He is possibly the most significant English playwright at work today: mercilessly perceptive, funny and honest. A man of the people. (But then, of course, there's David Hare).

*

Another time: Martin Connor and I put on a production of a very funny farce by Hugh Leonard, *Some of my Best Friends are Husbands*, at the theatre in Watford with Tony Britton and Rosemary Leach playing the leads. Martin acted in it, as did one of my clients, and it got rave reviews outside London. It so nearly made it into town, but that's another story. And then, a few years later, when Martin had been voted to lead The Actors' Company, I re-worked the red-blooded melodrama *Lady Audley's Secret* into a musical, using Gilbert and Sullivan numbers – with one of my clients playing the eponymous heroine. The point of my telling you this is to show that I tried to create work for my clients, not just be reactive. (Martin's still a great mate and now one of the directors of London's Guildhall School of Music and Drama).

*

Must tell you – extraordinary coincidence: my Martin and I lived together in various parts of London, and it was when we had to leave a basement flat in Notting Hill Gate (because it was just so depressing, with a huge mural of a Warhol scarlet mouth exhaling smoke painted on one wall) that we eventually found an apartment immediately behind Olympia Stadium – in the house where Ally had lived in the last years up to his death, where we'd laughed at the cartoon of the dustman's cart. Our flat was on the floor above his – we were there for ten years.

*

And so office life went on, with occasional changes of personnel, changes of address, eight hours of ringing and answering of telephones, and in the evenings going to the theatre to see clients on an average of once a month in London. More visits to the provinces, going to preview screenings in tiny cinemas, at BAFTA, or wining and dining useful contacts – hugely busy, usually fun. But not all of it.

I shouldn't have been surprised that some of my actors began to think I spent too much time on Miranda's career rather than looking after them. I was as out-of-my-mind proud of their successes, attended many award-giving ceremonies because of them, but it was true that her career did take me abroad to meet some of the famous in our business, people I admired from as long ago as being a drama student, and it was thanks to her I got to experience that world. A lot of my successful clients are now as familiar with that heady existence as I became, but throughout those years, I knew I was giving my all to all of them.

I'm not going to indulge in the Blame Game, but the more successful the agency became, due to the success of the actors I'd chosen, the more the clients, once they'd tasted fame, seemed to want even more *immediately*. Quote: 'Why did it take so long?' Answer: 'That's the way the cookie crumbles. Why didn't my partner turn up ten years earlier?' I should have realised of course, that as an actor, I'd wanted appreciation and to be loved *all the time* – now, being their carer, I could understand their dissatisfaction – with knobs on. The excuses for some of their final rejections of the agency, of me, were numerous, but in the end predictable: 'I'm so grateful for what you've done for me, you've been a wonderful agent, but . . .' I got to the point many years later of interrupting, 'Don't go any further, I've heard it all before.' (You don't get on with so and so who works in the agency; you don't think your career is going in the direction you think it should; your partner thinks you'd be better off somewhere else; you're breaking up with your lover and you want a clean slate; you're giving up the business and thought you'd just give it one more try with someone else; you don't expect ever to do as well again, yes, yes, yes . . .). The stuff in brackets I didn't say out loud, of course.

These fragile egos were leaving someone they loved, trusted and were grateful to – so they said. It was hard for them, they said. So what about me, I thought? I said I understood.

I tried not to sound sour when I told one of them: 'Jack Nicolson has had the same agent all his career, and it hasn't done him any harm.' She was nonplussed, but nevertheless left. She is supremely talented, so is still successful, but somewhat conceitedly I somehow doubt her career has been any better without me. Which also applies to some of the other big names I've represented.

Sadly, my relationship with Miranda soured ever so slowly. Our holidays together, her weekending in Martin's and my houses, searching for her cat in a neighbour's garden, the tennis, the laughter, throughout the nearly twenty years she was with me, all are to be savoured.

And, of course, our adventures in the Big Apple and LA, the fun and falsity of it all, I will always remember with astonishment – but less and less affection.

The nicest way to put it, I think, is to say we became detached, she and I. Our realities drifted apart probably because of my core belief in the responsibilities of an actor as a role-model, and we began to differ to the point where we no longer seemed to speak the same language. Well, you know that I believe in reality being essential to an artist because you've read about it earlier. We had huge fun and lots of success but came the time eventually when she treated me as hired help and the people in the office as her minions, so we parted company.

Her leaving the agency did knock some of the stuffing out of me. I knew all those years of hard work, love and care were being handed on to her next agent for free. Of course, I had some wonderful artists left, but just as when Bill Paterson joined, and his joining boosted my agency's reputation, Miranda's leaving took away some of the lustre.

Another one of my favourite artists, one with whom I'd had a very close relationship, one I'd found at drama school, and who had been with me for a long time, decided that she ought to look elsewhere for representation – which wounded me deeply, I must admit. (Well, they all did). Eighteen months later, I got a letter from her dog with words to the effect that he couldn't take any more of his mistress's moping, crying whenever she looked at a vase on the mantelpiece which we'd bought together in Crewe market when she'd been working there, and could I, *please*, put him out of his misery by taking her back into the agency. Please! Well, I can't resist any animal, particularly a dog, so of course I did, and she's still there. But hers was the exception that proved the rule. Once broken, trust can't be got back.

After twenty-five years I felt I'd outstayed my welcome on the agenting scene and thought maybe I should retire. I looked around without success for someone to take over the agency. The trade I was in was now in such a parlous state there was less and less imagination needed to further actor's careers – certainly my artful letters and phone calls were becoming less useful, fast emails and even faster texts taking over. In my casting around as to how best to look after my darlings, I thought there might be safety in numbers (hence Gardner, Skemp and Quick). For a short while I even thought to emulate the big supermarket agencies and take on more clients, using the scattershot effect: with so many clients offered to casting for each role, one of them would surely get it. But that would have been immoral. I made overtures to another successful one-man-band agent like myself, with the same number of clients, and we got to within touching distance of the altar before he got cold feet. I wasn't sure what would work, but for the sake of my loved ones, I had to try.

Throughout all this flailing about, the presence of Martin kept me from depression. We had a life away from the hurly-burly, and he helped me manoeuvre through the panic I occasionally felt just under the surface. However, I couldn't share my worries in detail because he would very quickly become more depressed than me.

At around this time, I heard from Claude, my French lover Marcel's younger brother. He thought I should know that Marc had died. Marc had retired from London to live in Exeter. I already knew that, as Marc and I had met in London a couple of times before he left. One of his younger hangers-on at the Cadogan Square flat had gone down to Exeter with his wife to look after him. Marc and I were planning on my going down there to meet up when I got Claude's letter. It seems my ex had gone out on a snowy morning to do some grocery shopping, let himself back into his house, and his snow-impacted shoe slid on the kitchen floor – he brained himself on the corner of the kitchen table.

My winding down did take another four years, some of it still fun but much less glamorous, and halfway through that period, in late 1999, I found someone, not just reliable but with a similar sense of humour to work with – Andy Herrity. I sold him half the company in 2006 and retired down to Dorset. A lot of the clients I'd had with me for those twenty-nine years stayed with him, so he immediately had an income – but I made sure I never gave those once-actors of mine any advice if they rang me. It wouldn't have been fair on him to maybe contradict something he'd advised.

Some of those admirable, lovely actors are still friends, and we get together, either in London or down here in Dorset. I still go and see their work, sometimes driving bloody miles across the country as in days of yore.

CHAPTER 16
Love Is Not All Peaches and Cream [4]

When I ran the agency, I rationed myself to four weeks' holiday a year. Two of those weeks would be in France at our barn and the other fortnight somewhere else in the world. Even when we went to Australia, we only took two weeks away. Yes, after all that mileage – and the price!

Barn in France? Didn't I tell you? Well . . .

Penny Brownjohn, a girlfriend of ours, went off on holiday to France and was away much longer than we'd expected. Because, it turned out, she'd bought a three-storey house in a small out-of-the-way town in the Auvergne. It was ridiculously cheap – ridiculous to us Brits, that is. What she paid for this property was probably about a tenth of what she would have had to pay for a bungalow in England. Of course, it needed doing up, but the daring of the whole enterprise fired my imagination. 'Martin, as we don't have the cottage in Norfolk now, what about getting somewhere in France instead?' I think my fella was too astonished at the proposition to object, so almost the next day we were on a plane to Toulouse (three-quarters of the way down France and a bit to the right of centre).

We so nearly bought a group of cottages with another of our girlfriends, Sue, in the Cognac area (the left side), but then her mother became incapacitated, so that venture came to nothing. In retrospect, thank heavens. Imagine owning one of a group of three or four houses and a friend in your commune being forced to sell up – and you find the new owner in your midst poisonous.

I was very keen we find somewhere miles away from the

---

4   'Was it Romeo or Juliet who said, when about to die? Love is not all peaches and cream' is a lyric by Cole Porter.

nearest habitation so that, as I put it to the various estate agents we met over there, we could play Mahler's Symphony of a Thousand at full blast at three in the morning without disturbing any neighbours. We were shown a lot of properties, some of them crumbling heaps where one particular agent would say, pointing at a stained wall with rotting woodwork, 'just a lick of paint' – which is a catchphrase we still use. It was this same woman who took us to a house on the edge of a village where you stepped down from the front door onto the road, and, when inside, she pulled at the shutter on the window to let in more light it came off in her hand, and, and, *and* in the tiny back garden there was a twenty-metre-high water tower. One ruined chateau we were shown was on the crown of a conical hill – with no access…

We had great fun looking, but we'd nearly given up when on our third visit, we found a new estate agent in Toulouse who understood what we wanted. He drove us forty miles to the west to a long two-storey rectangular barn, with a broken-backed Roman-tiled roof, standing in the middle of a vast tract of farmland with three mature chestnut trees close by and two rusting pieces of farm machinery leaning against its walls. It also had a working well and a largish open-fronted stone hen-cum-goat house to one side. The nearest habitation was a quarter of a mile away, and the town of Lectoure was strung along the ridge of an escarpment on the horizon.

Perfection!

To begin with, I think Martin thought I was mad and perhaps trusted I'd see the error of my ways, but he was clever enough not to pour cold water on my enthusiasm. However, I do think the adventure bug got to him somewhere on our touring around those different areas of France looking for the perfect spot – but never, even in his wildest imaginings, did he think this massive edifice was the sort of thing we should take on.

We went to look at the property on a couple more occasions – by which time I knew exactly where each switch, plug, flight of stairs, doorway, new opening for windows and new walls would need to be – and the last time, before we returned to England, we set up a meeting with the vendor. Two months later, we signed the deeds in the mayor's office. Monsieur Margoet, the farmer who had sold the barn to us, told us a few years after we'd finished building, he thought we were truly 'lunatics Anglais!'

The tiles on the roof were reputedly fashioned in Roman times on the thighs of young women – hence the tapering. We had to scour near and far to find sound tiles to replace our cracked ones. And then there were two of the massive supporting oak beams to strengthen. The cost of repairing the roof was the same price as the house – but even doubling the original cost, the place was way cheaper than anything of even quarter the size in England.

Penny, the sorceress who had inspired this dream of mine, knew of an English builder from Norfolk, whose name was Kerry Taplin. (Kerry, the first man I'd actually met with my Christian name – *and* he was from Norfolk). We employed him and his sons to create my imagined interior in this huge near-empty barn which, inside, was walled off into five sections. When we first saw it, there was hay in one, ancient garlic stalks hanging from racks in another, cattle stalls in a third, and farm machinery in the vast open one at the west end. The east end had once housed the woman who had many years before farmed the property. That, the smallest section, had a fireplace, a hanging flex without a bulb, and a sink with a tap. All it needed was a lick of paint!

Kerry and his two sons lived in tents during the work, where mice joined them in their sleeping bags, and Kerry was bitten by a rat when he was asleep.

We had local French workmen do the roof. We used as many local builders as we could for obvious diplomatic reasons.

I won't go into all the tribulations of getting the place habitable. A tiny example: the first septic tank was far too small – what did we know? It was made of plastic and having been delivered was blown half a mile away by the wind to the far side of the next-door field, so another, much larger concrete one was brought, dropped into the hole . . . and cracked, so we had to get a third. Of course, a much heftier supply of electricity had to be brought in from the B-road a good half-mile away – in France that didn't cost us a sou – and the same with the water supply, which was much easier to install as the farmer's water spigots irrigated the fields around us.

The spaces between the stones which made up the huge barn had to be plugged with mortar - otherwise the wind didn't just sweep across the plain, it swept through the house. The property boundaries were pegged out, and a wooden fence put in place, grass seed was sown, and we planted ornamental bushes, twelve saplings (six of them fruit trees) and *rosa banksiae* along the south wall. Fields everywhere are now huge and these ones in the Gers were arable (sheep could have safely grazed). Surrounding the building through the years, there was maize, garlic, flax, mustard, sunflowers . . .

We had to have a new ceiling put up over the old lady's rooms at the east end. And as that ceiling was also the floor of the cavernous space overhead, we used polished oak planks – because I thought we might use that roof space as a concert hall. Grandiose, eh? A Concert Hall! What I had in mind was to have maybe two or three of the best string-playing students from the Royal Academy of Music – I had contacts there – flown over for short all-expenses-paid holidays in the summer to play sonatas, trios, possibly quartets when we could afford it, maybe jazz – and advertise it locally. We certainly had the ground to park thirty or forty cars around about for the punters I anticipated.

In the twelve years we owned the place, that dream never came to fruition. Five or six years on, the surrounding area outside now covered in the coarse grass that can survive a baking summer, the saplings now looking treelike and all fruiting when appropriate, the *rosa banksiae* spreading over the south wall, we had a swimming pool put in. Martin was very thrilled with that. Never in his life had he imagined being the Owner of A Swimming Pool. But you've got to do things right.

The problem was the attendant care and attention the place

needed all year round was expensive, and the only way we could break even was to let the east and west ends we'd had adapted as living spaces to summer visitors – three bedrooms the old lady's end, two the other. Which meant that we couldn't stay there at the time of year we would most have liked to without damaging our bank accounts. But that said, we had the most wonderful holidays there in the spring, the early summer, autumn, Christmas and New Year. Being bang in the centre of the lower half of France, in Gascony, the winter weather could be really unfriendly: icy fogs which could last for days, so in January and February the place was uninhabitable to us pansies – but even then, it still needed cash for the supervision provided by a local English couple. (Had a waterpipe burst, was the roof leaking, etc.?).

At warmer, even hotter times of the year, if you could see the Pyrenees a hundred miles away to the south, it meant there'd be rain the next day.

If you imagine our barn, Vignaux de Bas (Lower Vines – we didn't name it – nor translate it for our friends) being in the centre of a vast saucer of countryside, our extended view spreading 360 degrees around us included Terraube, an ancient wee village on the west horizon ten miles away; and maybe only two miles away to the north on the escarpment, Lectoure. Lectoure had a four-and-a-half star Michelin restaurant in the majestic Hôtel de Bastard (eating outside in the courtyard of a warm evening with swifts and swallows swooping overhead was close to grown-up Disney). Condom, the cathedral town where the road signs were always being stolen, was maybe only twenty-five miles away; no English voices were heard in the bustling weekly markets we went to – until Terry Wogan bought a chateau not too far away, dammit! The fruit and vegetables, all locally grown and freshly picked that morning, were so much more characterful than the British 'ripen at home' stuff; the walks along the Grande Randonée routes, easily followed because of the unobtrusive markings, were uninterrupted by hazards (we must have trudged at least a hundred miles of it over the years); the Gers people themselves were inquisitive and generous of heart – after all the area had once been ruled by the English, hence their rather Anglicised patois.

And we could pick mouthfuls of figs, mulberries, grapes and the little yellow Mirabelle plums alongside the nearly empty roads and lanes. Why bother with a basket?

We made good friends there, not all of whom spoke English. Martin, the handsome Englishman who spoke their language fluently was the lure. My smattering of schoolboy French and my clowning was only used for decoration. Just to show how much I was bewitched by that beautiful corner of France, I once crumbled a tooth biting down on an olive pit and fell deeply in love with the French dentist who spoke only a word or two of English. So when at that first meeting she mimed I needed a root canal right there and then I was so smitten I agreed, nodding my head in ignorant infatuation. (Her husband was also a dentist, and the two of them with their two youngsters became good friends). And, of course, in France we got immediate medical attention for fourpence or less. (We were in the EU then).

I absolutely adored it – the house, the area, the people, everything. Martin loved it when he was there, particularly once there was no more building work to be done, but because he spoke the language like a native, he settled the bills, argued when need be with water and electricity boards, the telephone company et cetera, so he had an enormous concertina file of things that needed doing/ had been done – and as the years went by, he found that burdensome. I blithely arranged the sightseeing trips with visiting friends to the beautiful places of interest nearby. For instance, on a Saturday morning, I'd drive us fifty miles on nearly deserted roads to Nérac, the market town where the King of France's chateau overlooks the river with the town sprawled all around it, eating at a riverside restaurant under the awnings after we'd bought that evening's meal at the market stalls.

Martin's and my birthdays were three months apart (ten years difference, but only three months apart), so we split the difference the year of our fiftieth and sixtieth birthdays and had thirty people eating at four long trestle tables on the grass outside the barn, some from England (a few of them my actors), maybe a half-dozen French friends, one Parisian – I mention her separately because they really are a race apart – and our American friend, Joe Simon – sans ferret! It was hardly worth our visitors coming for just the weekend, so we spread the celebrations over four days, sleeping as many as we could in the barn, the rest in hotels and smaller 'gîtes' nearby. It was the most fun one could imagine, and we could make as much noise as we wanted. And did we ever!

With the performers there, mealtimes were sometimes hysterically camp; as when Roger Sloman (of *Nuts in May*) and Paddy O'Connell (*The Brothers*) brought the food to us, at the stretch of tables beneath the trees, as Long John Silver and Quasimodo. Lots of loutish *Oooh Aaar*-ing, grunts and whinnies and slapping down of plates. And Miranda using the well-known hand gesture in charades while acting out *Casablanca*: two syllables, second syllable sounds like . . . And then later, for the next phrase or saying (and I forget what it was), she found she was able to use that same wrist movement again. And there was dancing with balloons, swimming in the Three Lakes nearby – our pool hadn't been built then – Martin coming down the waterslide sitting bolt upright as though reading a newspaper – sightseeing . . . can't begin to tell you how utterly blissful those four days were.

One Christmas, there was the Incident of the Flaming Goose. My partner had probably the heaviest coat you can imagine. No, it wasn't the coat that was heavy, but its contents: scissors, penknife, lengths of string, a small roll of loo paper held together by a rubber band – well, you never know when, do you? – earplugs, paracetamol, loose change (he now kept his paper money in a fanny-pack concealed under his shirt – he'd been mugged in Holland Park), documents, probably a pack of cards, I don't know. I was never rude enough to ask him to empty his pockets. So when at Christmas I was cooking a goose and, after stuffing it, needed to close the aperture I looked about me for an answer (where were the skewers, did we have any skewers?), Martin produced a carpet needle and a spool of dental floss from his pocket. A little sewing later: Voila!

I put the goose in the oven and went to change. Getting back downstairs, I saw the oven in flames. And my brother, with great presence of mind, opened the oven door and threw the flaming goose into the snow. Perfect timing. Snow crisps up the flesh. Didn't you know?

And then I remember Ava, Fred Astaire's daughter, at our barn another Christmas with her husband. I didn't believe her when she said she couldn't dance for toffee – but she swore it was true.

(My fiftieth party was at Forrigan, without Naomi in attendance. You can see from the photo Imelda and her husband, Jim Carter were there, and Miranda and Billy. Martin wanted there to be a walk after lunch, and although we had asked people to come comfortably dressed, Penny, the house-witch, and her chap arrived in full Edwardian gear. Seeing them strolling the lanes was like looking at a clip from *The Go Between*.

I was given lots of presents, including a beautiful black leather attaché case, but the next day when I came back from London to collect the pile of goodies I'd dumped on a bed upstairs, I couldn't find the card to go with it. To this day, I've never been able to thank whoever it was who gave me such a wonderfully generous gift. If you are reading this, thank you so very much – and please forgive my lack of manners).

I think maybe, of all the regrets I've had in my long life, letting go of Vignaux de Bas has to be one of the greatest. But we had to. We found this house in Dorset, and it made no sense to have the burden of letting our property in the Gers while paying a mortgage here. The barn cost us a small fortune through those twelve years, but we sold it for almost exactly that amount. My partner, even though he loved being there, was mighty relieved when we gave it up.

*

During all the years we were together we went on the most amazing holidays, he and I. There were places he wanted to revisit, and places I wanted to discover, so he shared with me the astonishing Iguazú Falls on the borders of Argentina and Brazil, where he'd been before with his mother; and South Africa where his stepfather had been posted as a diplomat – and, incidentally, where his mother had died. One of his half-brothers, John (the one he met first when he was thirty) had an apartment in Cape Town, and we took the Blue Train from there to Johannesburg, driving along the southern Garden Route back to Cape Town.

We both wanted to go to Peru, particularly to Machu Picchu and, further up the Andes from there, the reed islands on Lake Titicaca. At Machu Picchu, we stayed the night before visiting the ruined village in the only hotel allowed in its National Park. Any time after daybreak, hotel guests can go onto the site – other tourists being bussed up from the valley below are not allowed in before ten. Cold and misty just after dawn, it was more than a little eerie wandering alone through those roofless dwellings, so perfectly preserved, with only the grazing alpacas for company, the strange conical mountains looming through the heavy cloud.

The Inca village had been so elevated the Spanish never found it – so it was saved from destruction. The Spanish conquerors razed to the ground everything religious they could find of the indigenous people to prove the superiority of their God. Our God. They built their Christian churches on the Inca temples' foundations, but at every earthquake, their churches collapsed. Up in Machu Picchu – as at every Inca monument we visited – the massive granite boulders were so perfectly honed you couldn't get a wafer between them. No mortar, just pressure held them together. In Machu Picchu, there is only one small displacement of two stones which happened during one of their frequent earth tremors.

We zip-lined through the tree canopies in Costa Rica; we went white water rafting along the bottom of the Grand Canyon (I'm a sissy now with heights); we took Naomi to Mauritius, and Madeira; we visited a friend in Sydney because the Millennium fireworks here in Dorset were rained-off and the next day on television I saw the magnificent display on the Sydney Harbour Bridge . . . *and*, as we would be paying so much to go so far around the world why not visit the Great Barrier Reef afterwards? . . . *and* while we were there we should learn to dive, shouldn't we? We did all that in the two weeks and got our Certificates for Open Water Diving at the reef – where one night I swam with sharks.

(These sharks were vegetarian, just in case you think I was ultra-macho. Mind you, if you attracted their attention by shining a torch in their eyes, they might take a bite out of you to see if you were edible. Or maybe that was just one of those jokes put about by the veterans on our boat to frighten newcomers – but I didn't want to prove them right).

I *had* to go that night because I only had three successful swims on my card and needed one more to get my certificate. I had bottled out on one of the final test dives, the waves were too rough, and I kept inhaling water before submerging fully – so I left my 'buddy' Martin to go on down with the instructor. Consequently, Mart was sure of his certification. The only dive left that could get me mine was the midnight one.

I remember every fraught day on that little cork of a boat, especially when one of the experienced divers on board was brought back in a motorised dingy, his spreadeagled body blue – and looking quite dead. We'd been taught to swim away from the boat against the tide, so our return would be that much easier. This guy had forgotten and done the opposite – and then not been able to swim back. He survived, but that extra frisson of fear only added to our already barely checked terror. It was all about survival that course, so it was one contrived fright after another. But we have our PADI certificates.

We went to Rio and stood under the outstretched arms of Christ on the mountain. Afterwards, we travelled up the coast and had a bit of a beach holiday. It was exactly that – a bit of a beach. After six feet of sand, you could wade out for a quarter of a mile into the ocean, and the water just about reached your knees. The hotel suggested hiring a fisherman to row us to another spot up the coast, which is what we did for the last few days. It was deserted of tourists – actually, almost any human creature – and it was lovely swimming there. Looking inshore from the water, we could see three or four tiny houses and a dilapidated chapel with a small clump of wild horses grazing around it. The hotel had given us packed lunches, and the boatman picked us up four hours later. Undiluted happiness.

We made friends with the sub-manager of the hotel, Bruno, who informed us by email that a week after we left – the season over so the hotel was closed for renovations – he had been held at gunpoint one night by three masked men who demanded money, but when he made them understand there was nothing of worth in the building as there hadn't been any guests staying for some time, they moved on to the hotel next door where there were still a few German tourists in residence. When the police arrived an hour later, there was a short gun battle ending in one of the young bandits being killed. At that point, the tiny gang gave up – and I imagine those holidaymakers gave up too, their unzipped suitcases emptying as they rushed for the exit. Holiday of a Lifetime!

Martin and I, and a good American friend of ours, Richard, stayed overnight (Richard in a covered wagon) on the rim of the Grand Canyon at a ranch where cowboys spun ropes, corralled a herd of cattle, shot clay pigeons out of the sky – and where us two English softies impressed the hell out of them with our marksmanship. Martin's a dead shot, and I'm pretty good. (Many years later, at a carnival in France, between us we won our lady companion two mammoth soft toys shooting ping-pong balls off jets of water). Early next morning, we were helicoptered down a crevasse to the Colorado riverbank by what looked like a fourteen-year-old pilot, and terrifyingly the blades seemed only inches away from the cliff surfaces on either side as we hurtled downwards. We corkscrewed onto a small beach, our stomachs in our mouths, and met the rest of the rafters and crew – maybe sixteen all told – who had already been on the trip down the Colorado river for three days (we were doing the last four). We were given our tents and sleeping bags, and strict orders as to the rules of the Grand Canyon: on no account to use ordinary soap, to keep an eye out for scorpions, and not to drop anything without picking it up – consequently the surrounds were pristine, looking no doubt much as it did to the original settlers. The vista was vast and majestic, the water icy cold and brownish because of the silt it carried. The second morning when we stopped for lunch, I thought I'd have a swim in this most glorious setting, and as no one else seemed keen, I jumped in alone – and tried not to scream. We had been warned the water was freezing but Wonder Man here didn't believe anything could be *that* icy without being cubed. I was wondering just how soon I could get out in a carefree way when I felt a sudden current of warmth around my body. Oh, that was better – I relaxed. This was beautiful – look at that view! And then I noticed a man on the bank upstream who was holding his wife just clear of the water, her dress hoisted up, so she could have a pee. I waded out as soon as I could muster nonchalance.

I'm here to tell you urine is warm and sterile and refreshing to bathe in. Ass's milk? Bah!

We weren't in the dories of old but in flat-bottomed rubber dinghies, three-a-side, each with a paddle, and with one of the firm's employees sitting in the stern at the rudder. And on that second day, we'd been through two rapids, obeying instructions and paddling like mad when shouted at, the river boiling through the rocks on either side – we were pioneers! – when a human head came swirling past me in the water, aimed at the rocks. And then it was gone.

Only just arrived and someone was going to die.

We caught up with the unfortunate man in the calmer pool below the maelstrom. We discovered later that this fellow, I suppose of about sixty, a podgy banker from Wisconsin, had toppled out of his dinghy without any difficulty and had miraculously escaped being shredded on his dash through the rocks. He was white-faced, shaken and stirred – but completely unharmed.

The next day he was strapped to what looked like a throne

at the front of the provisions raft, a much sturdier affair than our boats, and half an hour later, maybe at the third or fourth rapid as we strained with all our might on our paddles to avoid catastrophe, there was that detached head swirling past again heading for the rocks. It was going to be all right, wasn't it, it had been last time, and sure enough, there he was, the same man, being hoicked out of the water downstream.

That evening, all of us eating around a romantic but unnecessary campfire, the twice-immersed banker told us that on that very day, his decree nisi had come through – and as he said it, the back of his chair gave way and his legs shot up into the air. We were too startled to laugh, and he trudged off to his tent muttering that God must have it in for him. That finished us.

Another odd memory from that wild and wonderful trip: wherever we berthed, the toilet, a tall cylinder, was set some distance away from the camp in the middle of the bushes. The detached seat was the indicator as to whether the loo was being used or not. If we found the seat lying on the ground at the beginning of the crookedly path that led to the cylinder, it meant no one was perched on it, so the rim was ready. Carrying a loo seat under your arm through that idyllic scenery was weird. Even our faeces were carried downstream on the raft to be disposed of.

Oh, yes, the only night Martin and I didn't bother to set up our tent, the rain pelted down on us in our bedrolls out of what had been a cloudless sky. It was earlier that same evening Marty found a baby scorpion in his bedding – cuchi cuchi!

On our last afternoon in the loneliness of that breathtaking vista, someone played the flute. It brought tears to my eyes. The immensity of the surrounding mountains, the vast open spaces, the sound of paddles hissing in the water, the caress of the breeze, it all left you with the blissful certainty that you were the only people in the world – that the universe could accommodate you if you were happy to be infinitesimal.

There was a third time I felt that eerie sense of calm on our travels, and that was when we took a boat through Patagonia from the southernmost habitation in the world, Ushuaia, through the numerous islands, all with English names, to see the Perito Moreno glacier in Chile. Because vegetation is sparse, it barely supports any animal life, so almost nothing and nobody lives there (except, of course, the colonies of miniature penguins on the coasts). The mountains and lakes are seemingly untouched by man: no houses on the banks, no tourist buses or restaurants, just us on a small cruiser nosing through the quiet infinity of nature.

Venice of course is the exact opposite, the jewel in the crown of man-made fabrications. Once you leave the Plaza de Saint Marco with its hundreds of tourists, within five minutes you can be alone wandering through a miracle of gently decaying beauty. Tiny chapels littered with Titians and Tintoretto's; ornate rooms with glorious adorned ceilings; narrow canals with dinky little bridges; a creaky wooden opera house where Martin, driven mad by all the noise around us, made a loud *sssh* in the middle of the inaudible tenor's aria – his mouth was opening and closing so he must have been singing something – only to see a patron being carried away behind us by ambulance men. That opera house, La Fenice, burnt down later that same year. Then there are the gondolas, the cats, the Bridge of This and the Museum of That. I think every child in the world should be given a free pass to Venice at birth so that they can appreciate just how enriching to the soul a man-made creation can be.

Then there was the Mardi Gras in Tenerife; the boat down the Nile; barging along the Canal du Midi with friends; Bruges; two holidays in Cyprus; visits to the Keukenhof Gardens outside Amsterdam to see the tulips; chateaux on the Loire; loads of visits to Paris where Martin's friend Martha lives – last time we were there we got to see the unique Juliette Gréco, the French chanteuse I was in love with (a voice Marc had introduced me to), in one of her last ever performances at the Olympia; four visits to Barbados with various pals; Mexico and the Mayan temples; Florence, Rome and Naples (so, of course, the ruins of Pompeii); the wild animals on a Kenyan safari trip (including a white rhinoceros at the water hole at four in the morning); and Vienna for the New Year's Day concert. We paid for but cancelled two visits: one to the Gambia (where we'd stayed before, but this time persecuting homosexuals had become the new president's pastime), and another to Sri Lanka, where there were bloody riots in the north of the country the week before we were scheduled to go – there was no way one could order a drink on the beach in the south from a hotel employee whose family might live in the war zone. I really wanted to revisit India, but Martin, my sweet hypochondriac, was afraid of Delhi Belly. Of all the places we wanted to visit, we left the Galapagos too late because it seems the islands are now being ruined by tourism's detritus.

*

Once we'd moved to north Dorset, I worked only intermittently as an agent. I thought I could semi-retire by taking Mondays off and eventually Fridays as well, but it was a mistake. It meant the knowledge of what the clients had been up to was no longer at my fingertips. I had to scramble to keep up to date, *and* I was having to pay rent for a place to stay those working days in town. It kept me in a perpetual state of uncertainty, and although the staff were kind enough not to sigh outwardly when I asked them something for the second time while I tried to join up the facts of what they'd already told me, they surely found it a waste of their time. So I wasn't enjoying work, they weren't enjoying me, and I wasn't enjoying my new home as much as I could have.

This state of affairs lasted a year or so before I knew I had to commit to being retired. I told you I'd engaged quite the most interesting and bright guy a few years before, Andy Herrity, so I offered him a partnership and was able to leave the running of the agency entirely to him. He changed its title to Gardner Herrity.

Martin's and my cottage here in the southwest of England is fifty yards down a No Through Road, which means very little traffic goes past. It's a pretty, thatched, Grade II listed building. The back of the house has a really lovely view through an orchard across a valley.

The house itself is surrounded by well-established trees. The front garden is where we plant annuals. I suppose because of working those eons ago in the American Society for Psychical Research and my consequent realisation that plants feel pain when cut or uprooted I never cut the flowers, so they come out of the ground, grow and die back naturally. A bit like us, I like to think. (I even employ an outsider to come and prune when we are away for the day). We've kept the back as nature might have intended. I call it the orchard because until a hundred years ago, the whole of our side of the valley was famous for its cider apples, and we still have four gnarled, propped up apple trees outside, along with an oak and two sixty-foot ash to one side – so the view through these old trees is of the fields up the slope opposite.

A part of me worried that two men coming to live in rural Dorset might be met with covert prejudice, but if there is, or was hostility, it has never shown itself to our faces, and the numerous friends and acquaintances we have could have been bespoke for us two poofters.

Martin's uncle, Rod, died ten years into our lives together, and Mart used the money he inherited to go to college and get himself a degree in translating and interpreting. He found the latter too stressful, so has made a living translating from English (his mother tongue) into Spanish (his other mother tongue) and vice versa, for the law and the police, Customs and Excise, private companies and individuals. It's not uncommon for there to be a policeman sitting here on the sofa waiting for the translation Martin's working on to be ready so it can be taken back to London.

Only occasionally do I miss the gossip and behaviour of my showbiz friends, so I do go up to London to meet up with theatricals and see their performances, both on and off stage, while Martin works in his study here. The rest of the time, I can see them on screen or in nearby theatres (Bath, Salisbury or Poole). Living vicariously – the fun without the anxiety of predatory competition. Throughout our time together, my Mart enjoyed actors' company but eventually tired of the me-me chatter as the years went by. He wouldn't show his boredom, he was too polite for that – he just got quieter and quieter and got on with other things. But he was such good company I don't think any but our really good friends knew.

I intuited early on that plays and players needed to be really exceptional for him to enjoy them, so I would only take him with me to what I thought he was likely to find absorbing. That wasn't as difficult as it might sound. But occasionally, in the early days, I did get it wrong, and when I did, he could be caustic. There was one time, at the Edinburgh Festival, when I took him to a dance theatre company I'd never heard of before. (I always tried at these festivals – and I must have attended five or six as an agent, two as a performer – to not just go and see my clients work, but take in other plays, classical concerts, contemporary dance companies, or an opera, whatever appealed). So at this extraordinarily dull, endless show where dancers (ha!) crouched on chairs and hopped off only to menace other chair-huggers before pushing or sliding them off, I was startled to hear, at the end during the minimal applause, a sibilant hiss coming from somewhere not too far away. For the first time in our lives together, I realised Martin was showing his displeasure as it's done in Latin America: not booing but hissing. We went afterwards to a nearby restaurant for dinner, where he, without drawing breath, shredded the evening's performance for more than a minute, never repeating himself, and I started to laugh. His aptitude with words was such a privilege to be around.

*

I don't know when it came to me in my early years that I would just as soon be a dancer as an actor. I mean the Broadway hoofer-type dancer – 'gypsies' I think they're called over there. If you've ever seen Liza Minelli's number 'Arthur in the Afternoon' on YouTube, you'll know just the sort of male dancer I mean: swivelly, lithe and sexy as hell. So we go now to see the Matthew Bourne Company, Mark Morris and Balletboyz whenever they are in the provinces, and Alvin Ailey's dance troupe whenever they're in England.

Mind you, I also thought I'd like to be a concert pianist and an international tennis player. But six hours a day, every day, bashing things about? No, I'm too impatient. So I watch *Strictly Come Dancing*, starting about halfway through the competition by which time the non-dancers have cottoned on to what is needed, they've lost half a stone because of all the hard training they've had to do – I should know – and have not just grasped the rudiments of dance but are wringing it out. Except . . .

One year I watched open-mouthed with admiration the brilliant couple Alexandra Burke and Gorka Márquez, always getting top marks from the professional judges – and always relegated to the bottom two by the public's vote. It happened twice, confirming my suspicions that by and large, the British public is racist. Alexandra Burke is a stunningly attractive, brilliant performer on the dance floor – did I forget to mention she's black? By the time the finals came, I knew the public wouldn't allow her to win, and of course they didn't, they chose the Scot, the cheeky chappie Joe McFadden – big grin always ahoist – excellent dancer, very attractive, but not in the same league as those other two. I came to the sad conclusion early on that the consistently best dancing couple in the show that year couldn't win because although they could dance the socks off everyone else, one of the two was black *and* an uppity female. And the other was from some *foreign* country. I remembered my time in India as a boy, when the British wouldn't more than smile politely at the other white Europeans there and were kind to the darker skinned because we needed them to skivvy for us. We Brits have a built-in superiority complex – we are better than others. Bloody Upstarts! When did that happen? It can't have been when the Romans or the Normans were here, that's for certain! Elizabeth the First perhaps – all that pillaging of Spanish galleons at sea. Thinking along those lines, I realise sadly, that since mankind peeped out of caves it has always been suspicious of 'the other'. We have only come a short distance. We can deny being 'racist', but with a quick private phone call, express it anonymously. Nowadays, an anonymous tweet will do the trick.

*

I thought when I retired, I would love the relaxed life: the getting up late and going to bed at one, two o'clock, whenever. (My partner in bed by midnight. Always). I had thought gardening every day would help keep me fulfilled, but I had to have a back operation four years after leaving London, and that put an end to anything supple. I learned to cook, and thanks to Nigel and Nigella's recipes, I get congratulated for it, and I joined an art class. After six months of enjoyable idleness, I got bored. I needed to be useful. We still walked the dogs (Martin for the morning hour, and both of us in the afternoon), and then my right knee started to give. I don't want to make this an organ recital, but that joint is going to have to be attended to soon.

And, of course, taking Naomi's advice, our dogs have been poodles. Our first, an apricot bitch, I named Bosky. After ten years, we thought to get her a companion and found a chocolate brown puppy at a breeder not too far away in Somerset. She had a fancy Kennel Club name, as did Bosky (Call Me Madam), but her owners called her Pansy. Well, that certainly wouldn't do for two butch guys walking their dog in the nearby woods (imagine shouting out Pansy every time she disappeared), but we'd already decided it was Martin's turn to name our new pup. So what was it to be? He wouldn't tell me, and wouldn't tell me until the day came and we had her on the back seat of our car.

'So?'

'She's going to be called Jessie,' he said, and I nearly choked. Martin, coming from South America, didn't know that up in Scotland a Jessie *is* a Pansy. 'A Jessie . . . a big girl's blouse!' But we could shout, 'Jessie, come here,' without raising any English eyebrows – so that's what she was named.

Our latest, an apricot toy poodle, whose Kennel Club's name is Apricot Tart (the breeder called her Princess – another name two men don't want to shout out in public), is now named Biscuit for home consumption.

Nowadays, the woods ring out with the names of solicitors:

303

Buxton, Parker and Baxter, being called to heel. What happened to Bobby, Bella and Titch? Maybe not as upmarket, but just as good a firm!

*

I was looking for somewhere to hold our noughties double-birthday party when someone suggested we try the new building that had been put up in Sturminster Newton, The Exchange. It was going to be a theatre seating 300. What!!! A theatre down the road from where I lived? I got over-excited and joined the board – the building wasn't quite completed – but after volunteering to do this that and the other, it dawned on me my enthusiasm was being mistaken for smart-Alecdom. 'Comes up from London. Thinks he knows it all!' That wasn't said to my face, but that was the distinct impression I got, so I jumped ship. The thing is I don't know it *all*, but I do know a lot of it! After all, I've been in Entertainment/The Biz for the best part of fifty years. I have some knowledge and a few contacts.

So when David Conville, who lived locally and once ran the Regent's Park theatre, suggested I help him mount a production of a play he'd written, I was a happy man. We did a rehearsed reading of it at his house, and it went extremely well. That encouraged him to put on something else – any suggestions? 'What about Alan Ayckbourn's *Relatively Speaking*,' I asked, 'which might be the most perfect farce ever written.' (Notice I said, *might* be. I *might* be the only one who thinks so. Feydeau runs Alan a pretty close second – with Michael Frayn nose-to-nose). My offer to direct it was taken up. I found a small group of actors from around here, all of them trained at drama schools, all having had to give up a career in acting to make a living. But acting is like bicycling – the art is never completely forgotten. They were excellent, these ex-thesps, and the production was very well received. So I offered to do another Ayckbourn, *Intimate Exchanges*, a two-hander, and that too went down a treat. I knew that without any Name Actor, it would have to be the author who attracted the public – Ayckbourn, Coward, Stoppard or Rattigan, for example. Then, for another town nearby with a theatre, Shaftesbury,

I did a John Mortimer double bill: *Knightsbridge* and *The Dock Brief*. The actors were great, the performances very successful. We were asked to reprise *The Dock Brief* for a charity performance.

But these forays into my past world only kept me enthralled twice a year, so what else to do? A couple of local friends, Julia and Chris Boeree, and I formed a Limited Company: Dress Circle (Wessex).

I wrote to well-known actors I could call friends and others who might know of me, suggesting they come and do something at the Exchange because, early days, it very much needed promoting to attract public attention. Sturminster Newton used to have a centuries old cattle market that had closed not long before we arrived in the district – so the town was no longer the financial draw it had been. Stur was in danger of having no purpose. (It's even worse now – the three banks have closed, the garage is a Car Wash, and the Creamery which produced the well-known Sturminster Cheddar has long gone).

Actors are extraordinarily generous with their time, and I had no sooner asked Ian McKellen than he said yes.

A little segue here: Sir Ian McKellen must be one of the most generous human beings I know – and I don't know him well. I had been turned down by him early in my career as an actor when he directed, and I auditioned for – I can't believe this – a musical version of *Henry V*. Surely not. My memory must be playing tricks. (Was the musical *Chrysanthemum*?). Whatever, I sang, and he very courteously said no. I met him again when Merlith asked him to substitute for an incapacitated George Cole at a ceremony where a blue plaque was to be put on the house in Hampstead, where Ally had lived for so many years. Ian spoke, the local press noted down his witty speech, we all laughed and applauded, and he joined us family at a pub nearby for refreshment. He was such an easy bloke to talk to I asked him to come down here to Dorset and do something at the Exchange. Well, of course – he'd be pleased to! A few months later, Martin and I picked him up after his last performance of *Waiting for Godot* at the Theatre Royal in Bath, he slept the night here, and the next morning, Sunday, he introduced the first of the *Lord of the Rings* films to an auditorium of children who were ecstatic to be in the presence of Gandalf – even if he was in civvies. I'd asked him if he would like to present any film of his in the afternoon which he thought hadn't had the appreciation it deserved, and he chose the oddity *Neverwas*. He talked to the audience about the making of it before we screened it, telling us too about his film of *Richard III*, which we showed later that same evening. We ferried Sir Ian back home to London in time for an early supper. Serena's a wonderful guy!

Bill Paterson came for an afternoon's chat with me on stage and read excerpts from his book, *Tales from the Back Green*, pleasing the audience no end ('such a relaxed, delightfully funny, and intelligent man' – this sent to our website), after which there was a book signing.

John Gorrie, the fine director I mentioned earlier is also a writer of renown (he's a BAFTA winner for his television screenplays of *Edward the Seventh*), and he brought his entertainment to the Exchange: *Myra and Joyce 'Playing to the Gallery'*, about the friendship between Dame Myra Hess and Joyce Grenfell during and after the last war. It had Stephanie Cole and Pat Hodge as the leads. With Richard Sisson (one half of Kit and the Widow) playing some of Hess's more famous classical pieces on the piano and accompanying Pat singing some of Grenfell's funny songs, we had queues waiting for return seats. Unsurprisingly.

Lynne Truss, the author of *Eats, Shoots and Leaves* came, and along with Marion Bailey, James Fleet and Mike Leigh, performed four of her monologues for radio: *A Certain Age*.

Martin Brown, the illustrator of the *Horrible Histories*, made skilful use of his rapt young audience, demonstrating his cartoony genius; Moray Watson, after a long and varied acting career, told us some racy tales with *Looking Back and Dropping Names*; Kevin Moore did his one man show: *Crocodiles and Cream* – a portrait of Lewis Carroll; and I staged the children's opera, *Amahl and the Night*

Visitors by Menotti – the musical director, David Gostick, bringing some of his London contacts down to sing the 'Three Kings'. That and staging productions of two more of Alan Ayckbourn's plays, and a mini musical for kids written by a notable local, 'Hans and the Snowlady', brings us almost up to date. *Except . . .*

Eileen Atkins came down recently and was interviewed by the director Richard Digby Day. She is wicked fun. There is nothing like this Dame, that's for sure.

That's my tally of productions at The Exchange over the years we've been here in Dorset . . . so far! Any offers, thespians? We have a nice spare bedroom. It's hugely important to attract visitors to spend money in our shops and restaurants before Sturminster dies. And a thriving Exchange could help do that.

It still has a part-time public library, but for how much longer?

*

Of course, some of the nicest people we know down here vote The Wrong Way, but nobody's perfect, and they will keep liking us – which is difficult to turn down. Neither Martin or I hunt, shoot or fish – nor play bridge – so we are not on the social A-list, nor have we ever wanted to be. Mart was surprised to find a female cousin down here who, after asking us if we played bridge, said, 'Never mind, you'll be very useful for all our widows!' Doing what, exactly? Our A-list of good friends comprises musicians, singers, artists and the odd actor. Dorset seems packed with creative people, and it's a very friendly county – as against Norfolk, where the folk are much more reserved. If we hadn't moved from Norfolk and had had our noughties birthday party there we might have had, with luck, a dozen locals attending, whereas here, there were just under a hundred. Some of them admittedly were invited because we felt we should return invitations – and at least half of those we haven't kept up with – and then there were other dear people who had helped us in numerous ways through the years. And, of course, there were the friends from London, Paris and Los Angeles who came – so I suppose those would have been with us in Norfolk as well. OK, so in

Norfolk we'd have had two dozen people. But you get my point.

From the day Martin got his translating certification, he was at his desk at nine, Monday to Friday. That's diligence for you. But in the past ten years or so, translating work has dried up to a degree which worries me, but Martin seems unperturbed. Translations are being sent abroad and are almost always returned in a mangled form. These are then sent to bona fide translators here to be improved – at half the cost. Marty refuses: if a translation is to have his name on it, it's then his responsibility if there's any misinformation in it – and because what he gets to 'improve' is not always a nuanced version of what was originally sent abroad, why would he 'approve' it by signing his name to it? He'll get the blame if there's anything wrong with it.

And my day? Radio 3 is put on when I get up, around about nine nowadays, and on Mondays, I go to a watercolour art class with Jake Winkle – great name, great artist, and once the drummer in a boy band. On Thursdays, I travel to a one-to-one Pilates session just to try and keep my body from seizing up completely. (Martin is still lithe and supple, but he works hard at keeping his body in trim, while I'm turning into an avocado).

We take it in turns to cook dinner (lunch is on the hoof) and sometimes in the evenings go to the films or the theatres in the surrounding area. And we entertain a fair amount. Sunday afternoon is religiously kept for private play. As to my willy, that friend of many years standing? When I look down nowadays, I sometimes don't see it – and that's not because of my stomach. Then it's like searching for a cashew I dropped in the long grass.

What else about me haven't I mentioned that you might find interesting?

I've long thought of my body as a suitcase that contains the mind. To begin with, if you're lucky, you're given a shiny new pristine piece of luggage, and through the years, it gets scuffed a bit here, dented there, one of the locks won't work any longer, it loses a hinge until it bulges and looks in a pretty sorry state – but inside the mind is inviolate. So for longer than I can remember, I've believed that lending your suitcase, your body, to others is not immoral – the mind inside is capable of withstanding all sorts of vicissitudes and learning from them. Eventually, your suitcase is damaged beyond repair, is disposed of, and the mind is free to soar.

Anything else? More than anything I hate cruelty – to animals and children, in particular. Those two groups have no defence against so much of mankind's utter disregard as to their needs. Seeing or hearing of some acts perpetrated against them can shake me to the core with hatred.

*

I can still be relied on to shoot my mouth off before really thinking things through. However, I do believe in putting my hand up like a child to get my turn (so I have a few moments to examine my forthcoming pronouncement for obvious flaws) before, as a friend says, 'dropping hand grenades into the conversation'. But I trust my values to have got me to the point I'm trying to make, and that what I'm saying has a kernel of truth – to me, anyway. Maybe one day I'll learn to marshal all my facts before opening my mouth but if I did, I probably wouldn't get to speak before the conversation moved on to another topic.

If ever I find myself in front of the entrance to heaven, I hope my mind can be read, so I don't have to verbally justify myself.

'Excuse me, am I at the right auditions?'

Silence.

'"Pearly Gates", yes?'

Voice from the darkness: 'What have you got for us?'

'Well, um, I was born in Calcutta, Kolkata now . . . ah, but you know that, yes, of course you do, so, um – so what exactly is it you want? You know my background. My career? Didn't my agent send you my CV?'

Silence.

'I've got a piece of *Hamlet* if you'd like. 'To be or not to be . . .'

'Next.'

*

Perhaps because very soon after we met, I had discouraged Martin from sharing his grief with me, I thought that his naturally sanguine nature through all the following years meant all was well. It was maybe three years ago that I inferred all was far from right with Laila, Martin's half-sister in Buenos Aires. We had stopped over to stay there on our way down south to Patagonia and socialised with her. She was odder than I remembered. We met Dianna, her sister, only briefly. A bit like my mother, Dianna is good to look at and has married well (a mere three times for her) and lives in a large house in Pasadena, California, but she was in Uruguay when we were in Argentina, so we ferried over the River Plate to meet her – against Martin's inclinations as he never liked her – something about his mother's jewels going walkabout after her death. But I persuaded him we should, that she was nearby, and it was a pity to hold grudges. Silly me.

Laila trained as a doctor but for the past twenty years seemed incapable of holding down a job, even as a hospital orderly – not for any length of time, anyway. She would ring Martin at about five in the morning and chatter on for an hour. I'm not sure she could ever work out the time difference between the two countries or be bothered to remember it when she felt the urge to ring.

She had met and married an interesting, spiky, Irishman when she'd once been on holiday in Thailand, and they'd lived for a short while in London; but her hubby eventually had to leave her for the simple reason that he'd given up the booze (because he needed to hold down a job so as to pay their living expenses) and Laila kept him up all night talking, drinking Coke, and I suspect now, although he was too loyal to say, smoking dope. Waiting for the divorce, she returned to live in South America, where she led a very peripatetic life, spending whatever she made on helping drug addicts and doing good works. If everything she told us was to be believed, she was constantly being swindled by her patients, so was always short of money.

She had been given an apartment by an aunt who, for no

reason Laila could satisfactorily explain, suddenly became estranged (we did find out why later), so Martin and Dorian were constantly sending money to tide her over: to pay the electricity bills so she had hot water, to pay her overheads in the apartment block, to pay for her to live between the jobs she couldn't hold down for more than a few months . . . Over the years, it amounted to a considerable sum.

But then, one day, three years ago, Laila was found unconscious on her apartment stairs and rushed to hospital. We got word back from there that she was an alcoholic, and because she'd been a doctor and had been self-prescribing, she was now also a drug addict.

All the money her half-brothers had sent her had been squandered on her vices, and she had spent the winter without heat or hot water or nutrition and was badly in arrears with the rent in the block where she lived.

It was then that her younger sister, Dianna, came rushing to her rescue, like Mother Teresa on a unicorn, to look after her sibling. Laila had often said how much she disliked her sister (they were forever feuding), so being helpless and being looked after by Dianna must have been galling. And then, out of the blue, Martin, the softer touch of the two brothers, was being sent email after email on a daily basis by the sisters pointing out that by Argentine law, relatives had to look after any ill or indigent members of the family, there being no national health service. Oh, and had Dianna mentioned that she'd been involved in a car accident recently and it was suspected that the right and left halves of her brain were out of sync – so she wasn't going to be able to help financially, being incapable herself? Of course, all the emotional blackmail was rot: they were only Martin's half-sisters, and he lived in England and was British, but no amount of persuasion from me or his QC brother could convince him he wasn't one day going to hear a violent knocking at our front door and be hauled off to an Argentine gaol.

I'm sure he felt his mother would have wanted him to help her daughter, but he had his life, his dogs, his home, and friends here, and I, Kerry, told him he mustn't send another penny to Laila until she got herself a job – even if it was stacking shelves in a supermarket. We needed to know she was taking responsibility for herself. Giving an alcoholic money was preventing her recovery.

He found the situation intolerable, so he defected.

This is a favourite joke I used to ask Martin to tell as he was so much better at telling jokes than me.

A man goes on holiday to his villa in the South of France, leaving his butler to look after his house here. He has only been abroad a few days when he gets a telegram from England saying: 'Your cat is dead.' He rushes back and says to the butler, 'Jenkins, that was a terrible way to communicate the news. You know how much I loved that cat.' So Jenkins apologises and asks how he should have done it. 'Well,' says the man, 'your first telegram should have said something like: "Your cat is on the roof, and we are having trouble getting him down," and then you should have sent another telegram a day or so later, saying: "We have him down, but he's not well," and then a last one, saying what you did: "Your cat is dead."' 'Oh, right, sir,' says Jenkins. 'I'm so sorry.'

The house owner goes back to his place in France, and he's only been there a week when he gets a telegram from Jenkins: 'Your mother is on the roof.'

On 31 October, the day before our thirty-sixth anniversary, Martin, quite deliberately, climbed up onto the roof.

Not another waltz, no.

Author's Thanks

First and foremost, my thanks to Richard Tyler Jordan for his belief in my ability as a writer, his encouragement through the years, and his practical advice.

Hannah Boursnell for editing.

Foz Foster for his marvellous cover.

Roger Davenport, the author and actor, the first reader of the early script, for his example, observations and advice.

Chris and Julia Boeree for their enjoyment and their hands-on, constructive help.

Mark Daly of TimeSleuths for his discovery of my other family, which helps me end the book on an upbeat note.

Dominic (Mr Memory Man) O'Brien for pointing me in the right direction vis à vis publishing.

Penny Mountain, Liz Gardiner, Eliza Hunt, Sue Bovell, Pat O'Connell, David Delve, and James Dinsmore for their enthusiasm throughout.

John Heffernen for sending me the idea for the cover.

AND

For the past twenty or more years of my life, I've shared most of my days with Petroc Trelawny, Sarah Walker and Sean Rafferty, along with all those other friendly and knowledgeable music presenters dotted about on Radio 3. (Through Sean Rafferty I've met hundreds of music makers, and what a privilege that's been).

AND

I heard of James O'Brien maybe eighteen months ago and occasionally listened to his programme on LBC, but as I became more politically engaged, I started to listen to him at ten in the morning, and I now stay firmly at his side till one. Since Lockdown, I've begun to think of him as my best friend – my Bestie if you like. He has an extraordinary facility with words and unexpected phrases. He seems to mirror my feelings: my anger, my sense of injustice and the ridiculous – he makes me laugh a minimum of three times per programme! But, unlike me who's inclined to slosh about emotionally, he has a well of good sense and an inquiring mind which prevents him – and therefore, me – from despair and cynicism. He has been a saviour for me these past dire months. He speaks the truth as he sees it without being a know-all, he has a true need to understand when he's wrong, and his conversations with adults and children are an unselfconscious delight. Inside James O'Brien, you can often glimpse the Garden-of-Eden child. Latch on to him – he's essential to the equilibrium of the world.

In the afternoons, I return to Radios 3 and 4, my sensibilities having been shaken awake in the morning. Sadly at the weekends, there's a dearth of the man. But then there are new classical music releases on Saturday and Michael Berkeley on Sunday!

By the Way

I told you early on I wasn't that bothered to find out more about my antecedents, but through somebody else's doing, I found out just a few months ago.

If you remember, I wrote in the opening chapter that my mother had always told me my father was 'none of my business', so I knew absolutely nothing of him apart from the little I gleaned from what she'd let slip to my brother and friends. But I had no idea what he looked like, why he and my mother split up so soon after my birth, where he might be if he was alive . . .

About eighteen months ago, some local friends, Julia and Chris Boeree asked me to let them have a look at what I'd written, and I was flattered enough by their curiosity to let them see the first draft of this book. Not that long afterwards, Chris rang me to say he hoped I didn't mind but he'd shown Chapter One to their next-door neighbours' son, who happened to be down for the weekend. The son, Mark Daly, had his own company, TimeSleuths, which sometimes worked with Ancestry.com on some of their projects, and he had been so intrigued to hear about a woman who had married five times and had told her son nothing of his beginnings that he'd spent a few hours overnight researching her and would be happy to show me what he'd found out.

So…my mother hadn't been born in Gloucestershire but in India. Her mother, my gran, who had looked after me as a youngster, had been married twice, first of all to a Gomez, then to a Ferrier. Mark Daly couldn't be sure which of her three children might have been my mother without further investigation, because in the Gomez family tree there was a daughter called Peachy, and in the second, the Ferrier family tree, an Eline – either or both of which could have been her. (Incidentally, I was delighted my mother had gifted me the perfect name for a Drag Queen: Peachy Gomez! If you ever see that name advertised as performing at the Vauxhall Tavern, that'll be ME!)

She had two brothers, Clayton and Maurice – again never mentioned once throughout our lives together. That bit of information made me wonder where those two men were when my gran died alone in London – put into a pauper's grave for lack of any relatives because my mother and her had a row and my gran had apparently torn up all reference to her.

There's more to be found out about my mother, but I'm not sure I want to pry into the psyche of a woman who needed to hide her past in order to live her present. Was *she* unhappy as a child, perhaps? Whatever the reason for Alan Meek leaving her so soon after their marriage, she was barely twenty years old and must have been crushed – and consequently incandescent with fury. She certainly went on to become a rich woman later on when my father, Geoffrey Gardner, married her and sent me, her son, to school, but why did she need a cover version of herself for the world at large for those many, many years?

I had, I thought, finished the book when it occurred to me that we (you and I) might like a look at my father – my birth father, that is Alan George Meek – so I went back to Mark, and asked his help. A month later, he told me my half-sister, Georgina, would be emailing me from Australia to set up a meeting. I had a **sister**! She would surely have a picture of our dad.

(No, it seems I have two sisters, Georgina and Sylvia. But the two of them have been estranged for forty years, ever since the latter joined a cult and was persuaded that her mother had sexually abused her as a child! Similarly, one of my best friends has a daughter who was persuaded by an American cult that she'd been physically abused by her mother as a child. My friend now never sees or hears from her daughter or her grandchildren. It seems that the purpose of these cults is to wean children away from their family support, thus welding their emotional dependence onto a group of strangers. Presumably money changes hands).

Georgina, Georgie as she likes to be called, and I had a Zoom meeting, as this all has taken place while the world is in the grip of the Coronavirus pandemic, when 'Zooming' has become the norm. This handsome stranger in her seventies was so happy and tearful, whereas old Kerry here looked on dispassionately. I was moved that she was so moved. She'd been searching for me all her adult life, but of course couldn't find out anything because, aged six, my surname had been changed to Gardner. Everywhere she'd travelled, she'd asked for a local telephone book looking for a Kerry Meek. Being told all this, aged eighty-three, was like reading the new chapter of a book about someone I might have been. But wasn't.

It seems I was right when I surmised that my father had left my mother and me to return to his first love, Noreen. Apparently, they'd been engaged to be married, and he had broken it off because of her insistence that her mother live with them. He then married my mother Eline Therese, they had me, and then Noreen wrote and said she'd made a mistake. (See Chapter One). And yes, he was in the army, but later a mercantile assistant – although Georgie questioned that, as she'd always thought of him as an army man. I'll never know the reason my parents parted. I hate to think he just dropped my mother (and me) the moment his first (and maybe only) love relented and called him back to her side. It would explain my mother's determination to blank him out. Her hurt must have been overwhelming. But that's just a probability. Maybe far from the truth.

My father was offered a good job in Australia where he had relations (the Meeks were in England at the time), so he sold everything and moved there to start his new job – only to be told the job had fallen through. He never quite trusted the Australians after that, even though he lived there the rest of his short life. According to Georgie's husband, Garry, he remained a disappointed man to his dying day. He once remarked to Georgie: 'I've lost both my sons.' His second child, his first with Noreen, had been a boy who died in childbirth. I was, of course, the first. Apparently, he'd tried to find me for as long as he could, but – again – my change of name made that impossible.

Looking at his picture, I think I would have loved him if he'd been contactable. (Maybe not if my mother had been pouring vitriol in my ear, so maybe she was right to never talk of him). My mother's third husband, and the one I knew as my father, was always very civil and kind towards me, but we never exchanged feelings, even when I was at Marlborough and could have done with a bit of extra warmth. He was a good man Alan Meek, but just like my father, Geoff, an upright man not given to showing much emotion. Apparently, Noreen was much the same. But he was a loving father to his two daughters. He died on the golf course at the age of fifty-six of a heart attack. His wife was 102 when she died, so she survived him by forty-six years. You can see the photo Georgie sent me of his marriage to his second wife (my step-mother!). This took place in 1940, three years after I was born. So this photo is my very first sighting of my father.

Georgina's over the moon at finding me. Now in my eighties, I'm bemused, amused and touched by these discoveries, but not knowing a damn thing about any of it for so very long, does this perhaps-life do more than intrigue me? If this book gets published, it'll probably be a long time from now, so maybe I'll re-write that last sentence because I've become embroiled.

In the last nine months, I've gained aunts, uncles, nephews and nieces galore. Best of all, I've gained a sister, half or otherwise. I *think* life would have been more fun with a largish family, but I've heard too many Christmas-gathering stories to be sure that's what I'd have liked. The only sister likely to talk to me, Georgie, has been a nurse most of her life – and that makes me proud of her. She lives in a gated community in Australia not too far from Sydney, with her half-Dutch husband and dog (full marks!). If life gets back to normal, they might well get back to visiting his family in Holland, so that's just a hop and a jump over the water, and I'll get to actually meet them. Until then, we'll be Zooming.

*

Just a couple of things before I sign off. Thanks for the heads-up, Angel, that sales pitch you gave at the beginning, but you made no mention of how to cope when you're a twenty-four-year-old in an eighty-three-year-old body. I try now not to look at my face as I shave because it looks like I'm shaving my mother. That small whinge aside, I would like to thank you for a pretty good time down here. I've tried to do the best with what I've been given, I think. But you may disagree. I'll find out soon enough, I suppose. Cheers.